Perceptions of
Aging
in
Literature

Recent Titles in
Contributions to the Study of Aging

PERCEPTIONS OF AGING IN LITERATURE

A CROSS-CULTURAL STUDY

Edited by

Prisca von Dorotka Bagnell
and
Patricia Spencer Soper

PN
56
.04
P47
1989

Foreword by W. Andrew Achenbaum

CONTRIBUTIONS TO THE STUDY OF AGING,
NUMBER 11
Erdman B. Palmore, *Series Adviser*

GREENWOOD PRESS
NEW YORK · WESTPORT, CONNECTICUT · LONDON

Library of Congress Cataloging in Publication Data

Perceptions of aging in literature.
  (Contributions to the study of aging, ISSN 0732–085X ;
no. 11)
  Bibliography: p.
  Includes index.
  1. Aging in literature.   2. Old age in literature.
I. Bagnell, Prisca von Dorotka.   II. Soper, Patricia
Spencer.   III. Series.
PN56.04P47 1989   809′.93355   88-34723
ISBN 0–313–26292–6 (lib. bdg. : alk. paper)

British Library Cataloguing in Publication Data is available.

Library of Congress Catalog Card Number: 88–34723
ISBN: 0–313–26292–6
ISSN: 0732–085X

First published in 1989

Greenwood Press, Inc.
88 Post Road West, Westport, Connecticut   06881

Printed in the United States of America

The paper used in this book complies with the
Permanent Paper Standard issued by the National
Information Standards Organization (Z39.48–1984).

10 9 8 7 6 5 4 3 2 1

The Pillow Book of Sei Shōnagon. Translated by Ivan Morris. Copyright 1967. Courtesy of Columbia University Press.

Essays in Idleness. In *The Tsurezuregusa of Kenko*. Translated by Donald Keene. Copyright 1967. Courtesy of Columbia University Press.

Komachi at Sekidera by Zeami. In *Twenty Plays of the No Theater* edited by Donald Keene, translated by Karen Brazell. Courtesy of Columbia University Press.

Saigyō, *Mirror for the Moon*. Copyright © 1978 by William R. LaFleur. Reprinted by permission of New Directions Publishing Corporation.

The Zen Poems of Ryokan, selected and translated with an Introduction, Biographical Sketch, and Notes by Nobuyuki Yuasa. Copyright © 1981 by Princeton University Press. Selection, pp. 155–56, reprinted by permission of Princeton University Press.

The House of the Sleeping Beauties by Yasunari Kawabata, translated by Edward G. Seidensticker, published by Kodansha International Ltd. © 1969. Courtesy of Kodansha International Ltd.

The Sound of the Mountain by Yasunari Kawabata. Translated by Edward Seidensticker. Copyright 1970. Courtesy of Alfred A. Knopf, Inc.

Diary of a Mad Old Man by Junichiro Tanizaki. Translated by Howard Hibbett. Copyright 1965. Courtesy of Alfred A. Knopf, Inc.

The Decay of the Angel by Yukio Mishima. Translated by Edward Seidensticker. Copyright 1974. Courtesy of Alfred A. Knopf, Inc.

Tso-chuan in *Meng Ch'iu* by Li Han and Hsü Tzu-Kuang, translated by Burton Watson, and published by Kodansha International Ltd. © 1979.

Tz'u verse by Li Ch'ing-chao. In *Anthology of Chinese Literature,* edited by Cyril Birch, translated by Hsu Kaiyu. Reprinted by permission of Grove Press, Inc. Copyright © 1965 by Grove Press, Inc.

"Autumn Meditations," part 4, by Meng Chiao and translated by Stephen Owen; "Lament for Lu Yin" by Meng Chiao and translated by Kenneth Hanson; and an untitled poem by Han Yu and translated by Charles Hertman are from "The Pond in a Bowl." In *Sunflower Splendor*, edited by Wu-chi and Irving Yucheng Lo. Copyright 1975. Courtesy of Double-day, a division of Bantam, Doubleday, Dell Publishing Group, Inc.

"Autumn Meditations," part 5 of *The Autumn Wastes,* and *Yangtse and Han* by Tu Fu. In *Poems of the Late T'ang,* translated by A. C. Graham. Copyright 1965 by A. C. Graham. By permission of Penguin Books Ltd.

Journal by Wu Yu-pi. In *Personal Reflections on the Pursuit of Sagehood: The Life and Journal of Wu Yu-pi,* translated by M. Theresa Kelleher. Ph.D. diss, M. Theresa Kelleher, Columbia University, 1982. Courtesy of M. Theresa Kelleher.

Dream of the Red Chamber by Ts'ao Hsueh-ch'in. Translated by Gladys and Hsien-yi Yang. Copyright 1981. By permission of the Foreign Language Press.

To
Eduard von Dorotka,
who, in the ninth decade of his life, is still
the youngest, dearest, and most civilized man I know.

P. v. D. B.

and
To
my children
Carey, Chaz, and Joseph
who keep me young despite my years.

P. S. S.

Contents

Foreword: Literature's Value in Gerontological Research

In 1972, G. P. Putnam's Sons brought out an English translation of Simone de Beauvoir's *La vieillesse*. Old age, according to de Beauvoir, had been excessively romanticized for centuries. Writers denied the physical horrors of late life and ignored the social opprobrium of the elderly, she claimed, because of the cultural imperatives of a bourgeois society. "That is why the whole problem is so carefully passed over in silence; and that is why this silence has to be shattered. I call upon my readers to help me in doing so" (Beauvoir, 1972, p. 7). *La vieillesse* clearly was no mere scholarly tome; it was a quasi-autobiographical manifesto by one of the world's most influential intellectuals. After its publication—the book was an immediate best-seller in France when published in 1970—a new relationship between the humanities and gerontology began to take shape.

The Coming of Age, as the 585-page American edition was titled, received mixed reviews. Most critics were impressed by the copious research. To make her case, Beauvoir gathered data from anthropology, biology, psychology, and ethnology as well as literary, artistic, and historical materials. Nonetheless, many found Beauvoir's analysis of the record imbalanced because it was so grim. Reviewers were willing to grant that sentimental themes about age and aging were commonplace, but they also charged that the author overlooked evidence that did not support her argument. Critics described her tone as strident, even narcissistic. They faulted Beauvoir for equating old age with disease and characterizing it as a "problem." They disagreed with her view of the last stage of life as an insult rather than a phase of the complex process of human development (Butler, 1972; Coles, 1972; Woodward, 1983). For all its shortcomings, however, *The Coming of Age* had challenged readers to reexamine the nature and significance of pervasive and enduring attitudes toward growing older. Even if Beauvoir's assessment would not be the last word, her cri de coeur heralded a resounding chorus of new voices speaking about gerontological research in new ways.

Shortly after *The Coming of Age* was published (though probably not as a direct consequence of that event), American scholars began to investigate how inherited images, biases, attitudes, socioeconomic structures, and cultural processes affected people's present-day manner of defining and dealing with the assets and liabilities of senescence. Most humanists who have become interested in ideas about age and aging engage in what accurately—if awkwardly—can be described as comparative hermeneutics. That is, they interpret thoughts and feelings about growing older that are emboided in traditional vessels of culture (folklore, myths, magic, rituals, art, diaries, poetry, songs, proverbs, social mores, and legal codes) and comparatively modern modes of expression (the latest medical etiologies and therapies, novels, ethnic stereotypes, jokes, movies, and television programs). Once they have identified basic themes, nuances, metaphors, conflicts, and paradoxes within a particular piece, most investigators then compare specific bits of information with evidence from other speakers, writers, and artists (Philibert, 1979).

Scholars who turn to the humanities in doing gerontological research seem to be concerned primarily with accomplishing two objectives. On the one hand, they generally want to describe and explain continuities and changes in the meanings and experiences of being old and growing older. The universals of aging across place and over time fascinate them as much as the variations that result from parochial, ephemeral circumstances, those that reflect differences in race, class, or gender, and those that emanate from relatively recent gains in life expectancy (Achenbaum, 1985; Moody, 1981). On the other hand, humanists struggle to comprehend the nature and dynamics of the metastructure of ideas about age and aging. They seek to learn which prescriptions, images, and stereotypes are based on "realities" manifest in the human condition. They also try to understand how the concatenation of long-term and short-range sociohistorical forces can simultaneously reinforce prevailing ideas and create new notions, while permitting outmoded perceptions to remain robust.

Those engaged in blazing new intellectual frontiers have found the experience exhilarating. They have developed fresh ways of making the humanities vital to the aged. Biomedical and social gerontologists have increasingly referred to pioneering books and articles in the humanities in the course of formulating, executing, and reporting their own research projects. More than other types of inquiry into aging, humanistic gerontology has emphasized the extent to which modes of conceptualizing and expressing ideas have perennially shaped our viewpoints and conditioned our behavior. The contributions of specialists in the humanities are pertinent to anyone sensitive to the need to delineate and comprehend particular forms of expression, manifestations of style, continuities and shifts in context, and levels of meaning.

Yet attempts thus far to define the precise and complete relationships between the humanities and aging have been inadequate. No one has fully succeeded in saying what "humanistic gerontology" is, much less how it can be done most effectively. Researchers often employ different techniques with divergent objectives in mind. Furthermore, the uses of the humanities made by scholarly professionals and social-service deliverers are rarely the same. As a result, academic studies designed to fathom humanistic endeavors and traditions, no less than efforts to make the humanities accessible to the aging and the aged, often operate at cross-purposes.

Each discipline in the humanities defines its research agenda and goes about its business in distinctive ways. For example, historians so far have been preoccupied with mapping shifts in attitudes about old age expressed by predominantly middle-class, white male "professionals" and with generating quantitative analyses of changes in the elderly's modal demographic and socioeconomic patterns (Stearns & Tassel, in press). The scholarly output in reconstructing the history of "age" in the United States and Western Europe has far surpassed the number of published works by philosophers, literary critics, theologians, or rhetoricians.

This is not to suggest, however, that literary specialists have played only a minor role in promoting humanistic gerontology. Quite the contrary. The most original work in English has tapped an area of concern to gerontologists—the issue of "creativity" in late life—that no other cadre of humanists has pursued (Lehman, 1953). English professor Kathleen M. Woodward (1980) has pointed the way to a fresh approach. Through a critical analysis of T. S. Eliot's *Four Quartets,* Ezra Pound's *Pisan Cantos,* Wallace Stevens's "To an Old Philosopher in Rome", and Book 5 of William Carlos Williams's *Paterson,* she sought to explicate the satisfactions and experiences these poets expressed in late life. By comparing these works to their authors' earlier achievements, Woodward demonstrated how these men moved through verse toward a kind of closure to their individual life course.

In addition to studying the late works of distinguished novelists and poets, literary experts have been trying to increase our familiarity with materials in both high and popular culture that illuminate the moods and diversities of old age. One of the best examples of this genre is Ronald Blythe's *The View in Winter* (1979). This book consists mainly of the reminiscences, reflections, and recommendations of thirty-nine old Britons presented in a format that resembles the structure of *Canterbury Tales.* Blythe creates a realm in which "The District Nurse," "The Retired Engineer," "The Repairer's Widow," and "The Character-Actor and Fabian" speak, presumably, for all elements in society. Like Chaucer, Blythe gives the last word to religious people on the "prayer route." The vibrancy of *The View in Winter* comes from the author's ability to empathize with and take cues from his subjects. Thus, when Blythe notes that "old age is full of death and full of life. It is a tolerable achievement and it is a disaster. It transcends desire and it taunts it. It is long enough and it is far from being long enough" (p. 29), he offers an image of age's complexity that is faithful to, yet goes far beyond, his interviews. Indeed, Blythe's achievement underscores an obvious point, but one that bears stating: very often the relationship between the humanities and aging is most fruitful when people with different perspectives and intentions collaborate.

Indeed, more than researchers in any other discipline, students of Anglo-American literature and the Romance and Oriental languages have conveyed the universals of aging in all of its richness, ambiguity, and contrarieties. These specialists are sensitive to the levels of discourse and range of emotions transmitted in the words we use to describe the elderly and in the manner in which the old themselves characterize their circumstances and worldviews. Poets and critics have been able to amplify the sorts of observations made by historians, philosophers, and social scientists because they are so attuned to the importance of nuances: they are able to extract volumes of insight from a play's denouement, a novel's epigraph, or a poem's refrain. In so doing, they have made great works of literature available and comprehensible to those who want to broaden their own understanding of the process of senescence.

This volume underscores literature's value in gerontological research. It joins some fine anthologies and bibliographies in pointing us to major works in high and popular literature (Edwards & Flynn, 1982; Freeman, 1979; Moss, 1976). By offering a sample of literature from all corners of the earth, the work has ethnographic value. Many of the themes suggested here complement and illuminate issues being investigated by cultural anthropologists (Keith, 1979, 1981).

Perceptions of Aging in Literature: A Cross-cultural Study has a particularly attractive quality that makes it quite useful to researchers and practitioners in the field of aging: all of the authors write with assurance—they clearly are "experts." Yet they are honest enough to let us know when they are speculating or simply have not reached a definitive opinion about some issue. Their expertise and sensitivity to the need to relate their particular case study to the big picture thus give one confidence in mining this book for insights and hypotheses.

In asking Jon Hendricks to write the introductory chapter, the editors have guaranteed that scholars and practitioners throughout the aging network will take notice of this volume. Hendricks has a knack for expressing ideas in ways that transcend disciplinary turfs: he has a gift for making sense of complex theories and empirical realities. Reading the introduction prepares the reader for what follows. Accordingly, let me indicate some of the things I learned and recalled while reading this volume in manuscript. I organize my thoughts in response to several issues that were raised by Hendricks and Cynthia Leedham, and amplified by various contributors.

LITERATURE AS A REFLECTION OF SOCIAL CONDITIONS

"The thought of the inevitability of old age prompts feelings and images that reflect the local and share in the universal," observes Roger Allen at the conclusion of his critique in chapter 8 of old age as theme and technique in the Arabic world. Other authors made similar points: their analyses and examples remind us that old age is an age-old phenomenon with particularist qualities. The interaction of structural forces, culture, and individual life courses affect the shape of ideas in different ways at different times. Hence social conditions, Louis Roberts argues in chapter 2, were no less important than styles of rhetoric and prose in shaping portrayals of the elderly in classical literature. The contextual interplay of other enduring patterns of sociohistorical forces have an impact, of course, though here too, interesting variations are noted. Thus Robert H. Stacy hypothesizes, in the chapter on Russian literature, that the declining years of older women are perennially described in "abjectly forlorn and ugly" terms in Russian literature, whereas men by and large attain "a noble state of grace" in old age. How different this is from prescriptive images of women elsewhere. According to Myron Lichtblau, in chapter 7, Colombian Gabriel Garcia Marquez imbued the last years of the matriarch of the Buendia family with symbolic significance in *One Hundred Years of Solitude* (1967): Ursula "represents the legendary greatness of all womanhood, and in her old age is seen the maturity of Hispanic America."

Nor is the richness of experiences in later years any less vivid because the aged usually have been allotted marginal parts of books or treated as special cases. Older people, most critics concur, play secondary roles in British and American literature. Even so, as Richard Fallis shows (chapter 3), Anglo-American writers afford us "a rich gallery of characters where we can meet almost every imaginable human type, and they help us understand the nuances and textures of later life with great specificity and intensity." A comparable range of imagery and prescriptions exists in German literature. Gerd Schneider finds (chapter 5) that positive themes—such as the acceptance of old people by society and the fostering of intergenerational understanding—predominate. Precisely because the aged are not the center of attention in the masterpieces of literary history, the manner in which they are characterized enables writers to flesh out details and transform even mundane circumstances into compelling narrative.

Does it follow that Western writers have intentionally invoked themes that might lead a reader to conclude that old age is better than previous stages of life? Not necessarily. To cite just one obvious contrast, the dis-

tinguished social historian Peter N. Stearns (1977) has convincingly demonstrated that ageism is a central feature of French culture. It has pervaded
France for centuries. The animus against age heightened during the Industrial Revolution; only in the twentieth century, contends Stearns, have
more positive views come into vogue. One can accept the main lines of
Stearns's analysis, however, and still not grasp all of the pertinent dynamics of the Gallic history of old age. Important qualifications and elabora-
tions arise from a survey of literature. Paul Archambault, in chapter 4 on
French literature, shows us that for all the prejudice and disesteem they
suffered in premodern times, the elderly in France nonetheless wielded
considerable power over the young and transmitted seasoned (or is it hardened?) advice to the rising generation: "The aging crone, the cuckolded
husband of medieval fabliaux or of La Fontaine's *Contes,* and Molière's
aging lovers, misers, and notaries still remain a strong social force with an
elastic capacity for retaliation as well as an uncanny ability to transform
themselves from objects of ridicule to objects of fear." Such examples give
provocative insights into the distinction that Hendricks and Leedham draw
between "core" and "peripheral" characters in their introduction.

   This volume, moreover, provides additional evidence with which to test
the hypothesis that "modernization" has affected the meanings and experiences of growing older. Materials here bolster much that has been written about trends in Western civilization. It is interesting to note that older
people apparently gain greater prominence in twentieth-century literature
as their sheer numbers increase. But even more striking are several comments made about the connections between modernization and aging that
writers detected in literary patterns in the Orient. That the veneration traditionally accorded the old in the East has been undermined by rapid industrialization and urbanization is becoming a well-known gerontological
"fact." Anthropologists are not the only observers to comment on the
irony that the Japanese began to celebrate Respect for the Aged Day *(Kierō
no hi)* at precisely that moment in history when cultural support for such
esteem was waning: interpretations of the phenomenon seem analogous to
the debate over the intent and power of the Fourth Commandment that is
part of our Judeo-Christian heritage. Yet I was surprised to discover in
Virginia Skord's analysis (chapter 9) that views of aging in modern Japanese literature are so pessimistic, a stance that was not as evident centuries
earlier. Edward Gunn reports a similar trend in Chinese literature (chapter
10); the works he cites document "the rise of a youth culture, giving social
form to the tensions of the younger generation, moved at once to honor
and care for their elders and to instruct and triumph over them." In contemporary literature in the East, no less than in the West, it seems that the
aged's uncertain and fluid status is conveyed in all its ambiguousness and
dynamism (Ganschow, 1978). The range of symbolism is not invariably

more complex than it was in the past, but there have been marked shifts in emphasis and subtle changes in tone.

LITERARY CONVENTIONS AND INTERPRETATIONS OF OLD AGE

As one progresses through *Perceptions of Aging in Literature: A Cross-Cultural Study,* it is clear that the same sorts of figures appear and reappear in different localities and in every period, from the classical to the contemporary. Some characters—the bitter old man who is jealous of youth's sexual vigor and the poor widow finding through piety the strength and determination to go on—seem stereotypic to modern ears. Others—Ulysses, Job, the Wandering Jew, and Hänsel and Gretel's witch—are archetypal figures. Mythology, folklore, and everyday conversations, moreover, clearly serve as prototypes for stories about intergenerational rivalries and cooperations, for tales about the process of (dis)engagement in later years, and for reminiscences and prophecies uttered by elderly personae. In still other instances, images of aging complement the main story line; by staying in the shadows, older characters help to integrate themes into a central motif.

Yet to note that there appears to be a stock of common themes and images that writers employ to describe the elderly is not to discount the significance of some powerful and highly specific images, as shown by some of the examples the contributors have presented. I share Professor Fallis's opinion that *King Lear* is "the richest text in our language on the social forces in old age." Nor shall I soon forget emblems of aging from Eastern cultures—the withering cherry blossom, the plum, and the old warhorse—symbols and metaphors that are far more complex than I previously imagined. Indeed, the very richness of the historically particular and culturally specific imagery underscores the marked ambivalence of aging themes throughout literature.

The ambivalence that surrounds old age is of a different order than the Janus-like symbols that we associate with other turning points in the human life course (Erikson, 1979). Possibly the fuzziness reflects the fact that late life itself is such a nebulous existence of unpredictable duration. Conceivably it is old age's paradoxical nature that has invited authors to wax eloquent about the variegated "shades of gray." In this volume we see several examples of older people's keen perception of the joyful and sorrowful limits of the present moment—a sensibility tempered by their fondness for a past that no longer exists. Similarly, every critic reports that great literature and familiar artifacts of popular cutlure often seize upon the penetrating beauty of age amidst the ravages of physical decay. From the voices of the old recorded here, one repeatedly hears a curious admixture of spontaneity and deliberation coupled with candor and under-statement. Thus, when Virginia Skord suggests that the aged crone Ko-machi in a nō play displays "the delicate interplay of vital forces [that] operates in the elderly, hampered only by physical limitation," I believe that she has correctly seized on a timeless and ubiquitous quality of old age, which literature graphically embellishes.

What seems to have fascinated writers everywhere throughout the ages is the insistence of the old to remain true to—to (re)affirm—the basic truths of the human condition in their simple utterances, in their seemingly pe-destrian gestures, and in their very mien. What do the aged do to sustain the warp and woof of human nature? Why do they do what they do? Do they succeed? Why is their failure fraught with irony laden with tragic undertones? Such are the issues posed and recounted in tales that, at their best, settle not for some facile cliché but rather seize upon the amazing resilience of potential in later years. Good writers tend to develop this theme in admiring terms that are just a bit unsettled and unsettling. Such reflections lead in turn to a third major theme I detected in this volume.

CREATIVITY AND AGING

The ambivalence conveyed in literary conventions about old age carries over into interpretations of creativity in late life. By way of illustration, let us continue to refer to the central character in the nō play—"Komachi expresses the pleasure she takes in life even as death approaches and in composing poetry even though her creative vision has waned." The theme is hardly limited to characters in Japanese literature. Remember Brecht's "Unseemly Old Lady" who starts a new, unconventional life at seventy-two. Think of how Kazantzakis's Zorba the Greek or Tolstoy's old Cos-sack Eroshka embody virility and paganism.

Yet creativity in late life is not always viewed in world literature as a blessing. Entropy looms as a threat. Tillie Olsen emphasizes in *Silences* (1983) that the apparent absence of creative expression can cause pain and conflict. The price of social criticism, more often than not, is opprobrium: for creativity to flourish, it is sometimes necessary for persons of any age to demand (or seek refuge in) "a place apart"—in the interiority of one's mind or the loneliness of one's heart, to invoke motifs from classic Amer-ican literature (Warren, 1975, 1984).

I wish that the contributors to this volume had focused more on the creative styles of artists in their later years. Yeats bravely admonished older writers to "abandon nothing, transform everything." What the economist Joseph Schumpeter described as "creative destruction" is obviously rele-vant at this juncture. Very often artists reach new innovative heights in part because they must compensate for losses in stamina or acuity. Yet once again this is no place for Panglossian generalizations: one thinks of the shift in style that characterizes T. S. Eliot's later works or makes Robert Frost's poetry after World War II so painful to criticize (Pritchard, 1984). Wordsworth's later poems offer a stunning instance of stagnation. If we are to understand and realize the potential that is associated with the "third quarter of life," to use Alan Pifer's phrase (Pifer and Bronte, 1986, p. 402), we must systematically investigate the physical, intellectual, interpersonal, structural, and cultural factors that inhibit and facilitate growth in later years. Literature provides a wonderful laboratory for such gerontological research.

I was disappointed to find no chapter on African literature, and I would have preferred a fuller discussion of the relationship between (1) folklore and the argot of ordinary people and (2) the images of old age found in high literature. The time has come, I believe, for gerontologists in all specialties to be more precise in delineating the boundaries and acknowledging the shadows that encompass the realm of aging (from womb to tomb) and the sphere of old age. But I note these shortcomings merely to suggest some interesting avenues for future research. Suffice it to say that I learned much from this volume. It should serve as a treasure trove for researchers and practitioners in many areas. With its publication, literature's value to gerontology has been greatly increased.

W. Andrew Achenbaum

REFERENCES

Beauvoir, S. de. (1972). *The coming of age* (P. O'Brian, Trans.). New York: G. P. Putnam.

Blythe, R. (1979). *The view in winter*. New York: Harcourt Brace Jovanovich.

Butler, R. N. (1972). Review of de Beauvoir's *The coming of age*. In *Washington Star*, May 28, pp. G6–7.

Coles, R. (1972). Review of de Beauvoir's *The coming of age*. In *The New Yorker*, August 19, pp. 68–72.

Edwards, W. M., and Flynn, F. (Eds.). (1982). *A cross-national core list of significant works*. Ann Arbor: Institute of Gerontology.

Erickson, E. H. (1979). Reflections on Dr. Borg's life cycle. In D. D. Van Tassel (Ed.). *Aging, death, and the completion of being* (pp. 29–67). Philadelphia: University of Pennsylvania Press.

Freeman, J. T. (1979). *Aging, its history and literature*. New York: Human Sciences Press.

Ganschow, T. W. (1978). The aged in a revolutionary milieu: China. In S. F. Spiker, K. Woodward, and D. D. Van Tassell. (Eds.). *Aging and the elderly: Humanistic perspectives in gerontology*. Atlantic Highlands, NJ: Humanities Press.

Keith, J. (1979). The ethnography of old age. *Anthropological Quarterly, 52.*

Keith, J. (1982). *Old people as people*. Boston: Little, Brown.

Lehman, H. C. (1953). *Age and achievement*. Princeton: Princeton University Press.

Moody, H. R. (1981). Aging and culture policy. In *The arts, the humanities and older Americans*. Washington, D.C.: National Council on Aging.

Moss, W. (Ed.) (1976). *Humanistic perspectives on aging*. Ann Arbor: Institute of Gerontology.

Philibert, M. (1974). The phenomenological approach to images of aging. *Soundings, 57*, pp. 3–24.

Pifer, A. and Bronte, L. (1986). *Our aging society, paradox and promise*. New York: W. W. Norton.

Pritchard, W. H. (1984). *Frost: a literary life remembered*. New York: Oxford University Press.

Stearns, P. (1977). *Old age and European society: The case of France*. New York: Holmes and Meier.

Stearns, P. N. and Van Tassel, D. D. (in press) *The elderly in a bureaucratic world*. Westport, CT: Greenwood.

Warren, R. P. (1975). *Poetry and democracy*. Cambridge: Harvard University Press.

Woodward, K. M. (1980). *At last, the real distinguished thing*. Columbus: Ohio State University Press.

Woodward, K. M. (1983). Instant repulsion: decreptitude, the mirror stage and the literary imagination. *The Kenyon Review, 5*, pp. 43–66.

Preface

This volume belongs to the genre considered "humanistic gerontology" in the field of aging. It deals with a portrait of aging in a cultural and historical perspective illuminated by diverse national literatures.

The leitmotif of the work explores attitudes toward aging as expressed by society toward the aged and by the aged themselves. It outlines the cultural construction of old age with its social and psychological ramifications, which are often imposed upon the aged from without. It focuses on the status and treatment of old age, and how different cultures throughout time and within a specific place enhanced or demeaned the cross-cultural phenomenon called aging.

This volume also deals with the interaction of the older person with his or her physical, social, and cultural environment. It hopes to transcend the narrow observations on Western industrial societies most familiar to us by including excerpts from Eastern literatures as well. It delineates changes occurring in norms and values in the East and West through historical, political, and sociocultural influences on successive generations.

The various norms and values of aging that have been created by humans in the course of their history have been, in the main, ignored by gerontologists. They seem more interested in the objective laws that govern science than in the subjective experiences that contribute, in part, to the aging process.

Literature, like other art forms, has given us a portrayal of aging throughout history. In poetry, drama, novels, philosophical treatises, and essays, one can find conceptual attitudes toward aging. In a paper given at the annual meeting of the Gerontological Society of America in San Francisco in 1983, D. G. Kehl and G. G. Hall outlined how belles-lettres contributes to the study of aging by helping to stimulate interest in aging; to serve to dispel stereotypes about aging; and to appeal to the emotional, psychological, and spiritual by complementing the scientific, statistical, and technical emphases. It dramatizes in a human context the raw objective data and serves to evoke sympathy and understanding for the aging process.

The purpose of this volume is hermeneutical. It is an attempt to add to that body of knowledge that helps illuminate, explain, and bridge the dichotomy that still exists between the scientist and the humanist in the field of aging. It is a field heavily weighted in favor of the social and behavioral sciences, the developmental theories on the Freudian model, and the sociological role theory, so that aging has taken on its own gestalt, albeit an asymmetrical one. Michael Philibert states succinctly in "The Phenomenological Approach to Images of Aging" in *Aging and the Human Spirit* by LeFevre and LeFevre (1985):

A science of man which pretends to reject all normative considerations, to eliminate any consideration of values, to treat man as a pure object of science, becomes indeed an accomplice to the social practices that devalue man. *(P. 192)*

Sensitive gerontologists such as Philibert, Van Tassel, Erikson, and Freeman introduced a new thread into the history of gerontology by their work as humanistic scholars. Hendricks, Achenbaum, Cole, Moody, McKee, and others followed suit.

This book makes no pretense of presenting a comprehensive view of the portrayal of aging in literature. It hopes to complement other similar works such as Joseph T. Freeman's *Aging, Its History and Literature;* S. F. Spicker, K. M. Woodward, and D. D. Van Tassel's *Aging and the Elderly: Humanistic Perspectives in Gerontology;* Ruth Granetz Lyell's *Middle Age, Old Age: Short Stories, Poems, Plays, and Essays on Aging;* and Laurel Porter's *Aging in Literature.* Amongst the book's regrettable omissions are the rich portrayal of and sayings about old age in the Old Testament, the Indian *Laws of Manu,* and African literature. The objective of this volume is to continue to broaden the resources and objectives of gerontological interdisciplinary research to include the wealth of ideas, concepts, norms, and images found within the humanities, thereby fulfilling its role as contributor to the quality of life of older persons.

As an editor of this volume, I am pleased to pay grateful tribute to my fellow contributors, both in gerontology and literature, who gave so much of their time and expertise to bring this work to its fruition. This volume has been long in gestation, and I wish to give special thanks for their patience and understanding.

I was also lucky to find in my co-editor, Patricia Spencer Soper, the colleague with whom I could share the responsibility of editing this work.

We worked on the principle of the division of labor. The responsibility for the conception and the content of the volume is mine. Patricia Soper's contribution lies in the superb editorial work, the minutiae of checking all manuscripts and footnotes, without which this volume could not have been so consistent in style.

The editors are grateful to the All-Gerontology Center at Syracuse University, directed by Neal S. Bellos, for the financial and technical support provided for this project. Special thanks also go to Rose Tout, administrative secretary to the director, for her invaluable assistance in typing the manuscript and her willingness to aid with corrections and other details. Thanks also to Carey Soper who read and re-read the material. In addition the editors must note a special debt of gratitude to the reference staffs at the Liverpool Public Library and the Bird Library at Syracuse University who searched for data that seemed impossible to locate. Finally, the editors would like to express their appreciation to those at Greenwood Press whose courteous advice and continuing encouragement brought this project to completion: Loomis Mayer, Maureen Melino, Charles Eberline, and Alicia Merritt.

In general, each chapter provides an introductory essay on the broad perspective, followed by representative selections of literary pieces as well as a list of suggestions for further reading. Of particular interest to the reader is the index, which includes thematic entries in addition to the conventional author, title, and subject entries.

P. v. D. B.

REFERENCES

Freeman, J. T. (1979). *Aging, its history and literature*. New York: Humane Sciences Press.

Kehl, D. G. and Hall, G. G. (October 1983). *The study of aging through literature*. Paper presented at the thirty-sixth annual meeting of the Gerontological Society of America in San Francisco.

Lyell, R. G. (1980). *Middle age, old age: short stories, poems, plays, and essays on aging*. New York: Harcourt Brace Jovanovich.

Porter, L. and Porter, I. M. (1984). *Aging in literature*. Troy, MI: International Book Publishers.

Philibert, M. (1985). The phenomenological approach to images of aging. In C. LeFevre and P. LeFevre (Eds.). *Aging and the human spirit: A reader in religion and gerontology*. Chicago: Exploration Press.

Spicker, S. F., K. Woodward, D. Van Tassell. (Eds.). (1978). *Aging and the elderly: Humanistic perspectives in gerontology*. Atlantic Highlands, NJ: Humanities Press.

Perceptions of
Aging
in
Literature

1

Making Sense: Interpreting Historical and Cross-Cultural Literature on Aging

Jon Hendricks and Cynthia A. Leedham

Making sense of cross-cultural and historical literature on aging is a complex process, demanding a certain amount of theoretical sophistication. We need to be aware that we are dealing not with straightforward attempts to describe aging and its impact, but with literature as an art form, a fact that implies a number of considerations with regard to the nature of literature, its purpose and function, and various modes of interpreting literature that are found within traditions of literary criticism. We must bear in mind that while aging is a universal phenomenon, its impact and its meaning are mediated by economic, structural, and cultural factors. Interpretations of cross-cultural literature on aging will be a function not only of the orientation of particular authors of that literature, but also of the implicit or explicit theoretical models employed by the commentators.

Our basic thesis is that while aging may be a universal phenomenon, its process cannot be described without reference to social situational factors. Within the bounds of the physiological, the structural, and the cultural, a variety of individual interpretations and responses are possible. The ways in which aging is dealt with in literature to a certain extent reflect structural factors, to a degree represent cultural and individual reactions, and are in some measure a function of other considerations that we will mention in the course of our analysis.

BASIC ASSUMPTIONS

The Implications of Literary Conventions for Interpreting Literature on Aging

As noted, we are concerned here with literature in the sense of an art form, not scientific writing. We must, therefore, employ appropriate criteria for factuality, truth, objectivity, and meaning. It is essential that we be explicit about the multifaceted nature of literature and bear the following considerations in mind.

The purpose and functions of literature. What were the multiple functions of differing types of literature in the society under consideration? Who was it written for and why? Did authors, audiences, and those who commissioned, published, or marketed the literature see it as serving differing functions? In turn, what constraints might this place on the ways in which age and the aging process are presented? What function does a particular body of literature serve for people of other cultures when they read it?

Genre and style. Creative writers tend to observe more or less flexible conventions with regard to the form of their works and style of writing. Seventeenth-century classical French tragedy, with its insistence upon the unities of time, place, and action, is an extreme example of the limits imposed by genre, but even the stream-of-consciousness novel imposes certain limits by its form. Stylistic constraints are most obvious in poetry, particularly in traditions that make elaborate use of metre and rhyme. All literature, however, tends to draw on a variety of stylistic devices. These may be articulated as part of a philosophy of literature, as in the seventeenth-century French "précieux" insistence on avoiding "vulgar" language (which resulted in the loss to the French language of a vast wealth of terms open to sixteenth-century writers),[1] or the campaign by William Wordsworth and the English Romantics for a return to ordinary language (Wordsworth & Coleridge, 1963). Stylistic devices may arise as a result of the circumstances in which literary forms develop: in the Old French epic, for instance, which arose out of an oral form, descriptions of people's appearance follow a highly stylized configuration, with variations only in the details. This stylization serves the purpose of cuing the narrator's memory. In other cases, the use of style may be more eclectic and less self-conscious.

Genre and style have important implications for the way in which the world is presented. What an author writes may not be an attempt to re-create reality as he or she perceives it for purposes of everyday living, but rather a skillful use of style and genre to evoke a particular intellectual reaction or emotion in the reader. Before one takes comic portrayals of the foibles of the elderly as an indication of ageism, one should remember how often the rashness of youth has also been satirized. One should not, however, err too far in the other direction by considering what is said and the way it is said as simply a matter of technique. Literary conventions and the ways in which they are used may tell us something about what people consider important. In a related field, some art historians have claimed that medieval painters simply did not know how to incorporate perspective into their works. Others have suggested, however, that medieval artists were concerned with bringing out aspects of reality that overrode perspective. The use of tenses in the Old French epic seems haphazard and chaotic to the modern French reader, and some have suggested that their authors simply did not have a good sense of the relationship between tenses and time. A more careful reading, however, reveals that the different tenses are systematically used to convey different groups of immediacy and duration of action. To uncover the intended meanings of a piece of literature, then, takes a careful evaluation of genre and style.

The meaning of meaning. What do we mean when we talk about the meaning of a literary work? This issue has been hotly disputed among literary critics. Some would focus on the intention of the author and the meaning the text had for him or her. Others would claim that once written, the text takes on a life and meaning of its own, which may be discovered by those who explore it. Still others would interpret the text in terms of its meaning within the culture in which it was created. Some would claim that the text has new (and valid) meanings for each succeeding generation and for people of other cultures who read it.

Literature as a Data Base

In using literature as a data base for considering attitudes toward aging, we need to realize that we are dealing with a highly select and specialized data set. As Louis Roberts notes in chapter 2 of this book, the body of literature that is available to us will inevitably be but a small portion of all the literature produced by a culture. In societies in which the vast majority of the population is illiterate, literature will have been written for a select audience. In all cultures, in evaluating the ways in which age is portrayed in literature, we need to bear in mind the social position and age affiliation of author, audience, and subjects. We need to look at the intention of the author as it is expressed through literary convention. This means that in interpreting what an author has to say about age and aging, we need to look at it in the context of the work as a whole, as well as taking account of the tone in which it is said. In Shakespeare's *Hamlet,* Polonius is often cited as a satirical portrayal of a sententious old man. One should remember, however, that in Rosenkrantz and Guildenstern we have an equally satirical portrayal of foppish youth. Furthermore, what literature has to say about old age per se does not constitute all that it has to say about old people. Old age may serve as a symbol rather than as an accurate indicator of attitudes toward old people. One also needs to look at the way in which old people are portrayed as people in literature, as characters in the action who just happen to be old and who are engaged in the flow of events.

Finally, as noted before, we need to be aware that the culture in which we participate, the theoretical models we espouse, and our own perceptions and predilections influence what we read into literature. Depending upon our orientation toward the interpretation of literature, we might say that this means that our interpretations tend to be biased and thus to distort the intentions of the author and/or the intrinsic meaning of the text; or, alternatively, that our perspective offers valuable new insights regarding its meaning. An intermediate position—one that we would tend to favor—would hold that an unreflective interpretation of a foreign literary work in terms of one's own conceptual categories, without any attempt to get at the intentions of the author or the cultural and literary traditions within which he or she is writing, tends to lead to a distorted interpretation. An interpretation may, however, lead to new insights if one makes a conscious effort to be aware of one's own cultural perspectives, conceptual categories, and theoretical models; to understand the author's intentions and the social, cultural, and literary context within which they arose; and then to analyze the meaning of what the author had to say for one's own perspectives. This general hermeneutic approach to textual analysis has found broad application in the social scientists' search for objective meaning (Bernstein, 1976; Bleicher, 1982; Ricoeur, 1971).

The Quest for Objectivity

Georg Simmel once said that "objectivity towards other people often hides the most boundless solipsism" (Simmel, 1950, p. xx). A lack of awareness of our own contextuality can lead us to unreflectively read our own biased interpretations into the lifeworld of others. We cannot attain objectivity by standing on a fixed point outside the world. We can, however, develop an awareness of our own contextuality and that of others that leads in turn to a widening of our horizons. Indeed, this has traditionally been one of the primary functions of literature. By writing about the reader's world in a relatively detached way, authors such as Jane Austen have led the reader to see the world in a different, more critical light. Perhaps, in using literature as a data base for looking at attitudes toward age and aging, we should strive not for objectivity in the sense of seeking "the truth" or "the Greek view of aging" (a vain pursuit, as noted by Roberts), but rather for an enlightened intersubjectivity that enables us to appreciate the richness, complexity, diversity, and ambivalence of attitudes toward aging. In seeking to go beyond our own lifeworlds and our own biases to understand the lifeworlds of others, we will need to bear in mind all of these dimensions if we are to use literary literature as a data base.

Sanchez-Barba (1973; 1978) distinguishes three levels of history: *(a)* "encapsulated history," which refers to the accounts people give of events (for instance, in the press or in talking to each other), *(b)* the "existential ideal," by which he means the official version of events, what people think ought to be happening, something like that which is represented by Goffman's idea of "face work" (Goffman, 1959); and *(c)* "living existence," which refers to events as they happen and the varying potentialities that they contain. For Sanchez-Barba, history contains a certain element of choice in the sense that although one is constrained by circumstances, one may realize varying potentialities within them. In a sense, one might say that certain types of literature (journals, for instance) represent encapsulated history (which tells one at least as much about the people who write it as it does about events). In another sense, some literature may give voice to an existential ideal. Robert Stacy's chapter highlights this aspect of the treatment of aging in Russian literature by authors such as Tolstoy. In some cases, the existential ideal portrayed in literature may represent shared cultural norms, rooted in the sense-making strategies of ordinary people. In other cases, the existential ideal may represent a worldview or ideology indirectly imposed by those in power, who act as gatekeepers to the means of production and dissemination of literature.[2] Above all, literature can make people aware of living existence, of the fact that things can be otherwise and not just so: they are not inevitable (Weber, 1949). In some cases, this is done directly by the presentation of differing interpretations and disparate lifeworlds. In other cases, however, it is done indirectly by satire that makes the reader poignantly aware of what might have been. Analyses of literature from a social structural viewpoint, provided that they are careful to take account of the cultural context, conventions, and intended meanings of literature, are representative of a type of analysis that can provide new perspectives on literature as reflective both of structural constraints and of the potentialities inherent in a situation.

In statistical studies, generalizability implies that the attributes in question may be found in that particular form in a majority of the population at large. It is a matter of identifying widely distributed traits in the interests of large-scale planning. Generalizability in the study of literary lifeworlds might, however, be considered in a somewhat different sense. Rather than looking for the norm, for what is most frequently found, we might look for interpretations and lifeworlds, the principles of which can be understood by people in different situations. Rather than looking to cross-cultural literature on aging for some kind of universal picture of what it means to be old, searching for the lowest common denominator, we should expect to find a series of sketches of what aging means for a variety of particular people in diverse situations and cultures and thus come away with our perception of the potential meanings of aging enriched.

Sociocultural Factors and Cross-cultural Literature on Aging

Aging as a Universal, Yet Culturally Specific Phenomenon. According to the anthropologists, age is a universal criterion employed in every known society to differentiate and rank persons. That is, while age is a biological fact of life, it is never merely that. It is also a cultural attribute that colors social definitions of people and things they do. Silverman and Maxwell (1982) note that three age levels—childhood, adulthood, and old age—are inevitably, though not invariably, found in all human societies. Obviously, the criteria employed to discriminate among and distribute roles will change as the broad parameters of the context change.[3] As far as being old and being granted respect are concerned, each is a reflection of societal values in general and the underpinnings of the prestige hierachy in particular. In short, old age, esteemed or denigrated, is socially produced. Rich and poor, scholar, laborer, merchant, or businessman, sick and healthy—each will find a different old age depending on his or her relative position vis-à-vis dominant value frameworks; and according to their own particular orientations and life histories, individuals may develop their own style in interpreting and living out the relative positions in which they find themselves, with all their liabilities and assets.

In making sense of the status accorded the elderly in various contemporary cultural contexts, it is crucial to remember that present-day preindustrial societies may not bear a great deal of resemblance to their historical counterparts. While each may be said to be moving toward industrial or postindustrial social systems—although even that is disputed by some—the fact that the latter already exist and exert influence over the former may make all the difference in the world.

By looking at the meaning of age through an analysis of a society's literature, it is possible to distinguish general motifs from those specific to particular subcultures. The intertwining of the two manifests itself through a series of achieved statuses that reveal a broad pattern as well as variations on that theme. Regardless of how diversified the criteria for membership in status groups may be, they not only determine the broad contours of people's lives but also imply what is held up as valuable within that culture. A reflective use of literature as a mirror to divine these patterns provides a valuable and potentially insightful method of analysis.

Despite the heterogeneity and the cultural relativism, just what can be said? What common threads characterize the human condition over the life course? What impact do scientific method, as a worldview, and industrial capitalism, as a mode of production, have on the allocation of age-appropriate roles for older persons? Do these latter two dimensions infuse old age with qualities not present prior to their development?

In puzzling out the social history of old age, cross-cultural research has pointed to the importance of personal resource inventories in determining status accorded. Regardless of the stage of societal development, cross-cutting themes emphasize the importance of resource control as a means of insuring access to opportunity and, in turn, prestige. In a word, where older persons exercise control over valued land, information, goods, and services, we tend to find an ideology that maintains that they are worthy of respect. Filial piety is a sterling concept, but one that is nearly always undergirded by an ironclad control over whatever younger people aspire to. Principles of veneration are likely to result from the leverages older people have to ply and therefore often mask what closer scrutiny suggests may have been an outright power relationship (Stearns, 1982), though we should not automatically assume that this was always based on purely material or economic considerations.

Seemingly, an ideology of respect is most pronounced among societies that are isolated or insulated from external influences. In these groups, tradition reigns strongest. Older people, having the greatest experience with tradition, are therefore active and sought-after experts. Whether they are the proprietors of oral information or own the land or the machinery of production, they are the gatekeepers (Silverman & Maxwell, 1982). In these situations, it is not surprising that an ideology of respect—along with satire and other forms of reaction to their power and the abuse of it—is contained in the literary record.

In terms of interaction, so long as the benefits to be gained are greater than the disadvantages that might accrue from a lack of respect, younger persons are likely to remain deferential. If the influence older people are able to wield is debased for whatever reason, a realignment of behavior and values is likely to occur. It must be stressed, however, that the normative values regarding the elderly derive from structural characteristics, mediated by varying cultural interpretations, and are not merely a consequence of individual attributes. Similarly, it must be borne in mind that there is not an exact congruence between structure and values. Change may occur in one while the other may lag, only to undergo transformation somewhat later; and the interaction between them is mediated by cultural interpretations of the meaning and significance of life.

Viewing Aging in Cross-cultural Perspective. In approaching analyses of cross-cultural differences in aging, we should also be aware of the conceptual orientations of the analysts, which may either illuminate or unduly simplify the issue. Whether implicitly or explicitly, commentators addressing aging in literature carry with them an orienting model that prompts them to highlight certain dimensions while underplaying others. Social scientists' perspectives on societal stages and the relative role accorded the elderly may lead the literary analyst to look longingly at a bygone era as a case of what might have been. Alternatively, visions of the past may be debunked: the theorist may consider it high time to put to rest the myths regarding a world that never existed. Finally, the world of the elderly may be seen as an ambiguous place, one in which their well-being is relative to property rights, production processes, forms of inheritance, and cultural norms left over from a particular past.

Like literary analysis of the situation of children prior to Rousseau, analyses of the role of the elderly in preindustrial or contemporary nonindustrial societies have followed the developing orientations of social historians. Only recently has consensus finally emerged regarding the pitfalls of reification and generic categorization (Stearns, 1982). What has become clear in the last decade is the variability of the mechanisms utilized in various contexts to buttress or undermine the status of those considered to be old. The historians Laslett (1976) and Stearns (1982) both caution that cross-cultural or historical investigations into the status of old people make an error if they only look for what may have caused either a fall from grace or an enhancement of the position of a group's elderly. Sources of power, control, and status maintenance must be identified before and after any perceived change. If the elderly had scant power to wield in the first place, it makes little sense to point a finger at the process of modernization as undercutting those of advancing years. To the extent that our literary analyses do suggest a decline in status for old people, caution must be exercised to see if that elevated status was extended to all members of the older age categories or only to those not shackled by poverty, ill health, or a fragmented worldview. However grim the age-old questions of old age may seem, as a rule, only the favored classes manage to make it into the literary record.

The Relevance of Structural Factors to Literary Analysis. The distribution of power and wealth indeed exerts a powerful influence on the lives of the elderly through access to nutrition and health care, to personal control over their lives, and to other opportunities. In cases where the literary portrayal of aging is done for symbolic or other purposes, structural factors may have no immediate import for the way in which it is depicted. In other instances, however, they may be relevant to the characterization of aging in two ways: (1) they may be indirectly reflected through their impact on the lifeworlds of characters and authors; and (2) literature may bring to life a variety of ways of interpreting and reacting to essentially similar structural conditions.

In seeking a paradigm for analysis of the impact of structural factors on the portrayal of aging, we would warn against rigid and exclusive adoption of one template, since any theoretical model is at best partial in its orientation and prone to distort reality, if relied upon too heavily. Such was the case with sweeping applications of modernization theory (Parsons,

1964), which held that "the status of the aged . . . is inversely proportional to the degree of modernization of the society" (Cowgill, 1972, 1979) and led to a pervasive and recently critiqued nostalgia for the "world we have lost" (Laslett, 1965; see also Achenbaum, 1978; Achenbaum & Stearns, 1978; Cohn, 1982; Hendricks, 1982; Quadagno, 1982; Stearns, 1976; Stout, 1975).

We would, however, suggest that perspectives arising from dependency theory, if applied with due regard for the specific historical dynamics of the situation, may yield new insights, while allowing one to remain open to the richness and diversity of reality. Grounded in an adapted version of the worldsystems approach (Langholm, 1971; Wallerstein, 1973), dependency theory holds that certain particular locales—because of geographic, economic, or political advantage—serve as a core or central place from which innovations emerge. Beyond these centers lies a periphery region, less advantaged, and perhaps set apart by distinct language, government, agricultural production, religion, and related social patterns. In the course of economic development, a symbiotic relationship develops between core and periphery, based on the exchange of raw materials or markets for finished products. This relationship is, however, structured to the advantage of the core, with cash crops replacing subsistence agriculture, and the growth in production of material goods concentrated on those produced, designed, and destined for the core (Hechter, 1975; Hoogvelt, 1977; Portes, 1976). Disadvantages for the elderly, arising in the course of industrialization, are thus seen as stemming from interest-group politics and deliberate structural arrangements brought about by those who control new components of industrial production (Dowd, 1980; Myles, 1980; Neysmith & Edward, 1984; Tigges & Cowgill, 1981). They may thus redound to the detriment of the elderly in the periphery, but not necessarily of those in the core. Similarly, dual economic theory (Bluestone, Murphy, & Stevenson, 1983; Calasanti, 1988; Gordon, 1972; Hendricks & McCallister, 1983) examines the ways in which the life chances of people as they age differ according to the work-life position of individuals in the core of peripheral industries of the economy. Attention to the structural location of the aged in these terms will make for a much more differentiated picture of the portrayal of aging in literature.

While the self-image of the elderly and images of aging are powerfully influenced by structural factors, it is also important to bear in mind that these influences are mediated by culture. In societies that place primacy on youth, beauty, sensual pleasures, and a life of productive activity, age will be devalued, making it difficult for the elderly to have a positive self-image. Where, on the contrary, experience, wisdom, and human understanding are valued, the elderly will tend to be seen in a more positive light. Images of aging thus result from a complex interplay of structural and cultural factors. Furthermore, within the constraints imposed by

structure and culture, there are varying potentialities and room for individual creativity in dealing with the contingencies of life. Purely sociological analyses may cast light on structural factors and their dynamic influence on people's lives. Perhaps part of what literature has to offer,
particularly literature drawn from a variety of traditions and cultures, is to
make us aware that structural factors are precisely something to which we
can react in a variety of ways, rather than allowing ourselves to be pas-
sively shaped by them. In some cases, this may be by presenting particular
ways of interpreting and dealing with opportunities and problems implicit
in aging in a social context, drawing on cultural perspectives and/or individual creativity. In other cases, it may be through satire or through sympathetic portrayals of the lifeworld of the disadvantaged elderly that alert
us to social policy issues.

INTERPRETING THE ARRAY OF CROSS-CULTURAL
LITERATURE ON AGING

The selections included in this volume cover a wide time span, from
ancient China, Greece, and Rome to the twentieth century; a plethora of
geographical and political units, including the Far East, the Middle East,
Europe, and the Americas; a variety of cultural contexts, from Uruguayan
pampas to the highly industrialized societies of Europe and the United
States and from the intellectual seriousness of the German Enlightenment
to the frivolity of the Japanese court; and a range of social classes, from
the *demi-monde* inhabited by François Villon to the Chinese elite portrayed
in Ts'ao Hsüeh-ch'in's *Dream of the Red Chamber*. They thus express a rich
variety of themes, which vary with the social position of authors and subjects, cultural and subcultural values, the historical context, and the type
of literature in which they are expressed. In this section, we will illustrate
ways in which the perspectives offered in this introductory chapter may
be used in making sense of this diversity.

Literature on Aging as Reflective of Structural Factors

Some of the selections in this volume are illustrative of differing perspectives on aging in periphery and core. François Villon was a kind of
vagabond who lived on the fringes of fifteenth-century courtly society.
Often in trouble with the law, he was sentenced to death at the age of
thirty, though this was later transmuted to ten years' exile from Paris. He
had a wry sense of humor, and his writings are expressive of the sentiments of people who live on the periphery of society. His *belle heaulmière*,
once the mistress of Nicolas d'Orgemont, the archdeacon of Paris, was a
courtesan whose fortunes in youth depended upon trading her charms to
men of position (Villon, 1961, p. 59). Her physical beauty gone, what was

left to her? At one level, her lament might be taken as expressive of the plight of women who, without resources in their own right, are treated as sexual objects, then discarded. How different she is from Brecht's old women, who, with resources and creative talents of their own, are engaged in activities and social networks, and who savor life to the last crumb—or from the Matriarch who rules over the household in Ts'ao Hsüeh-ch'in's *Dream of the Red Chamber*. Sanchez's *Down the Gully* represents the plight of the elderly who are dispossessed in a modernizing Uruguayan society. His hero, Don Zoila, sees his world destroyed by the onrush of modern society bringing new ideas to the pampas and new ideologies to his children. In this proud old gaucho, who throughout his life has fought against the imposition of rules and regulations by the central authority in Buenos Aires, may be seen a tragic example of the results of the encroachment of the interests and ideas of the core on the periphery. His drama is one of a number of readings that illustrate the tensions between adult children and their parents in rapidly changing societies. The sergeant's outcry, "When a man goes broke, folks don't bother with surnames," may be taken as symbolic of the plight of those who are dispossessed through social change (Lichtblau, chapter 7). Mahfuz's "An Old Photograph" in the chapter on Arabic literature traces the different ways in which a group of people in an old school photograph have aged. Through the stories of these individuals, Mahfuz shows us the lifestyles of people who have a variety of relationships to periphery and core, as well as participating in a variety of cultural value systems. A close reading of the Mahfuz selection provides a ready example of the vagaries of the process of aging in the social worlds of those who are both central to and on the fringe of a developing society.

Cultural Mediation of the Approach to Aging

The character of the varying cultural systems in which author and subjects participate comes out as one of the factors that profoundly influence the attitudes toward aging expressed in this volume. In the writings of German authors such as Schopenhauer, Stifter, and Hesse, we have examples of a culture that places primacy on wisdom and insight and views old age as a time when one is freed from the passions of youth and gains a maturity that enables one to see life more objectively. In Goethe, for example, who asserts that immortality of the soul is accorded only to those who remain active into old age, and Brecht, who, as Schneider (chapter 5) notes, renders two of the most life-affirming portraits of old women in literature, we find a belief that the old should remain engaged in the creative activities of life. In contrast, Sei Shōnagon's *Pillow Book* is expressive of a subculture that values youth and elegance and scorns the elderly who put creature comforts before the rules of court etiquette. In the Japanese

Tale of Genji, we find a contrasting ideal of disengagement: the Buddhist ideal of nonattachment that views the achievement of longevity as an indication that one is too attached to the things of this world. Skord (chapter 9) notes that the narrator intimates that the old should keep to themselves and fade away as quickly and quietly as possible.

Aging and the Lifeworld of the Individual

Some of the selections exemplify the relevance of personal attributes and perspectives for operating within structural constraints. Again, Mahfuz's "An Old Photograph" is an interesting illustration, since the varying fates of his characters depend not only on structural factors, but on the ways in which they have negotiated the system. Brecht's spirited "unseemly old woman" exemplifies a refreshingly different response to the possibilities open to her. She represents those elderly persons who actively manage their world by whatever means are available and have the courage to make a new beginning at the "end" of their lives. Herman Hesse sees being old as "just as beautiful and holy a task as being young" and holds that old people, like the young, have a part to play that gives meaning to their lives. His Siddhartha finally attains inner harmony and peace in old age through the belief that love provides the underlying unity for all things.

Cross-cultural Literature on Aging as Literature

Clearly the selections in this volume are taken from a variety of literary traditions and genres. It is vital, therefore, to consider statements regarding aging in the context of the works of which they form a part and in light of the literary conventions and the tone in which they are expressed. Roberts, for instance, notes the importance of taking account of literary conventions in interpreting Greek and Roman literature on aging, citing the caricatures of old age in Greek Old Comedy as an example of this. While we would agree with Fallis (chapter 3) that T. S. Eliot had a sharp sense of the bleakness of old age, we would also note that it is important to remember that Eliot was preoccupied with mystical experience, and even though for him, old age was only bleak, he had hope for redemption (Eliot, 1962).

In looking at the broader context of his work, we see that Eliot was not so much concerned with the bleakness of age per se as with the need for redemption. Julia, in *The Cocktail Party,* is portrayed at the beginning of the play as a rather foolish old woman. As the action progresses, however, we come to see her as a capable person, à la Eric Erikson, of great spiritual insight who, with the other Guardians, deftly guides the characters toward a confrontation with the major conflicts and issues in their lives (Eliot, 1972).

Regarding tone, we would agree that the portrayal of the elderly by the naturalistic French novelists of the nineteenth century was grim, but we would also suggest the possibility that they were written precisely in such a tone as to arouse an indignant reaction against a social system that created such suffering. A more complete evaluation of the role of the elderly in cross-cultural literature, which would go beyond the scope of this volume, would require that we look more closely at old people as people in literature: do we find people in positions of power, or engaged in the action in other ways, who, while they are not used as symbols of old age, just happen to be old?

Setting Cross-cultural Literature on Aging in Context

In order to exhaustively evaluate the treatment of aging and the elderly in literature, one should set the exercise in context not only of the work and literature within which it appears, but of the circumstances of its creation and of the culture and society where it was generated. This involves answering a number of the questions raised at the beginning of this chapter with regard to the varying functions and meanings of literature for authors, publishers, and audiences, the shared assumptions on which the lifeworlds portrayed in literature rest, and the ways in which these mesh with the overall value and meaning systems and systems of production and consumption prevalent in the society under study. Since cross-cultural literature on aging is extensive and diverse, it is obviously beyond the scope of a chapter of this type to tackle such an undertaking, and many of these questions will have to go unanswered here. Readers will find hints at answers to some questions as they peruse the contents of this book. It is hoped that these glimpses will stimulate further investigation of both the literature and the culture.

Can we then offer no conclusions about the contents of this volume? If, by conclusions, one means a few pat statements that pretend to summarize so rich a variety of literary experience, then the answer is no. We would rather invite the reader to adopt the perspectives developed in this introduction and use them to explore for himself or herself the many and varied responses found in the selections to the contingencies of aging and to its social and cultural context: the physical disabilities that hamper some elderly; relations between the elderly and their adult children; love and sexuality; the economic and political context of aging; social change and conflict or continuity between generations; and engagement or disengagement in the life of society, to mention but a few. It is hoped that in exploring these responses, the reader may gain a deeper understanding of the lifeworlds of others, an increased self-reflectiveness leading to a sharpened sensitivity for both the structural and cultural constraints on the lifeworlds of the elderly and the varying possibilities for response and action within and against those constraints. One of the fears expressed by the critics of mass culture is that the stereotyped formulae of the mass media will preempt the vivid presentation of alternative lifeworlds. It is important that we ask whether this is indeed happening, and if so, what can be done to encourage alternative forms of literature. Reading literature is one of the ways in which we may become conscious of the structural forms and cultural assumptions implicit in our lives, begin to question them, and enter into the lifeworlds of others.

In this spirit the reader should regard this volume not as any kind of definitive statement, but as an invitation to reflection and to a continuing exploration of the contexts of others' lives. Skord indicates that aging necessarily involves ambivalence, both personally and socially, offering all the possibility and contradictions of life itself. We invite the reader to explore that possibility and those contradictions, to try to gain an inkling of others' lifeworlds from the inside, and thus to develop new horizons.

NOTES

1. See Molière's *Les précieuses ridicules* (1956) for a parody of the "précieux" approach to language and literature.

2. See Horkheimer and Adorno's "The Culture Industry" for an analysis of literature in this tradition.

3. See, for example, Philipe Aries's *Centuries of Childhood* (1962) for a discussion of the historical development of the meaning of childhood in Western European societies.

REFERENCES

Achenbaum, W. A. (1978). *Old age in the new land.* Baltimore: Johns Hopkins University Press.

Achenbaum, W. A., and Stearns, P. N. (1978). Essay: Old age and modernization. *Gerontologist 18,* 307–312.

Aries, P. (1962). *Centuries of childhood: A social history of family life* (R. Baldick, Trans.). New York: Knopf.

Bernstein, P. (1976). *The restructuring of social and political theory.* Oxford: Blackwell.

Bleicher, J. (1982). *The hermeneutic imagination: outline of a positive critique of scientism and sociology.* Boston: Melbourne & Henley.

Bluestone, B., Murphy, W. M., & Stevenson, M. (1973). *Low wages and the working poor.* Ann Arbor: University of Michigan, Institute of Labor and Industrial Relations.

Calasanti, T. (1988). Participation in a dual economy and adjustment to retirement. *International Journal of Aging and Human Development, 26*(1), 15–29.

Cohn, R. M. (1982). Economic development and status change of the aged. *American Journal of Sociology, 87,* 1150–1161.

Cowgill, D. O. (1972). A theory of aging in cross-cultural perspective. In D. O.

Cowgill & L. D. Holmes (Eds.), *Aging and modernization* (pp. 1–13). New York: Appleton-Century-Crofts.

Cowgill, D. O. (1979). Aging and modernization: A revision of the theory. In J. Hendricks & C. D. Hendricks (Eds.), *Dimensions of aging* (pp. 54–67). Cambridge, MA: Winthrop.

Dowd, J. (1980). *Stratification among the aged.* Monterey, CA: Brooks/Cole.

Eliot, T. S. (1962) Little Gidding. In *The complete poems and plays* (p. 141). New York: Harcourt, Brace.

Eliot, T. S. (1974). *The cocktail party* (Nevill Coghill, Ed.). London: Faber & Faber.

Goffman, E. (1959). *The presentation of self in everyday life.* Garden City, NY: Doubleday.

Gordon, D. M. (1972, Winter). From steam whistles to coffee breaks. *Dissent,* pp. 197–210.

Hechter, M. (1975). *Internal colonialism: The Celtic fringe in British national development, 1536–1966.* Berkeley: University of California Press.

Hendricks, J. (1982). The elderly in society: Beyond modernization. *Social science history, 6*(3), 321–345.

Hendricks, J., & McAllister, C. E. (1983). An alternative perspective on retirement: A dual economic approach. *Ageing and society, 3*(3), 279–299.

Hoogvelt, A. M. M. (1977). *The sociology of developing societies.* Atlantic Highlands, NJ: Humanities Press.

Horkheimer, M., & Adorno, T. W. (1972). *Dialectic of enlightenment.* New York: Herder & Herder.

Langholm, S. (1971). On the concepts of center and periphery. *Journal of Peace Research, 8*(3), 273–278.

Laslett, P. (1976). Societal development and aging. In R. H. Binstock & E. Shanas (Eds.), *Handbook of aging and the social sciences* (pp. 87–116). New York: Van Nostrand.

Molière. (1956). *Les précieuses ridicules.* In *Oeuvres complètes* (Vol. 1, pp. 219–244). Paris: Gallimard.

Myles, J. (1980). The aged, the state, and the structure of inequality. In J. Harp & J. Hofley (Eds.), *Structural inequality in Canada* (pp. 317–342). Englewood Cliffs, NJ: Prentice-Hall.

Neysmith, S. M., & Edwardh, J. (1984). Economic dependency in the 1980's: Its impact on third world elderly. *Ageing and Society, 4*(1), 21–44.

Parsons, T. (1964). Evolutionary universals. *American Sociological Review, 29,* 339–357.

Portes, A. (1976). On the sociology of national development: Theories and issues. *American Journal of Sociology, 82*(2), 55–85.

Quadagno, J. (1982). *Aging in early industrial society.* New York: Academic Press.

Ricoeur, P. (1971). The model of the text: meaningful action considered as a text. *Social Research, 38*(3), 529–562.

Sanchez-Barba, H. M. (1973). *Dialectica contemporanea de Hispano-America.* Madrid: Ediciones Jose Porrua Turanzas.

Sanchez-Barba, H. M. (1978). *Historia y literatura en Hispanoamerica (1492–1820).* Madrid: Editorial Castalia.

Silverman, P., & Maxwell, R. J. (1982). Cross-cultural variation in the status of old people. In P. N. Stearns (Ed.), *Old age in preindustrial society* (pp. 49–69). New York: Holmes & Meier.

Simmel, G. (1950). *The sociology of Georg Simmel.* (K. H. Wolff, Ed. and Trans.), Glencoe, IL: Free Press.

Stearns, P. N. (1976). *Old age in European society: The case of France.* New York: Holmes & Meier.

Stearns, P. N. (1982). *Old age in preindustrial society.* New York: Holmes & Meier.

Stout, H. S. (1975). Culture, structure, and the "new" history: A critique and an agenda. *Computers and the Humanities, 9,* 213–230.

Tigges, L., & Cowgill, D. O. (1981). *Aging from the world system perspective: An alternative to modernization theory.* Paper presented at the meeting of the Gerontological Society of America, Toronto, Ontario, Canada.

Villon, F. (1961). *Oeuvres* (A. Longnon, Ed.). Paris: Librairie Honore Champion.

Wallerstein, I. (1973). The rise and future demise of the world capitalist system: concepts for comparative analysis. *Comparative Studies in Society and History, 15,* 199–226.

Weber, M. (1949). Critical studies in the logic of the cultural sciences. In E. A. Shils & H. A. Finch (Eds. and Trans.), *Max Weber on the Methodology of the Social Sciences* (pp. 113–118). New York: Free Press.

Wordsworth, W., & Coleridge, S. T. (1963). *Lyrical Ballads.* New York: Barnes & Noble.

2

Portrayal of the Elderly in Classical Greek and Roman Literature

Louis Roberts

A remarkable aspect of the Hellenic cultural achievement was the ability of the Greeks to perpetuate the artistic and intellectual concepts that they had evolved. Despite the Greeks' notorious condescension toward the "barbarians," they managed to transmit their own vision of beauty and truth, including attitudes on old age, among these alien peoples. They ensnared an individual, Alexander, and an empire, Rome. Through Alexander they managed to influence the world of the Middle East and Byzantium; through Rome this vision captured modern man as well. We pay the Romans their tithe by speaking of the "Greek and Latin classics" as if they were somewhat identical, which they are not.

A brief chapter on any subject that stretches over a thousand years in antiquity cannot hope to present more than an outline of how the men and women of Greek and Rome viewed old age. Even in the two most productive literary classical periods, there were major differences in the way old age was viewed in each particular Greek *polis* and Italian municipality. Beyond the particularly Greek or Roman perceptions of aging, attitudes varied from family to family and from person to person. Hence this arrangement of material is intended merely to suggest some possible ways in which selected Greek and Roman authors thought about old age.

GREECE: LITERARY AGING

Plato in the *Timaeus* (1969) records an anecdote to the effect that Solon once went to Egypt and fell into conversation with an aged priest, who said, "O Solon, Solon, you Greeks are always youths; no Greek man is ever old." The Egyptian priest was projecting the popular notion that the

Early Hellenic world admired and respected only that which was aesthetically pleasing. What was ugly, including the physical aspects of old age, the Greeks ignored. The literature, however, does not reflect this view, even though the physical aspects of aging for some Greeks were gruesome. Nestor in the *Iliad* (Homer, 1902) can no longer participate in boxing and wrestling matches, because "grievous old age" weighs him down. Alcman, in a poetic fragment, laments that age has made him weak and incapable of joining in with the whirling round dances of the choruses and with the dancing of the maidens:

> Maidens whose honied voice is so loud and clear,
> my limbs can no longer carry me. Would, Oh would God
> I were but a lark, such as flies fearless of heart with the
> halcyons over the bloom of the wave, the Spring's
> own bird, purple as the sea.
>
> (Alcman, 1867)

Another Greek, Mimnermus, wishes to live no longer than sixty years, and those years he wishes to be free from worry and illness. He complains about his "painful and ugly old age," all the while "longing for precious youth" (Mimnermus, 1866). Anacreon complains about what he sees in the mirror: his withered locks, hoary temples, decaying teeth, and the near touch of death (Alcman, 1867).

Later in Greek literature, Pindar, the most famous of the choral poets, finds in old age just the reverse of Mimnermus's view. For Pindar, old age brings a period of calm satisfaction stemming from the knowledge that the gods have granted glory and a goodly store of wealth; he notes the belief that one's descendants continue to win favor and that this too can give strength to combat the aging process. Even so, in *Nemean IX,* we find a hint of mortal weakness:

> If anyone having wealth and excelling others
> in beauty of form show strength by his athletic
> prowess, let him remember that the limbs he
> engorges are mortal and that in the end he
> will put on dust.
>
> (Pindar, 1930)

The dramatic poets represented a variety of attitudes toward old age both by presenting the aged on stage and by commenting on old age. They also testify to the problem of generalizing about old age in classical literature. Only a tiny fraction of that literature has come down to us. The names of some 150 Greek authors of tragedy are known, but apart from odd scraps quoted by later authors and anthologists, the plays of only three tragedians from fifth century B.C. Athens are extant. Aeschylus wrote 82 plays, of which 7 still exist; Sophocles reportedly wrote 123 plays, of which we have 7; Euripides wrote 92, of which we can read 18 or 19. Presumably, what we have is a selection of the best—or at least a cross section.

The chorus of Aeschylus's *Agamemnon* is composed of Argive elders who are no longer able to go to war. Their aged frames are supported on their triple feet because they have "strength like that of a child."

The old men receive a tongue-lashing:

> Old as you are, you shall learn how bitter it is
> for one so old to be taught when prudence is the lesson
> to be learned. Prison and hunger pains are the
> best teachers of wisdom even for the old.
>
> (Aeschylus, 1972a)

On the other hand, even the gods have respect for their elders. Athena in Aeschylus's *Eumenides* (1972b) addresses the chorus of old dames and says that she will endure the elders' anger simply because they are old. In Aeschylus's *Persians* (1972c), members of the chorus tear out the white hair of their aged heads in anguish. Clearly, old age for the Greeks was a life stage of mixed blessing, creating ambivalence in the aged and the young.

The picture of decaying old age is nowhere presented in Greek dramatic literature with greater concern than in Sophocles' portrait of the aged Oedipus (1975b). The former great king, weakened by lack of strength, exiled, and blind, drags out a powerless, friendless, desperate existence, miserably clothed, and carrying a thin purse to resist the pangs of hunger. In the *Antigone,* Creon addresses another chorus of elders:

> Cease now, before you fill me up with rage;
> don't talk like an old fool, old though you are.
>
> (Sophocles, 1975a)

And this same aged chorus sings:

> Of happiness the summit and crowning part
> is wisdom, and to hold the gods in reverence.
> This is the law: that, beholding the stricken
> heart of pride brought down, we learn only when
> we are old.

Euripides in the *Heraclidae* places the aged Iolaus on the stage. Iolaus refuses to be cheerful because he is weak from the ravages of age.

This shock's too much for me, and everything
is becoming dark. Hurry, children, prop me up:
Let me sit down and cover me with this.
To ignore the oracle would be the end of all
of us; although the choice is sorrowful,
nevertheless, it is the lesser evil of the two.

(Euripides, 1968c)

Earlier this same Iolaus had been advised not to fight with Eurystheus, for it often happens that though one's spirits are young and eager, one's body is old and weak (Euripides, 1968c). Interestingly, in early Greek literature, it is the foot that acts as the first, and later most intense, harbinger that old age has made its appearance. In the *Ion,* the old teacher summons his aged foot to be active, urging:

Old foot, come now, assume a youthful strength
for effort, though the years deny it to you.

(Euripides, 1968d)

In Euripides' *Phoenissae* (1968e), Jocasta, as an extremely old woman, trembling with age, drags her steps inside the house, where she talks about her despairing old husband to her son. Elsewhere in the play, Euripides has the characters talk of Oedipus's strength as that of a dream, and Creon asks his son, Menoeceus, to guide the failing steps of the old seer Teiresias, for an old man, whenever he travels, requires help from others. Another father, Pheres, advances to Admetus's house "on aged foot" (Euripides, 1968a). In Euripides' (1968b) *Hecuba,* the old woman soliloquizes to her tired feet, later lamenting her condition, childless, without a *polis,* destitute; fallen from her royal position.

Conversely, we have other images that show the aged as persevering, almost spry. In the *Anthologia Graeca,* edited by Stadtmueller in 1906, is recorded the remarkable case of an old man who went to Hades without a staff to support him. Callicrates mentions an old woman of 105 years whose steps never required resting on a staff (Theognis, 1971).

As today, poverty is frequently given as the accompaniment of old age. Theognis names poverty and hoary old age as the two great evils of men:

Fever and grey old age downed good men:
But, Kurnos, nothing masters a gentleman
more damnably than Poverty.

(Theognis, 1971)

Quite as important as social conditions in understanding the portrayal of the elderly are the literary conditions that furthered the development of conventions and shaped the poet's attitudes and interests. Old Comedy, for example, particularly the work of Aristophanes, often presents a caricature of old age. The chorus of his *Lysistrata* consists of twelve old men and twelve old women; that of the *Plutus,* of old country people; and that of the *Knights,* of old dotards, easily deceived. The chorus of the *Acharnians* signs of the weight of years and arthritic joints; the chorus of *Birds,* possessing the power of prophecy associated with old age, propounds counsels for feeble mortals. Individuals too provide caricature: Chremylus and Blepsidemus are two old "partners in nonsense and folly." Strepsiades in the *Clouds* has a bad memory, is dull of comprehension, and is too old to learn the subtleties of philosophical argument.

We are all disappointed when we read Greek lyric poetry, not because the poetry is unimpressive—it is supremely beautiful, even in its powerful evocations of the problems of old age—but because it exists for us only in shreds and tatters. The corpus of Greek lyric, meagerly augmented from time to time by the sands of Egypt, survives in ruins, but such fragments as the following from Simonides sadly convey a sense of the end of life:

> For all things reach at last
> one sickening void,
> our shining virtues and shining wealth.
>
> (Simonides, 1975)

This sense of the end of life imbued every facet of classical antiquity, but a fragment of Sophocles (1917) reads, "Old age teaches all things along with the wearing of time," introducing a more hopeful theme common in Greek prose authors.

Thucydides (1966) reports that the Athenian embassy begged the Lacedaemonian assembly to take time to deliberate, reminding the elders of their superior knowledge and informing the young of what lay beyond their experience. Certain qualities, such as prudence, discretion, and mature judgment and thought, are natural inheritances of old age. The opening scene of Plato's *Republic* (1969c) gives an ideal picture of a man who can enjoy, even revel in the delights of his old age. Dionysius of Halicarnassus (1889) argues that the perfect grasp of all things in all their relationships belongs to a matured understanding of an age disciplined by gray hairs. Plato, in *Laws* (1969a), presents the Athenian stranger who did not understand the nature of the universe as a young man, but once he is older he can explain it in a short time. Similarly, Socrates suggests that Protagoras should know more because he is older (Plato, 1969b). Plato (1969a) gives Nestor, the paradigm of the wise old man, the qualities of power and wisdom and temperance, and Quintus of Smyrna (1968) notes that Nestor did not mourn over Antilochus's corpse because the wise man's soul endures bravely.

Greek culture generally reflected the belief that in matters pertaining to law, older men have better judgment; only those over fifty years of age are called on to address the Assembly first (Aeschines, 1908). But Aristotle (1973) argues that old age of itself does not bring prudence, but must be accompanied by experience. Philo (1929–1962) went so far as to affirm that gray hair that is not accompanied by good judgment is a reproach, and Solon (1979) says that old age itself does not bring wisdom, but one must continue to learn in old age. This same Solon supposedly was asked on what protection he relied during Peisistratus's attempt to establish his tyranny, and Solon replied, "On my old age" (1979).

Some Greeks who were heavily involved in public life lamented other features of the aging process. Xenophon (1979) himself hesitated to live a longer time lest he be forced to pay the penalties of old age—to see and hear less keenly and to fail in intellectual capacities. Demosthenes (1968) chose exile instead of imprisonment, both because the latter would be disgraceful and because on account of his many years he could not endure the bodily pains and privations. Even Homer (1908) had Odysseus weep when he sees his father "worn down by age and with great grief in his mind." Lucian in his *Dialogues of the Dead* (1953) portrays the most cynical view of the troubles of old age and the worse fate that follows. In general, however, the period between the fall of Alexandria (30 B.C.) and the closing of the University of Athens by Justinian (529 A.D., which was also the year of the founding of Monte Cassino), was a period of gradual fossilization, brought on not only because the principles of rhetoric achieved a stranglehold, but also because the world of ideas was gradually changing with the irresistible advance of Christianity and other influences from the East.

ROMAN IMAGES OF AGING

Like Greek literature, Latin literature has come down to us as but a fragment of what was written. Even more than in the case of Greek writings, Latin literature was addressed on the whole to a highly educated audience, generally conversant with Rome, her history and institutions, and Greek ideas and literature. Just as much Greek as Latin literature continued to be written throughout the period of the Roman Empire, both pagan and Christian. In addition, the Roman of Rome itself was one personality; the Roman who was a Spaniard or African or Italian might have been a very different person in temperament and feeling. These cultures did not necessarily share the same attitudes toward old age. Literature manifests different strains deriving from many racial sources, blended in varying degrees, but always fused with something that is peculiarly Latin. To all Romans, however, moral essays were of great appeal. Discourses on such themes as friendship or old age were popular, but, as will be illustrated in the selections by Cicero and Plato in the final portions of this chapter, the ideas and literary forms are borrowed from the Greek.

The best known Latin commentary on old age is Cicero's dialogue, *De senectute* (On Old Age) (1909), a piece that remains relevant and read. The dialogue deserves to be read in its entirety and is readily available in translation, but some sense of its significance may be gleaned from excerpts. Cicero dedicated the work to his friend Atticus, and because it is in the literary form of a dialogue, Cicero then sets the rest of the book in the household of Cato the Elder, where "the words of Cato himself will completely unfold to you my own views on old age" (1909).

Even didactic poetry contained reflections on old age. Lucretius fears that creeping old age will loosen his hold on life before he can explain his theme fully (Lucretius, 1953). In a story by Seneca (1942) about how he failed to recognize his old playmate, he clearly illustrates the callous attitude of antiquity to old age generally, and servants or slaves in particular, especially in the immediate tour of inspection of an estate by a master not seen for a long time. Pliny (1963), in his *Epistlae,* reflects a somewhat less callous attitude in his concern for his old nurse.

Fragmented as it may be, the writing of antiquity provides a rich diversity of perceptions of old age. In one of his plays, Laberius (1897) shows us an old man standing before Julius Caesar, defending himself capably. In his ironic, erotic swan song, the poet Horace (1919) promises to attain "the dimension of stillness" appropriate to a serene old age in his *Odes and Epodes.* Juvenal (1979), the satirist, wrote sixteen satires that are among the most powerful examples we have of this Roman genre; in the tenth, "On the Vanity of Human Wishes," he paints a sordid portrait of old age. The first great Christian Latin poet, Prudentius (1961–1969), provides the biography of an old man looking back upon his life, while the poet Claudian (1961), sometimes called the last pagan Latin poet, gives yet another picture.

Obviously, further examples of the literary treatment of old age in antiquity could be given, but what I have chosen in this chapter is intended to be representative. A final word of caution is in order. No generalizations about how the elderly are portrayed in classical literature can be accurate. The amount of this literature that survives is itself so small, compared to what once existed, that it provides the strongest admonition against making any broad conclusions. What does emerge, however, is the sense of the importance of the elderly throughout all periods and social strata of ancient society.

SELECTIONS FROM GREEK LITERATURE

Sophocles (496–406 B.C.)
from *Oedipus Coloneus*

Sophocles was one of the three great Athenian tragedians. The vividness with which he portrays his persons and their motives and conflicts reinforces the notion that tragic drama first and foremost represents persons. The chorus sings about the aged king.

> Not to be born surpasses thought and word.
> Next best is to have seen the light of day
> And then to return whence we came.
> Once the light foolishness of youth is past,
> What trouble is beyond the range of man?
> What heavy burden must he not bear?
> Jealousy, faction, quarreling, fighting—
> The bloodiness of war, the grief of war.
> And in the end he comes to a strengthless age,
> Abhorred by all men, alone, without friends,
> Lonely in that complete twilight
> In which he must live with every bitterness.
> This is the case, not just for me,
> But for this blind and ruined old man.
> Consider some desolate northern beach;
> The breaking waves make flow
> This way and that in the storms of winter;
> So it is with him;
> The wild force breaking over him
> From head to foot, and on and on forever;
> Now from the setting of the sun,
> Now from the noonday glow;
> Now from the night and the north.

(Sophocles, 1975b)

Mimnermus (seventh century B.C.)

An early elegiac poet who was well known around 630 B.C., Mimnermus hated old age and death, as is clearly illustrated in this poem.

> O Golden Love, what life, what joy but yours?
>   Come death when you are gone and make an end.
> When gifts and presents are no longer mine,
>   Nor the sweet intimacies of a loved one.
> These are the flowers of youth. But painful old age,
>   The bane of beauty, following swiftly on,

Wearies the heart of man with sad foreboding
  And removes his pleasure in the sin.
Hateful is he to maiden and to boy
  And moulded by the gods to our sorrow.

(Pindar, 1930)

Aristophanes (445–385 B.C.)
from *Birds, Acharnians*

Aristophanes was the greatest poet of the Old Attic Comedy. This selection provides a caricature of old age as the chorus of *Acharnians* sings of the problems of aging.

Alas and woe for my years! Would that
I had back my youth when carrying my load
of coals I kept pace with Phayullus . . .
Now since my joints have stiffened and my shins
are no longer youthful,
And the legs of Lacrateides are weighted and sore with
old age, he has escaped us. But we
shall pursue. He shall not boast that
he escaped from the aged Acharnians, even
though they are truly old.

(Aristophanes, 1904)

Euripides (485–406 B.C.)
from *Hecuba*

Euripides shows us Hecuba appealing to her feet—a common theme—as a portrayal of physical decline in the elderly.

O helplessness of age!
Too old, too weak to stand—
Help me, ye women of Troy.
Give this slave those helping hands
You formerly proffered her
When she reigned as queen of Troy.
Prop me up with your arms
And help these useless
Stumbling legs to walk.

(Euripides, 1968b)

Plato (429–327 B.C.)
from *Republic*

Plato is one of the few Greek authors whose entire known corpus has come down to us. In the *Republic,* he gives a picture of an old man who can enjoy, even delight in, his old age. Socrates says to the aged Cephalus that there is nothing he enjoys more than conversing with old men. "For I consider them as travellers who have gone a journey which I, too, may have to go, and of whom I ought to ask whether the way is flat and easy, or rugged and hard." In this scene, Socrates asks whether life as an old man is harder and what Cephalus thinks about it. The old man replies:

"I will tell you, Socrates, what I think of old age. Men of my age flock together. We are birds of a feather, as the old proverb has it; and at our reunions the constant story of my companions runs, 'I cannot eat; I cannot drink; youth's pleasures, sex, and love are gone. Life is no longer worth living.' Some complain of the slights that they must endure from relatives, and they will tell you over and over again how many evils old age causes. But to me, Socrates, these complainers seem to blame that which is really not the cause. For if old age were at fault, I too as an old man, and every other old man also, would have felt as they do. This is not my own experience nor that of many others whom I have known. I remember well the old poet Sophocles, when in answer to the question, 'How are you when it comes to sex, Sophocles? Can you still make love to a woman?' 'Peace,' he replied, 'most gladly have I escaped from this mad and furious tyrant.' His words have frequently come to my mind since, and they seem as good to me now as when he first uttered them. For a great peace and freedom from these things comes with old age. After the passions relax their grip, then, as Sophocles says, we are freed from the hold not of one mad master only, but of many. As regards both sex and complaints about relatives, there is but one cause, Socrates. It is not old age but men's characters and temperaments; for the man who has a calm and happy disposition will scarcely feel the pressure of age. The man who is of the opposite disposition finds that both youth and old age are equally troublesome." I listened in admiration, and wanting him to go on and expatiate, I said, "Yes, Cephalus, but I rather suspect that people generally are not convinced by your statement. I rather suspect that people generally think old age sits lightly upon your shoulders, not because of your cheerful disposition, but because you are rich. Wealth is known to be a great comforter."

"You are correct," he answered. "They are not convinced. There is something in what they claim; not, however, so much as they think. I might answer them as Themistocles answered the Seriphian who was abusing him and saying that he was famous, not on account of his own merits but because he was an Athenian: 'If you had been a native of my country or I of yours, neither of us would have been famous.' And to those who are not rich and are impatient of old age, the same answer may be given. For to the good poor man old age cannot be a light burden, nor can a bad rich man ever find peace with himself." . . .

"Let me tell you, Socrates, that when a man thinks himself to be near death, fears and cares enter into his mind that he never had before. The tales of a world below and the punishment that is demanded there for what one has done here once constituted something to laugh about. But now he is tormented with the thought that they may be true, either from the weakness of age or because he is now approaching that far place—for these reasons he enjoys a clearer view of such things. Suspicions and alarms crowd quickly upon such a man, and he begins to reflect and ponder what wrongs he has done to others. When he finds that the total of his transgressions is large, he will often like a child start up in his sleep out of fear. He is overwhelmed with dark fears. To the man who is conscious of no sins, sweet hope, as Pindar beautifully says, is the kind nurse of his old age: 'Hope cherishes,' he says, 'the soul of the man who lives in justice and holiness, and is the nurse of his age and the companion of his journey; hope that is mightiest to sway the restless soul of man.' How admirable are his words!" (Plato, 1969c).

from *Laws*

Plato selects the ideal guardians.

The guardian of law shall not hold office longer than twenty years, and shall not be less than fifty years of age when elected; or if he is elected when he is sixty years of age, he shall hold office for ten years only; and upon the same principle, he must not think that he will be allowed to hold such an important position as that of guardian of the laws after he is seventy years of age, should he live so long. (Plato, 1969b)

SELECTIONS FROM ROMAN LITERATURE

Manilius (first century A.D.)
from *Astronomica*

Manilius wrote this didactic poem on astrology under Augustus and Tiberius. Of the man himself we know nothing. Five books of his astrological work survive. The following lines from the opening of the first book show his consciousness of old age.

> Why do we waste a life of worried years
> Tortured by fears and a heavy wish for wealth?
> Old from eternal care, we pursue long life
> But lose it, and without any happy times
> From answered prayer, we play the role of men
> Who will live forever—but we never live.
> . . . All time is marked by order flux.

Our death is fixed at birth;
Our end comes from its source.

(Manilius, 1977)

Decimus Laberius (c. 115–43 B.C.)

A Roman knight, Laberius is represented only by fragments. In the following mime, he appears as himself, a brave old man facing up to Caesar.

To what point have you cast down, almost to his wit's ends,
The man whom neither flattery nor bribery
Could as a young man avail to shove him from his post?
Look how easily an old man falls, and shows—
Struck by the complacent, a submissive, fawning speech!
Not even to an emperor could the gods deny—
Who then would allow one man to contradict him?
I who lived sixty years without blemish,
A Roman Knight who left his ancestral acres,
Now return home a mime. Certainly on this day
I have lived one more day than I should have lived.
Fortune, unbridled in prosperity and in pain,
Were it your pleasure with the lure and praise of learning,
To break the very point of my good name,
Why when I prospered, when my limbs were green and
    callow,
When I could satisfy an audience and such a man,
Did you not bend my liber self and spit on me?
Now you sent me—Where? What have I brought to the stage?
The ornament of beauty, dignity, and body,
Fire of spirit, the music of a pleasing voice?
As twining ivy squeezes the strong heart of the tree,
So senility in time's embrace has destroyed me,
And like a sepulchre I have only a name.

(Laberius, 1897)

Horace (65–8 B.C.)
from *Odes and Epodes*

Horace was born at Venusia in Apulia. This selection from his odes gives the sense of his view toward the years that are beginning to lie heavily upon him.

Wars long suspended, Venus, now
    Again you threaten. Spare me, I pray you, I pray.
I am no longer what I was when good
    Cinara ruled my heart. O wild devotion of
Delightful Cupids, try no more
    To force a man whose will these fifty years have steeled

To assume your delicate yoke—
  Go where the suave young men entreat your expertise. . . .
  Neither woman nor boy can please,
Nor any gaudy hope of love that's mutual,
  Nor sharing wine with my friends,
Nor gladdening my locks with garland of fresh flowers.
  Why then, Ligurinus, why
Do these infrequent fears dishonor my resolve?
  And why should this eloquent voice
Grow stupid in its speech and falter and be dumb?
  Throughout the long night and its dreams,
Now I embrace you, and now after you I speed,
  Swift as you spirit the fields—
Now, O friend, as you glide swift through impalpable waves.

(Horace, 1919)

Lucius Annaeus Seneca (4 B.C.–65 A.D.)
from *Epistolae morales*

Seneca, born in Cordoba, Spain, took his own life at Nero's orders. Here he provides insight into slave labor, an aspect of old age ignored in most literary references.

Wherever I turn, I find indications that I am getting old. I was visiting a suburban estate of mine and complaining about the expense of the dilapidated building. My caretaker told me that this was not the fault of neglect on his part—he was doing everything, but the fact was that the building was old. In fact this house was built under my own supervision—what will happen to me, if stones of the same age as myself are in such a crumbling state? I was upset at what he said and took the next suitable opportunity for an outburst of anger. "These plane-trees are obviously not being looked after," I said. "There are no leaves on them; the branches are all knotted and parched, and the bark is flaking off those squalid trunks. That would not happen if someone was digging round them and giving them water." He swore by my own soul that he was doing whatever possible, that there was no respect in which his efforts were falling short—but they were old. Between ourselves, I planted them myself; I saw their first growth of leaves. I went up to the entrance. "Who," I said, "is that decrepit fellow? How suitable that he should have been moved to the door—he is clearly waiting to move on. Where on earth did you get hold of him? What possessed you to steal a corpse from someone else?" But the fellow said to me, "Don't you recognize me? I am Felicio—you used to give me puppets at the Saturnalia. I am the son of your manager Philositus; I was your playmate when I was little." "The man is absolutely mad," I said. "Now he has turned into a little boy and playmate of mine. It could be true, though—he is as toothless as a child." (Seneca, 1942)

Pliny (62–113 A.D.)
from *Epistolae*

A somewhat less callous attitude is reflected here as the writer gives his old nurse the gift of a little farm.

I thank you for taking over the running of the little farm that I had presented to my old nurse. It was worth 100,000 sesterces when I originally gave it to her; but afterwards the income declined. . . . You must remember that it is not trees and soil with which I have entrusted you (although I have done that, too), but rather with a gift that I have made, and that it is as important to me who gave it as to her who received it that it should be as profitable as possible. (Pliny, 1963)

Cicero (106–43 B.C.)
from *De senectute*

The best known commentary on old age in Roman references is Cicero's dialogues, *De senectute* (On Old Age), a work dedicated to his friend Atticus.

Now, however, I think it good to write something on old age to be dedicated to you. For I would want to ease somewhat our burden of old age, which, if it is not already pressing hard upon us, certainly is fast approaching. . . . For me, writing this book has been so delightful that it has not only erased all the petty annoyances of old age but has also made old age soft and pleasant.

Because the work is in the literary form of a dialogue, Cicero then sets the rest of the narrative in the household of Cato the Elder. Scipio remarks that old age is never burdensome to Cato, to which Cato replies:

You seem to marvel at something scarcely difficult. To those who have not within themselves the means of a virtuous and happy life, every age is a burden. On the other hand, to those who seek all good from themselves, nothing can seem evil that the laws of nature inevitably impose. Old age belongs to this class. . . . No lapse of time could provide solace or make a fool's old age easy.

· · · · ·

I have often heard the complaints of my peers, and according to the old proverb, birds of a feather . . . complaints made also by the ex-consuls Gaius Salinator and Albinus, who were almost my equals in years, in which they were wont to lament, now because they were denied the sensual pleasures without which they thought life not worth living, and now because they were scorned by the people who had formerly paid them court. But it seemed to me that they were not placing the blame where it belonged. For if the evils of which they complained were caused by old age, the same evils would befall me and all other men. But I have been acquainted with many men who were of such a nature that they bore their old age without complaint, who were not unhappy because they had been released from the chains of passion, and who were not scorned by their friends. As regards all such complaints, the blame rests with character, not with age.

. . . . .

Indeed, when I reflect on this topic, I find four reasons why old age appears to be unhappy: first, that it takes us away from active pursuits; second, that it makes the body weaker; third, that it deprives us of almost all physical pleasures; and fourth, that it is not far removed from death. Let us, if you will, examine each of these reasons separately and see how much truth they contain. (Cicero, 1909)

Cicero provides typical answers to each of the four objections. In the course of this argument several quotations from other authors and poets are given.

from *Plocium,* by the comic poet Caecilius

In truth, Old Age, if you did bring no evil
But this one alone, it would be enough for me: that one
By living a long life sees much that he wishes not to see.
The saddest part of old age, to be sure, is this:
Old men feel in their age they are hateful to the young.

Cato continues:

But bear well throughout this entire discussion the thought that the old age I am praising is one that has its foundation well laid in youth. So it follows—as I once said with the approbation of all who heard—that old age is wretched that needs to defend itself with words. Nor can wrinkles and gray hair suddenly seize upon influence; but when the preceding part of life has been well-lived, old age gathers the fruits of influence at the end.

The dialogue concludes:

Moreover, old age is the final act, as it were, in the play of life, from which we should escape when it grows boring and certainly when we have had our fill. Such, my friends, are my views on old age. May you both attain it, and thus be able to prove by experience the truth of what you have heard from me. (Cicero, 1909)

NOTE

Most translations are my own, based on the original Greek or Latin texts. References cite the original versions. It would be cumbersome to list the same works in other English versions, but they are readily available. The complete set of Loeb Classics contains almost all the works referred to in this chapter.

REFERENCES

Aeschines. (1908). *Timarchus*. In *Orationes* (F. Blass, Ed.). Leipzig: Teubner.

Aeschylus. (1972a). *Agamemnon*. In *Septem quae supersunt tragoedias* (D. Page, Ed.). Oxford: Oxford University Press.

Aeschylus. (1972b). *Eumenides*. In *Septem quae supersunt tragoedias* (D. Page, Ed.). Oxford: Oxford University Press.

Aeschylus. (1972c). *Persians*. In *Septem quae supersunt tragoedias* (D. Page, Ed.). Oxford: Oxford University Press.

Alcman. (1867). In *Poetae lyrici Graeci* (W. T. Bergk, Ed.). Berlin: Weidmann.

Anthologia Graeca. (1906). H. Stadtmueller (Ed.). Leipzig: Teubner.

Aristophanes. (1904). *Birds, Acharnians* (Loeb Classics). Oxford: Clarendon Press.

Aristophanes. (1968). *Clouds, Acharnians* (Loeb Classics). Oxford: Clarendon Press.

Aristophanes. (1973). *Ecclesiazusae, Comoediae* (Loeb Classics). Oxford: Clarendon Press.

Aristotle. (1973). *Ethics* (J. Burnet, Ed.). New York: Arno Press.

Cicero. (1909). *De Senectute* (E. S. Shuckburgh, Ed.). New York: Macmillan.

Claudianus, Claudius. (1961). *Carmina* (T. Birt, Ed.). Berlin: Weidmann.

Demosthenes. (1968). *The letters of Demosthenes* (J. A. Goldstein, Trans.). New York: Columbia University Press.

Dionysius of Halicarnassus. (1889). *Opera* (H. Usener & L. Radermacher, Eds.). Leipzig: Teubner.

Euripides. (1968a). *Alcestis*. In *Euripide* (F. Chapouthier, Ed.). Paris: Les Belles Lettres.

Euripides. (1968b). *Hecuba*. In *Euripide* (F. Chapouthier, Ed.). Paris: Les Belles Lettres.

Euripides. (1968c). *Heraclidae*. In *Euripide* (F. Chapouthier, Ed.). Paris: Les Belles Lettres.

Euripides. (1968d). *Ion*. In *Euripide* (F. Chapouthier, Ed.). Paris: Les Belles Lettres.

Euripides. (1968). *Phoinissae*. In *Euripide* (F. Chapouthier, Ed.). Paris: Les Belles Lettres.

Homer. (1902). *Iliad*. In *Opera* (D. B. Monro & T. W. Allen, Eds.) (Vols. 1–2). Oxford: Clarendon Press.

Homer. (1908). *Odyssey*. In *Opera* (T. W. Allen, Ed.) (Vols. 3–4). Oxford: Clarendon Press.

Horace. (1919). *Odes and epodes* (P. Shorey, Ed.). Chicago: B. H. Sanborn.

Juvenal. (1979). *Satires* (J. E. B. Mayor, Ed.). New York: Arno Press.

Laberius, Decimus. (1897). In *Scaenicae Romanorum poesis fragmenta* (O. Ribbeck, Ed). Leipzig: Teubner.

Lucian. (1953). *Dialogi* (M. D. McLeod, Ed.) (Vol. 7). Cambridge: Harvard University Press.

Lucretius. (1953). *De rerum natura* (J. Martin, Ed.). Leipzig: Teubner.

Manilius. (1977). *Astronomica*. Cambridge: Harvard University Press.

Mimnermus. (1866). In *Poetaelyrici Graeci* (W. T. Bergk, Ed.). Berlin: Weidmann.

Philo. (1929–1962). *Opera* (T. Mangey, Ed.). (Vols. 1–10). London: Heinemann.

Pindar. (1930). *Pindare* (A. Puech, Ed.). Paris: Les Belles Lettres.

Plato. (1969a). *Eryxias* (J. Burnet, Ed.). Oxford: Clarendon Press.

Plato. (1969b). *Laws*. In *Opera* (J. Burnet, Ed.) (Vol. 5). Oxford: Clarendon Press.

Plato. (1969c). *Republic*. In *Opera* (J. Burnet, Ed.) (Vol. 4). Oxford: Clarendon Press.

Plato. (1969d). *Timaeus*. In *Opera* (J. Burnet, Ed.) (Vol. 4). Oxford: Clarendon Press.

Pliny. (1963). *Epistolae* (R. A. B. Mynors, Ed.). Oxford: Clarendon Press.

Prudentius, Clemens Aurelius. (1961–1969). *Opera* (H. J. Thomson, Ed.). London: Heinemann.

Quintus of Smyrna. (1968). *The war at Troy*. Norman: University of Oklahoma Press.

Seneca. (1942). *Epistolae morales* (R. M. Gummere, Ed.). Cambridge: Harvard University Press.

Simonides. (1975). In *Epigrammata Graeca* (D. Page, Ed.). Oxford: Clarendon Press.

Solon. (1979). *Poetae Elegiaci*. Leipzig: Teubner.

Sophocles. (1917). *Fragmenta* (A. C. Pearson, Ed.) (Vols. 1–3). Cambridge: Cambridge University Press.

Sophocles. (1975a). *Antigone*. In *Tragoediae*. Leipzig: Teubner.

Sophocles. (1975b). *Oedipus Coloneus*. In *Tragoediae*. Leipzig: Teubner.

Theognis. (1971). *Theognis et Phocylidis fragmenta et adespota*. Berlin: Walter de Gruyter.

Thucydides. (1966). *Opera* (J. Classen, Ed.) (Vols. 1–8). Berlin: Weidmann.

Xenophon. (1979). *Memorabilia* (J. R. Smith, Ed.). New York: Arno Press.

FURTHER READING

Bonner, C. (1937). Some phases of religious feeling in later paganism. *Harvard Theological Review, 30,* 119–140.

Cicero. (1971). *Cicero on old age and on friendship* (F. O. Copley, Trans.). Ann Arbor: University of Michigan Press.

Lattimore, R. (Trans.). (1949). *Greek lyrics*. Chicago: University of Chicago Press.

Lattimore, R. (1962). *Themes in Greek and Latin epitaphs*. Urbana: University of Illinois Press.

Lesky, A. (1965). *Greek tragedy* (H. A. Frankfort, Trans.). New York: Barnes & Noble.

Oates, W., and O'Neill, E., Jr. (1938). *The complete Greek drama* (Vols. 1–3). New York: Random House.

Ogilvie, R. M. (1980). *Roman literature and society*. Brighton, Sussex: Harvester Press.

Richardson, B. E. (1969). *Old age among the ancient Greeks*. New York: Greenwood Press. (This book still contains the most complete account of Greek views on old age and the aging process. The literature is covered, as well as the corpus of Greek art.)

3

"Grow Old along with Me": Images of Older People in British and American Literature

Richard C. Fallis

In one of Robert Browning's best-known poems, the speaker, an aged rabbi, invites his listeners to "grow old along with me! / The best is yet to be" (Browning, 1895, p. 338). But growing old has not been a particularly welcome invitation to many writers in Britain and America: genius flowers in youth, not in old age. The optimistic assertion that "the best is yet to be" has also not been one many writers shared. Thus, while literature in the English language is full of older characters, they have often been on the periphery of the action in novels and plays or have been secondary voices in poems. One can readily think of only a few works—until recent years—in which the focus was primarily on older people. On the other hand, the images of older people in British and American literature are so numerous and varied, even when they play secondary roles, that they could well deserve a book-length anthology unto themselves. In a few pages, I can only point to some especially striking figures and offer a few interpretive generalizations. If, until recently, the old have stood on the sidelines in books or have been treated as special cases, that has simply reflected the facts of life in our culture.

Even so, the most striking figures, whether created six hundred years ago or only recently, speak to us with urgency, insight, bitterness, or humor about themselves, their experiences, and their situations. It is, all told, a rich gallery of characters where we can meet almost every imaginable human type, and they help us understand the nuances and textures of later life with great specificity and intensity.

These qualities of specificity and intensity make generalizations difficult. On the one hand, some kinds of figures appear and reappear in almost every period from the medieval to the modern. The bitter old man who is jealous of the young and their futures can be found at any time, as can the older woman whose sensuality has not diminished with age, or the persnickety of either sex who are always too willing to judge present behaviors by yesterday's standards. At times, these figures become stereotypes, but it seems to me useful to go beyond the idea of stereotyping to try to understand that there is an elaborate and persistent cast of older figures in our literature. This is not the place to try to analyze all the elements in this typology of the old, but let me try to point to a few of its most important elements.

This cast of older characters has its roots in such sources as the Bible, the classics, and folklore, the great sources of so much in our serious literature as well as popular culture. Thus a really thorough study of images of the elderly in English would have to pay careful attention to show the figures—and stories—of Abraham, Moses, Job, Aeneas and Anchises, Ulysses, Socrates, Hänsel and Gretel's witch, the Flying Dutchman, the Wandering Jew, and a host of others have been interpreted and reinterpreted.

An adequate typology would also have to note how certain situations are told and retold: the tensions between parents and adult children; tales of engagement and disengagement from life situations; and occasions of the retrospective insight and visionary power old age can bring, to name a few. One would have to note, of course, that much of the imagery around the old reflects physical decay. Old age is the season of late autumn to winter; its landscape is of bare trees, windswept plains, and empty cities. One would also have to take into account a sense of basic hostility toward the old and the literary modes used to express this. To some extent, all this can be explained by some obvious facts: writers tend to be younger than the aged characters they create; and older people tend to be a threat to the young, or to seem so, as they try to control their lives or, more subtly, come to symbolize an inevitability the young would prefer to ignore. Conversely, younger people often seem determined to make the old conform to preset patterns. A Stoic tradition in our literature is very strong, at least in regard to the old, and it blends easily with Christian emphases on the acceptance of divine will. This may express itself in praise for the older person who accepts his or her fate; it may also take the form of satire against those who do not know "their places." This attitude expresses itself not only in the characters or speakers chosen for presentation but in the literary modes in which the presentations are made: satire, caricature, encomium, and pathos.

While certain ways of portraying the old seem common to every period and movement of British and American literature, each period also found special ways of seeing the old to meet its particular cultural needs. Medieval writers, for example, were often extremely ambivalent. With their sharp awareness of mortality and frequent commitment to the belief in a divine purpose in life's journey, they sometimes praised the old for accumulated wisdom, but often seemed dismayed by the fact of longevity. To be old was to be an oddity, a threat. On the other hand, for sentimental writers of the eighteenth and nineteenth centuries, the portrayal of the old was often the occasion for emotional outpourings about loss and diminution of powers. Some nineteenth-century novelists were especially alert to the pain of being old in a rapidly changing industrial culture to which the aged could make no important economic contribution and in which they only had skills industrialization had rendered superfluous. In contrast, "tough-minded" writers in our own century have often seen in the old pointed examples of the isolation and meaninglessness of modern existence.

In almost every period, at least until quite recently, the old have been seen as threats or burdens. American literature, if anything, has been harsher than British in this. Perhaps our rootlessness, emphasis on youth, and obsessions with success have always led to impatience with the slowness of age, fear of its conservatism, and disdain for its hard-won lessons. It is a sign of a culture in which longevity is becoming the norm that recently sympathy has begun to replace the satiric or patronizing attitudes of earlier times. Yet even in recent North American novels, the sympathy is still often with the older person who has been cast into an extreme situation. But none of these generalizations will take us far; the images of the old are simply too varied, too rich, too particular. So let me point to some specific examples a reader may find interesting.

We might begin with a most ancient figure, the Anglo-Saxon warrior of about the tenth century who speaks to us from an anonymous poem, "The Wanderer." His lament is of loneliness in a tough, bleak world where a man found definition in family and community. But he has had to learn the pain of exile in crossing "the woven waves, winter-sad, downcast for want of a hall . . . where I might find one . . . who should know of my people, or would comfort me friendless, receive me with gladness" ("The Wanderer," 1979, p. 84). This lament helps establish one major theme—loneliness and exile. The lament supposedly spoken by a Gaelic woman of about the same time helps establish a countertheme of old age as the time of loss of physical pleasure: "Year on year has worn my flesh / Since my fresh sweet strength went gray" ("Old Woman," 1959, p. 36). The Old Woman of Beare, like the Wanderer, speaks to us from a time and through a language remote from our own. Their concerns, however, can be found wherever the old are found.

But before we begin to think that every medieval portrayal involves only loss and pain, turn to Chaucer and his marvellous sketches of fourteenth-century pilgrims en route to pray at the shrine of St. Thomas at Canterbury. For the aging knight, there is modest satisfaction in a life well used. At a less exalted level, we have an elderly landowner, the Franklin, who is such a gourmet that his house "snowed" with meat and drink. Best of all, there is Chaucer's Wife of Bath, lusty, loud, and very definitely on the lookout for a sixth husband. There is pathos in the tale she tells the pilgrims of the young man who marries, by necessity, an ancient hag who is then magically transformed into a beautiful young woman, but Chaucer brilliantly balances this inner myth of the Wife's emotional insecurity against an external portrait of forceful self-assurance.

We might then turn from Chaucer's sketches to the extraordinary images of the old in Shakespeare. One thinks immediately of King Lear, of course, but let us put him and his play aside for a moment to look at other figures: dying John of Gaunt, who must watch his nephew-king waste the patrimony of "this scepter'd isle" of England; Polonius in *Hamlet*, full of wise sayings and stupid behaviors; Juliet's garrulous nurse; all those *senex* figures who would see the young miserable or even dead rather than disobedient. But against these killjoys, consider the Falstaff of the *Henry IV* plays, perhaps the greatest of all portraits of old age denying its situation in comic terms. A lord of misrule and confessed "coward on principle," Falstaff does all he can to assert his relentless vitality, heedless of the consequences. Prospero, the wise old magician of *The Tempest*, has to deal with consequences, in this case what happens when his old enemies come back into his life and the time comes for him to give up his beloved daughter. Prospero is a mythic figure of one kind of aging: self-assured, self-knowing, and gifted with special powers but ready to give them up in due time.

This kind of wisdom Shakespeare's Lear begins to earn only with the greatest difficulty, and the sheer harshness of the situations in that play helps put it among the greatest portrayals of old age in Western literature. At the beginning, Lear is a domineering monarch, ready to give up power's appearance but not its substance. His evil daughters shrewdly realize that "he hath ever but slenderly known himself." *King Lear,* then, is a mythic statement of the pain of education, especially in old age. Lear must learn that children can turn on parents for no apparent reason, that plain speech means more than praise, that madness is only a step beyond wisdom (or perhaps a step on the way to it), and that even purification by suffering may not be enough to sustain one's self in a world where deprivation is the norm. In short, *King Lear* is the richest text in our language on the social forces in old age: the consequences of physiological change, dependency, disengagement, and the results of retrospection.

The late seventeenth and eighteenth centuries are especially full of portraits of the old. The long-lived Samuel Johnson probably has the most to tell us, both in his own writings and in the great biography of him by James Boswell. Particularly aware of the "vanity of human wishes," Johnson came to old age sustained by religious faith and philosophical wisdom.

Yet to be intellectually ready for old age was not the same as being able to handle all its rigors, as Johnson's prayers and meditations show us. Against the inner Johnson of his own writing we can place an outer man drawn masterfully by Boswell, who knew his subject best toward the end of his life. Thus Boswell's biography is astonishingly rich in its anecdotes: "We talked of old age. Johnson (now in his seventieth year) said, 'It is a man's own fault, it is from want of use, if his mind grows torpid in old age' " (Boswell, 1982, p. 338).

Beside Boswell's Johnson we might put the comically irascible Matthew Bramble of Tobias Smollett's *Humphry Clinker,* forced by fashion to travel and take in new sights that generally bore or disgust him. We might also consider the virtuous, aging clergymen who appear in much eighteenth-century fiction, such country squires as Fielding's Allworthy, or the comic older men and women in the plays of Congreve and Sheridan. Common to many of these is the security and self-validation they could find in assured positions in the closed societies of villages and small towns and the unchanging facts of rural life.

For the poor, as some Romantic writers remind us, there were fewer certainties. The ancient farmer of George Crabbe's *The Village,* physically as broken as the dying tree he climbed as a boy, asks: "Why do I live, when I desire to be / At once from life and life's long labor free?" (Crabbe, 1834, vol. 2, p. 82). And no figure better catches the pathos of old age than the ancient Michael of Wordsworth's great pastoral poem by the same name. Blessed like the biblical patriarchs with a son in his old age, Michael has had to send him away to the city. Before the boy left, the two of them began to build a sheepfold together as a covenant of their love, but the boy has gotten into trouble and will never return to his father's farm. Michael, broken by grief, is said to go each day to sit by the incomplete sheepfold where he never again adds so much as one stone, leaving at his death a memorial to an unfinished fold and a broken covenant (1936, pp. 131–138).

Among the English novelists of the nineteenth century, none is more effective in portraying old age's mannerisms than Charles Dickens. With his eye for the grotesque and the absurd, Dickens can sometimes seem superficial, but one needs to turn to only one of his novels, *David Copperfield,* for a remarkable gallery of older figures: Aunt Betsy Trotwood, full of vitality and plans; old Mr. Wickfield, lost in memories and alcohol; Mr. Dick with his simple idée fixe; and all the rest. In Dickens, the old are often victimized by industrialization and its results, especially when they have to live in the disorder of a city. In contrasting ways, two other Victorian novelists, Anthony Trollope and George Eliot, were most acute in seeing the old in the tradition-enriched contexts of villages and closed communities. With George Eliot, we find an especially sharp psychologi-

cal insight into the ways in which the old and young can interact, be it in
Silas Marner's redemption by a child or Dr. Casaubon's inability to comprehend his young wife's emotional needs.

The more idealized images of old age in the nineteenth century come to
us in poetry. Tennyson's Ulysses has "not now the strength which in old
days / Moved earth and heaven" but is still "strong in will / To strive, to
seek, to find, and not to yield" (Tennyson, 1899, p. 207). His King Arthur, going away to the mystic land of Avalon, looks on the wreck of his
kingdom of chivalry with philosophic wisdom:

> The old order changeth, yielding place to new,
> And God fulfills himself in many ways,
> Lest one good custom should corrupt the world.
>   (Tennyson, 1889, p. 406)

So Browning's Rabbi Ben Ezra has also gained a kind of wisdom from
a rich life experience, though this scholar speaks in more complex language than Tennyson's departing king.

As recollection, retrospection, and summing up are important themes
for these old speakers, so we find the same in a different key in Thomas
Hardy's poem on his eighty-sixth birthday, "He Never Expected Much."
There life reminds the poet that "I do not promise overmuch, / Child;
overmuch; / Just neutral-tinted haps and such" (Hardy, 1976, p. 652).

With Hardy the poet, we have come to a modern temperament, and in
our own century the poets have often been best at commenting on the
retrospective view. William Butler Yeats, in "The Wild Swans at Coole,"
gives us such a view that is the more moving for being understated. Yeats,
however, was not always a poet of understatement; his long retrospective
poem, "The Tower," is full of violence and anger. One of his favorite
voices as an old poet was that of "Crazy Jane," who insists that the most
valuable lessons are learned "in bodily lowliness / And in the heart's pride"
(1963, p. 294). Few things in Yeats's work are more moving than "After
Long Silence," a brief lyric to a woman who had been his mistress thirty-
five years before when "young / We loved each other and were ignorant"
(Yeats, 1963, p. 301).

Because Yeats lived to seventy-three, his poetic powers undiminished,
he presents a particularly interesting example of a Romantic lyricist whose
life experience goes far beyond the youthful things most often celebrated
in that style. T. S. Eliot, conversely, had virtually ceased writing poetry,
except in plays, by his sixtieth year, but even as a younger man he had a
sharp sense of the bleakness of old age and its uncertainty. Ancient Ger-
ontion lives in fear that his world of memories and bitterness may be
invaded by some life-giving supernatural force. Eliot's ancient magus re-

members his journey to Bethlehem to see the Christ Child as a difficult, frustrating trip from which, spiritually, he has never recovered.

If I have put the emphasis in these comments mostly on books from past centuries, it is because I think that the most striking images of the old in modern literature are already fairly well known and that it is important to remember that some of the most challenging images come from the more distant past and earlier forms of our literary culture. British and American fiction and drama in our own century have been, of course, immensely rich in figures of the old. One immediately considers Santiago in Hemingway's *The Old Man and the Sea* or Willy Loman in Miller's *Death of a Salesman*. A bit farther back, one can learn a good deal from the aging Lambert Strether of Henry James's *The Ambassadors,* and one should remember that James was especially adept with figures of aging people—men in particular—who came to realize in later life just what they had missed. Though their modes are sharply different, Samuel Beckett shares with James a special ability to call up for us the risks of retrospection in old age and the sense of futility it frequently offers, a theme also found sometimes in the plays of Harold Pinter.

Finally, I wish to note the increasing emphasis in recent years on fully rounded, fairly realistic images of older people in fiction. Muriel Spark's novel *Memento Mori* of 1959 may eventually be seen as signalling the beginning of a new and persistent concern with aged characters seen at the center of things rather than on the periphery. Kingsley Amis's brilliant and bitter *Ending Up* is not superficially sympathetic to its characters, all six of them over seventy. The hero of Saul Bellow's *Mr. Sammler's Planet* is about their age. Blessed by more capacity to grow toward understanding himself and his family, he is also almost corroded by his inability to make commitments. Less well known, but equally rewarding, is Constance Beresford-Howe's *The Book of Eve,* the story of a Montreal housewife who, when she begins to get her old-age pension, leaves her husband to find the life she has missed in years of service to him and his illness. In *Poorhouse Fair* and *As We Are Now,* John Updike and May Sarton have written brilliantly of the rigors of closed communities of the old, nursing homes, and the venality and cruelty that sometimes surround them. May Sarton, in fact, has given us a number of fine portraits of older women: Miss Caroline Spencer in *As We Are Now;* Hilary Stevens, the aging writer of *Mrs. Stevens Hears the Mermaids Singing;* and Christina Chapman in *Kinds of Love.*

Perhaps the most striking thing about recent fiction is its ability to bring aging characters to the center of awareness, away from the periphery. It is no longer surprising to find a novel with an aged central character or a play cast entirely with older persons. Now, more than ever in the past, writers seem to be responding to the implications of Rabbi Ben Ezra's invitation to "grow old along with me." Stereotyped figures remain, of course, and I suspect that the influence of literary tradition is so strong that aged figures may always remain something of a special class for writers. But whether on the edge of our awareness as readers or at the center, the most striking older figures in British and American literature do speak to us all, young and old, with special intensity and an insistence on being understood.

SELECTIONS

Anonymous Irish poem
from *The Old Woman of Beare*

> I, the old woman of Beare,
> Once a shining shift would wear;
> Now and since my beauty's fall
> I have scarce a shift at all.
>
> Plump no more I sigh for these
> Bones bare beyond belief;
> Ebbtide is my present grief;
> I am ebbing like the seas. . . .
>
> For my hands as you may see
> Are but bony wasted things,
> Hands that once would grasp the hand,
> Clasp the haughty neck of kings. . . .
>
> And O God,
> Once again for ill or good
> Spring will come and I shall see
> Everything but me renewed.

("Old Woman," 1959, p. 36)

William Shakespeare (1564–1616)
from *King Lear*

In this scene, Lear realizes that his evil daughters, Goneril and Regan, mean to strip him of even the last appearances of kingship, the twenty-five knights who follow him. Though the children here are inordinately evil, the giving up of the last signs of adult authority is a universal human situation.

Lear: I gave you all—

Regan: And in good time you gave it. . . .
Goneril: Hear me, my lord.
    What need you five-and-twenty, ten, or five,

To follow in a house where twice as many
Have a command to tend you?
Regan: What need one?
Lear: O, reason not the need! Our basest beggars
 Are in poorest things superfluous:
 Allow not nature more than nature needs,
 Man's life as cheap as beast's. Thou art a lady;
 If only to go warm were gorgeous,
 Why, nature needs not what thou gorgeous wears't,
 Which scarcely keeps thee warm. But, for true need,—
 You heavens, give me that patience, patience I need!
 You see me here, you gods, a poor old man,
 As full of grief as age; wretched in both!
 If it be you that stirs these daughters' hearts
 Against their father, fool me not so much
 To bear it tamely; touch me with noble anger,
 And let not women's weapons, water-drops,
 Stain my man's cheeks! No, you unnatural hags,
 I will have such revenges on you both,
 That all the world shall—I will do such things,—
 What they are, yet I know not; but they shall be
 The terrors of the earth! You think I'll weep;
 No, I'll not weep:—
 I have full cause of weeping: but this heart
 Shall break into a hundred thousand flaws
 Or e're I'll weep. —O fool, I shall go mad!
         (Shakespeare, 1900: 2.4)

from *As You Like it*

In this well-known speech, Jacques the cynic reflects on the aging process and the roles people play.

Jacques: All the world's a stage,
 And all the men and women merely players:
 They have their exits and their entrances;
 And one man in his time plays many parts,
 His acts being seven ages. As, first the infant,
 Mewling and puking in the nurse's arms.
 And then the whining schoolboy, with his satchel
 And shining morning face, creeping like snail
 Unwillingly to school. And then the lover,
 Sighing like furnace, with a woeful ballad
 Made to his mistress' eyebrow. Then the soldier,
 Full of strange oaths, and bearded like the pard,

Jealous in honour, sudden and quick in quarrel,
Seeking the bubble reputation
Even in the cannon's mouth. And then the justice,
In fair round belly with good capon lined,
With eyes severe and beard of formal cut,
Full of wise saws and modern instances;
And so he plays his part. The sixth age shifts
Into the lean and slipper'd pantaloon,
With spectacles on nose and pouch on side;
His youthful hose, well saved, a world too wide
For his shrunk shank; and his big manly voice,
Turning again toward childish treble, pipes
And whistles in his sound. Last scene of all,
That ends this strange eventful history,
Is second childishness and mere oblivion,
Sans teeth, sans eyes, sans taste, sans everything.

(Shakespeare, 1900: 2.7)

Alfred, Lord Tennyson (1809–1892)
from *Ulysses*

The speaker here is the hero of the *Odyssey*, a Ulysses grown old and tired of living in a world without challenges great enough for his own imagination.

I cannot rest from travel: I will drink
Life to the lees. All times I have enjoy'd
Greatly, have suffer'd greatly, both with those
That loved me, and alone; on shore, and when
Thro' scudding drifts the rainy Hyades
Vext the dim sea. I am become a name;
For always roaming with a hungry heart
Much have I seen and known; cities of men
And manners, climates, councils, governments,
Myself not least, but honour'd of them all;
And drunk delight of battle with my peers,
Far on the ringing plains of windy Troy.
I am a part of all that I have met;
Yet all experience is an arch wherethro'
Gleams that untravell'd world whose margin fades
Forever and forever when I move.
How dull it is to pause, to make an end,
To rust unburnish'd, not to shine in use!
As though to breathe were life! Life piled on life
Were all too little, and of one to me
Little remains: but every hour is saved

From that eternal silence, something more,
A bringer of new things; and vile it were
For some three suns to store and hoard myself,
And this gray spirit yearning in desire
To follow knowledge like a sinking star,
Beyond the utmost bound of human thought
        . . . Come, my friends,
'Tis not too late to seek a newer world.
Push off, and sitting well in order smite
The sounding furrows; for my purpose holds
To sail beyond the sunset, and the baths
Of all the western stars, until I die.
It may be that the gulfs will wash us down;
It may be we shall touch the Happy Isles,
And see the great Achilles, whom we knew.
Tho' much is taken, much abides; and tho'
We are not now that strength which in old days
Moved earth and heaven, that which we are, we are;
One equal temper of heroic hearts,
Made weak by time and fate, but strong in will
To strive, to seek, to find, and not to yield.

                           (Tennyson, 1899, p. 207)

Robert Browning (1812–1889)
from *Rabbi Ben Ezra*

Grow old along with me!
The best is yet to be,
The last of life, for which the first was made:
Our times are in His hand
Who saith, "A whole I planned,
Youth shows but half; trust God: see all nor be afraid!"

Not that, amassing flowers,
Youth sighed, "Which rose make ours,
Which lily leave and then as best recall?"
Not that, admiring stars,
It yearned, "Nor Jove, nor Mars;
Mine be some figured flame which blends, transcends them all!"

Not for such hopes and fears
Annulling youth's brief years,
Do I remonstrate: folly wide the mark!
Rather I prize the doubt

Low kinds exist without,
Finished and finite clods, untroubled by a spark. . . .

Rejoice we are allied
To that which doth provide
And not partake, effect and not receive!
A spark disturbs our clod;
Nearer we hold of God
Who gives, than of His tribes that take, I must believe.

Then, welcome each rebuff
That turns earth's smoothness rough,
Each sting that bids nor sit nor stand but go!
Be our joys three parts pain!
Strive, and hold cheap the strain;
Learn, nor account the pang; dare, never grudge the throe!
                                        (Browning, 1895, p. 338)

Matthew Arnold (1882–1888)
Growing Old

What is it to grow old?
Is it to lose the glory of the form,
The lustre of the eye?
Is it for beauty to forego her wreath?
—Yes, but not this alone.

Is it to feel our strength—
Not our bloom only, but our strength—decay?
Is it to feel each limb
Grow stiffer, every function less exact,
Each nerve more loosely strung?

Yes, this, and more; but not
Ah, 'tis not what in youth we dreamed 'twould be!
'Tis not to have our life
Mellowed and softened as with sunset-glow,
A golden day's decline.

'Tis not to see the world
As from a height, with rapt prophetic eyes,
And heart profoundly stir'd;
And weep, and feel the fulness of the past,
The years that are no more.

It is to spend long days
And not once feel that we were ever young;
It is to add, immured
In the hot prison of the present, month
To month with weary pain.

It is to suffer this,
And feel but half, and feebly, what we feel.
Deep in our hidden heart
Festers the dull remembrance of a change
But no emotion—none.

It is—last stage of all—
When we are frozen up within, and quite
The phantom of ourselves,
To hear the world applaud the hollow ghost
Which blamed the living man.

(Arnold, 1890, pp. 227–228)

Robert Frost (1874–1963)
An Old Man's Winter's Night

All out-of-doors looked darkly in at him
Through the thin frost, almost in separate stars,
That gathers on the pane in empty rooms.
What kept his eyes from giving back the gaze
Was the lamp tilted near them in his hand.
What kept him from remembering what it was
That brought him to that creaking room was age.
He stood with barrels round him—at a loss.
And having scared the cellar under him
In clomping there, he scared it once again
In clomping off;—and scared the outer night,
Which has its sounds, familiar, like the roar
Of trees and crack of branches, common things,
But nothing so like beating on a box.
A light he was to no one but himself
Where now he sat, concerned with he knew what,
A quiet light, and then not even that.
He consigned to the moon, such as she was,
So late-arising, to the broken moon,
As better than the sun in any case
For such a charge, his snow upon the roof,
His icicles along the wall to keep;

And slept. The log that shifted with a jolt
Once in the stove, disturbed him and he shifted,
And eased his heavy breathing, but still slept.
One aged man—one man—can't keep a house,
A farm, a countryside, or if he can,
It's thus he does it of a winter night.

(Frost, 1958, p. 135).

May Sarton (b. 1912)
from *As We Are Now*

The passage clearly illustrates that Caroline Spencer has become a person completely at the mercy of Harriet, the supervisor of the home where she has gradually deteriorated.

Days have gone by. It must be October, mid–October I think, because the leaves are flying fast. The great maples are skeletons against the sky. The beeches are still a marvelous greenish-yellow, a Chinese yellow, I have always thought. Pansy, now the nights are cold, sometimes comes to sleep with me, and slips out (clever cat) before anyone has stirred. The only time I weep is when she is there, purring beside me. I, who longed for touch, can hardly bear the sweetness of that little rough tongue licking my hand.

There is nothing to say any longer. And I am writing only because Lisa is to bring Eva today. Harriet doesn't want them to see me as I was— dirty hair I hardly bothered to comb, an old woman, a grotesque miserable animal. She washed my hair and it is drying now. This time she was gentle, thank God. I suppose she can be because I am just a passive bundle. She brought me a clean and, for once, properly ironed nightgown. I do not dress very often any more. I feel safer in bed.

. . . . .

It must be mid–November. The leaves are all gone. Harriet found Pansy on my bed and now locks her out every night. The walls close in on every side. I do not remember things very clearly . . . is my brother John still alive? Where has Anna gone? (Sarton, 1973, pp. 108, 115)

REFERENCES

Amis, K. (1973). *Ending up.* New York: Harcourt Brace Jovanovich.

Arnold, M. (1890). *Poetical works of Matthew Arnold.* London: Macmillan.

Bellow, S. (1969). *Mr. Sammler's planet.* New York: Viking Press.

Beresford-Howe, C. (1973). *The book of Eve.* Boston: Little, Brown.

Boswell, J. (1982). *The life of Samuel Johnson.* New York: Oxford University Press.

Browning, R. (1895). *The complete poetical works of Robert Browning* (G. R. Strange, Ed.). Boston: Houghton Mifflin.

Chaucer, G. (1957). *The Canterbury tales.* In F. N. Robinson (Ed.), *Works of Geoffrey Chaucer* (pp. 17–265). Boston: Houghton Mifflin.

Crabbe, G. (1834). *The village*. In *The poetical works of the Rev. George Crabbe* (Vol. II, pp. 2–216). London: Murray.

Dickens, C. (1972). *David Copperfield*. Baltimore: Penguin Books.

Eliot, G. (1963). *Silas Marner*. Baltimore: Penguin Books.

Eliot, G. (1965). *Middlemarch*. Baltimore: Penguin Books.

Eliot, T. S. (1962). *The complete poems and plays*. New York: Harcourt, Brace.

Frost, R. (1958). *Complete poems of Robert Frost*. New York: Holt, Rinehart, and Winston.

Hardy, T. (1976). *The complete poems of Thomas Hardy* (J. Gibson, Ed.). New York: Macmillan.

Hemingway, E. (1952). *The old man and the sea*. New York: Scribner's.

James, H. (1970). *The ambassadors*. Baltimore: Penguin Books.

Miller, A. (1967). *Death of a salesman*. Baltimore: Penguin Books.

The old woman of Beare. (1959). In F. O'Connor (Ed. & Trans.), *Kings, lords, and commons* (pp. 34–37). Dublin: Gill & Macmillan.

Sarton, M. (1965). *Mrs. Stevens hears the mermaids singing*. New York: W. W. Norton.

Sarton, M. (1970). *Kinds of love*. New York: W. W. Norton.

Sarton, M. (1973). *As we are now*. New York: W. W. Norton.

Shakespeare, W. (1900). *The works of William Shakespeare*. New York: Oxford University Press.

Smollett, T. (1967). *The expedition of Humphry Clinker*. Baltimore: Penguin Books.

Spark, M. (1959). *Memento mori*. Philadelphia: J. B. Lippincott.

Tennyson, A. (1899). *The works of Alfred, Lord Tennyson*. London: Macmillan.

Trollope, A. (1976). *The warden*. Baltimore: Penguin Books.

Trollope, A. (1978). *Doctor Thorne*. Baltimore: Penguin Books.

Updike, J. (1959). *The poorhouse fair*. New York: Knopf.

The wanderer. (1979). In M. H. Abrams (Ed.) & E. T. Donaldson (Trans.), *The Norton anthology of English literature* (Vol. 1, pp. 84–86). New York: W. W. Norton.

Wordsworth, W. (1936). *Poetical works*. Oxford: Oxford University Press.

Yeats, W. B. (1963). *Collected poems of W. B. Yeats*. London: Macmillan.

FURTHER READING

Beckett, S. (1958). *Endgame*. New York: Grove Press.

Cary, J. (1944). *The horse's mouth*. New York: Harper.

Clarke, A. (1976). *Selected poems*. Winston-Salem, NC: Wake Forest University Press.

Faulkner, W. (1930). *As I lay dying*. New York: Random House.

Jonson, B. (1962). *Volpone*. New Haven: Yale University Press.

Laurence, M. (1964). *The stone angel*. New York: Knopf.

Morris, W. (1971). *Fire sermon*. New York: Harper & Row.

O'Connor, E. (1956). *The last hurrah*. Boston: Little, Brown.

Olsen, T. (1961). *Tell me a riddle*. New York: Dell.

O'Neill, E. (1956). *Long day's journey into night*. New York: Grove Press.

O'Neill, E. (1970). *Desire under the elms*. New York: Random House.

Sackville-West, V. (1931). *All passion spent*. Garden City, NY: Doubleday.
Swados, H. (1974). *Celebration*. New York: Simon & Schuster.
White, P. (1973). *The eye of the storm*. New York: Viking Press.
Wilson, A. (1964). *Late call*. New York: Viking Press.

4

From Centrality to Expendability: The Aged in French Literature

Paul J. Archambault

France's oldest and most famous epic ends with the scene of a two-hundred-year-old emperor who has just finished the most recent of innumerable military campaigns against the Saracens and barbarians, and who would now like to take a much-deserved retirement. As Charlemagne sits and broods about his old age, wishing that death would overtake him, Saint Gabriel appears to the old emperor to tell him that God will not yet allow him to surrender to old age; there are further campaigns to be waged, and enemies to be subdued. Having "small heart" for such tasks, Charlemagne cries out to God that he is too tired. Weeping, the old king "plucks his flowing beard of white" (Sayers, 1969, p. 315).

There is nothing exceptional about Saint Gabriel's rousing a very old king from his sleep in order to tell him that he is not only socially useful but militarily indispensable. In much of French literature extending from the early medieval period to the Industrial Revolution, the elderly frequently, if not usually, play key political, military, and familial roles no matter what their age; indeed, the importance of the role is often directly proportional to the venerability that their ages inspire. Whether they are aging husbands or guardians, cuckolded spouses, authoritarian fathers, or old hags; whether they are peasants, burghers, or aristocrats, they inspire a mixture of reverence and fear. In comedies, they might inspire ridicule, but even so, they will never be discarded. Not only do they have the social advantage of owning land, holding the purse strings, and controlling the politics of their societies, they are also known for their strong sense of authority, which in the tragedies of Corneille, Racine, Voltaire, or Reynard still makes the earth tremble. In French comedy from Molière and Marivaux to Beaumarchais and Musset, whether they are jealous husbands, misers, or misanthropes, the aged are not without a few tricks of their own.

One could, of course, counter with a generalization as sweeping as the foregoing one and point to a whole series of texts in French literature between 1100 and 1800 depicting old age as something ridiculous, disgusting, and worthy of mockery. There is, in French literature, many an old man comparable to the aged knight January of Chaucer's *Canterbury Tales,* who, despite the countless electuaries, cannot avoid ridicule or humiliation on the wedding night. The sexuality of old men is often depicted as an object of disgust or ridicule. Even more so is the depiction of the sexuality of old women. There is in French literature, even of the popular sort, an ancient mixture of Gallic cynicism and Christian misogyny that makes of the aging woman's body the very symbol of decrepitude and disgust. On the other hand, the impotence of Villon's aging male burghers does not detract from their dignity as barristers, notaries, or churchmen. The sexual decline of the once lovely *belle heaulmière* (helmet-vendor) is a picture of ravaged sexuality:

> This is what human beauty comes to:
> The arms short, the hands shriveled,
> The shoulders all hunched up.
> The breasts? Shrunk again
> The buttocks gone the way of the tits.
> The quim? aagh! As for the thighs,
> They aren't thighs now but sticks
> Speckled all over like sausages.
>
> (Villon, 1977, p. 59)

In spite of mockery, ridicule, or disgust, however, the elderly in French literature up to the Industrial Revolution continue to play key social roles. That old helmet-vendor of Villon's is depicted with a hint of tender compassion, and she remains awe-inspiring even in old age; she is still able to transmit her somewhat-hardened advice to younger shoe-fitters, sausage-fillers, and bonnet-makers of her sex, urging them to make good while they can of their capacity for sexual control of the male:

> Take what you can right and left
> Don't spare a man I beg you
> For there's no run on old crones
> No more than cried-down money.
>
> (Villon, 1977, p. 61)

The aging crone, the cuckolded husband of medieval fabliaux or of La Fontaine's *Contes,* and Molière's aging lovers, misers, and notaries still remain a strong social force with an elastic capacity for retaliation as well as an uncanny ability to transform themselves from objects of ridicule to objects of fear.

In serious French literature from 1100 to 1800, then, the elderly are considered anything but obsolete. Michel de Montaigne (1533–1592), France's greatest essayist, may have thought himself as slipping into old age at the age of forty, but he wrote his greatest essays when he was well past fifty. Despite chronic illness and the psychological discomfort derived from his growing awareness of declining health and sexual energy, Montaigne took comfort from his ancient masters, the Stoics and Epicureans, and, more pointedly, Cicero, whose *De senectute* he venerated. He undisputedly thought of his own old age as the intellectual crowning of his life, at a time when, despite bodily infirmities, the mind reaches its fullest capacity for synthesis of a lifetime's experience. Montaigne has given French literature some of its finest and frankest pages about the onset of old age with its solitariness, both dreaded and aspired to, its reminiscences of youthful triumphs, and its recurrent sexual fantasies.

If the aged fathers of Corneille's tragedies, especially in *Horace* and *Le Cid,* consider themselves too old to fight to avenge their family names and prefer to exhort their sons to do it instead, old age seems to confer on the heroes and heroines of Racine an added measure of acrimony, aggressiveness, ferocity, cruelty, and, in the best instances, venerability and wisdom. Nero's sinister and brilliant elderly mother Agrippina (in *Britannicus*) does not hesitate to dispatch her first husband, Claudius, in order to put her son Nero on the throne. As a young emperor-to-be, Nero is himself flanked by two aging and sententious mentors, Byrrhus and Seneca, who together seem to represent the polarization of Nero's personality. And who can forget the fierce but majestic figure of Athalia? Here is one of the sublimest and bloodiest of the "cruel" old figures of Racine's theatre, a woman who once ruled over Israel with her husband Joram and must acknowledge her failed attempt to destroy David's line in the person of her grandson Joash.

Until 1830 or so, Romantic French literature was to a large extent a reminiscence of or a nostalgia for the past. Even in their youth, poets like Musset tried to sound like burnt-out rakes who had drained the cup of life to the dregs. One might say, without causticity intended, that it was fashionable in Romantic poetry to be old as quickly as possible: Musset's *Tristesse* (1840) was written when that poet was only thirty years old. After 1830, and even more so toward the end of the July Monarchy and the beginning of the Second Republic (1848), the more active of the French Romantic poets, Lamartine and Hugo in particular, became involved in politics, looking forward to a future lighted by democracy, progress, and brotherhood. In December 1852, both poets deplored the retrogressive coup d'état that ushered in the Second Empire and Napoleon III. Victor Hugo went into an eighteen-year exile to assert his dissent from the authoritarian politics of Napoleon's nephew, whom Hugo described in his poetic masterpiece *Les châtiments* as the worst possible punishment that God could have inflicted on the shades of the great emperor. By the time they reached a graceful old age, both of these matured Romantics realized that old age had made them more active, alert, and progressive in their outlook than they had ever been in their tired, melancholic, and backward-looking twenties. The mature works of Lamartine and of the aging Hugo (like those of the greatest of French Romantic prose writers, Chateaubriand, a generation earlier) are far younger in spirit than the works of their twenties when they thought they were bearing all the weltschmerz of the world. The acquisition of age seems, then, to result in the acquisition of an appreciation of youthfulness that translates into youthful writing. A compilation of poems written between 1846 and 1877, Victor Hugo's *L'art d'être grand-père,* is one of the most playful of Hugo's collections of poetry, and it was typical of that aging titan that some of his most jestful poems were his very last. "Do not elevate me to the rank of God," the patriarchal grandfather warns his admiring grandchildren with a gleam in his eye (in a poem written on June 26, 1875), for "I'd be a good guy if I were the Good Lord" (Hugo, 1974, p. 628).

Schematically, then, it would seem that sometime in the nineteenth century the image of the elderly in French literature evolved slowly from a traditional image of venerability, authority, and social utility to one of exploitability and expendability. The first great watershed is perhaps the realistic literature that arises from the spread of a commercial urban class in France and the consequent importance that liquid cash acquires as a means for social mobility. In Balzac's novels, money and bank accounts suddenly acquire an even greater importance than land, and cash flow is more important than a château in the country. Père Goriot's daughters, the Comtesse de Restaud and the Baronne de Nucingen, take full advantage of the savings that their father has accumulated as a vermicelli merchant in order to consolidate their newly acquired positions as aristocrats in the highly mobile society of Louis Philippe.

The second great watershed seems to be the industrialization of France after 1850 and the rise of an urban industrial proletariat. In the naturalistic novels and short stories of Maupassant, the Goncourt brothers, and Zola, an unfortunately familiar image of the elderly enters French literature, that of the exploited elderly, direct descendants of Balzac's Goriot. These images reveal victims of capitalist exploitation or that of their own families, victims who cease to be socially useful and who are mercilessly discarded, when they are not simply murdered like old Père Fouan of Zola's novel, *Earth.* These elderly are miserable and socially alienated, and whenever their children give them any attention, it is only out of interest for their inheritance.

The bleak attitude of the naturalist writers toward aging could not continue indefinitely without inspiring some reaction. Henri Bergson's brilliant analysis of time and human memory, begun in his essay *Les données immédiates de la conscience* (1889) and continued with *Matière et mémoire* (1896), represented a philosopher's reaction against a dark vision of the universe as static, purposeless matter, and of human aging as the mere degeneration of a higher organism. In the French literary world, Proust's masterpiece, *Remembrance of Things Past* (1922), without being construed as a mere application of Bergsonian ideas, was the product of seed that had sprouted and fermented in Bergsonian soil. When, in *Time Recaptured,* the aging narrator, Marcel, trips against a flagstone on his way to a reception at Madame de Verdurin's, a great revelation occurs to him— that the past, far from receding from us like a train in the distance, is ever present in human memory and can be called back, sometimes in its entirety, in privileged moments of involuntary reminiscence. By no means a religious writer, Proust was unwittingly rediscovering some of Saint Augustine's deepest intuitions about the human soul in *Confessions,* Book 2. In this regard, Proust's vision of aging was more positive than that of André Gide, who eschewed all religious or aesthetic consolations in old age and entitled his last little book *So Be It,* or, *The Chips Are Down.*

In the late twentieth century, France has become an aging society. The pyramid of age groups is slowly becoming inverted, with the tip on the bottom and a broad base of elderly on the top. In the past fifty years, the French elderly, particularly those of the middle class and even the few remaining peasants, have seen various forms of social legislation sheltering them from the type of exploitation that afflicted Zola's mine workers and peasants or Maupassant's petty bourgeois with their small fortunes or legacies. Poverty and oppression have, of course, not disappeared entirely from French society. From Jean Giono's short stories about the disinherited and aged poor of Provence during the days of the great depression to Bernard Clavel's novels about the slow disappearance of the one-family farm where the young refuse to continue, the image of the miserable, oppressed, or discarded elderly has continued to be a theme for French novelists writing in this century.

One real problem in French literature in the latter half of the twentieth century, however, has been not exploitation, but literary and sociological indifference to old age. As old age has become a more common phenomenon in French life, far from becoming a widespread theme in literature, it has tended to receive an indifferent treatment, like the condition itself. Most people would really like to forget it or call it by another name. Talk of old age, like talk of death, has become one of France's characteristic taboos. In a masterful essay, *La vieillesse* (The Coming of Age), Simone de Beauvoir admits that she once raised a furious outcry at the end of the third and last of her autobiographical volumes *(La force des choses)* when she spoke of herself as entering old age:

Society looks upon old age as as kind of shameful secret that is unseemly to mention. There is a copious literature dealing with women, with children, and young people in all their aspects: but apart from specialized works we scarcely find any reference whatsoever to the old. A comic-strip artist once had to redraw a whole series because he had included a pair of grandparents among his characters. "Cut out the old folks," he was ordered. When I say I am working on a study of old age, people generally exclaim, . . . "What a dismal subject." (Beauvoir, 1972, p. 1–2)

Simone de Beauvoir may be overstating matters in order to correct what she considers the "conspiracy of silence" against old age. It may be, too, that the relative absence of old age as a theme in current French literature can be interpreted as a sign that on the sociological level, at least, many problems that afflicted the elderly as a result of the Industrial Revolution and modern urbanization—poverty, exploitation, ill health, poor pensions—have to a certain extent been resolved through social legislation. But the psychological problems, particularly isolation and (given the weakening of traditional family bonds) the feeling of uselessness, remain in twentieth-century French society. The French elderly may not feel the pangs of isolation, uselessness, and society's indifference as acutely as millions of their American counterparts, yet these problems are current today in French society. They have nonetheless failed to inspire the French novel in the past twenty-five years.

SELECTIONS

Pierre de Ronsard (1524–1585)
from *Pièces posthumes*

The poet is conscious of the slow disintegration of his body.

> I've no more than my bones, a skeleton I seem,
> Unfleshed, unnerved, unmuscled, unpulped,
> Whom the arrow of Death without pardon has struck.
> I daren't look at my arms for fear I shall tremble.
> Apollo and his son [Aesculapius], two great masters combined
> Wouldn't know how to cure me; their medicines deceive me.
> Farewell, pleasant sun; my eye's all stopped up.
> My body is going where things disassemble.
> What friend, seeing me stripped to this degree,
> Will not bring back home a sad and tearful eye,
> Consoling me in bed and kissing my face,

While wiping my eyes which Death has put to rest.
Farewell, dear companions, farewell my dear friends.
I'm going down first to prepare you a place.

(Ronsard, 1938, p. 634)

The pain, then the resignation, of having to leave everything behind.

I must leave houses and orchards and gardens,
Dishes and vessels etched by the engraver,
And sing my own obsequies in the manner of the Swan,
Who laments his own leaving on the shores of Meander.
It is done. I've unwound the thread of my days.
I have lived. I have made a name for myself.
My quill soars to heaven to be there a spirit,
Far from the world's lures, which entrap keener souls.
Happy the man who never was. Happier yet who returns
To the dust whence he came. Happier still who sojourns,
Of man made an angel, in the bosom of Christ.
Allowing his earthly remains to decay,
The plaything of Fortune, of Luck and of Chance,
Freed of the body's bonds, a spirit at last!

(Ronsard, 1938, p. 637)

Michel Eyquem de Montaigne (1533–1592)
from *Upon Some Verses of Virgil*

Montaigne on his sexual need in old age.

I have no other passion to keep me in breath. What avarice, ambition, quarrels, lawsuits do for others who, like me, have no particular vocation, love would much more commodiously do; it would restore to me vigilance, sobriety, grace, and the care of my person; it would reassure my countenance, so that the grimaces of old age, those deformed and dismal looks, might not come to disgrace it; would again put me upon sound and wise studies, by which I might render myself more loved and esteemed, clearing my mind of the despair of itself and of its use, and reintegrating it to itself; would divert me from a thousand troubled thoughts, a thousand melancholic humors that idleness and the ill posture of our health loads us withal at such an age; would warm again, in dreams at least, the blood that nature is abandoning; would hold up the chin, and a little stretch out the nerves, the vigor and gaiety of life of that poor man who is going full drive toward his ruin. But very well understand that it is a commodity hard to recover: by weakness and long experience our taste is become more delicate and nice; we ask most when we are being least, and are harder to choose when we least deserve to be accepted; and knowing ourselves for what we are, we are less confident and most distrustful; nothing can assure us of being beloved, considering our condition and theirs. I am out of countenance to see myself in company with those wanton young creatures. . . . They have the strength and reason on their side; let us give way; we have nothing to do there: and these blossoms of springing beauty suffer not themselves to be handled by such benumbed hands nor dealt with by mere material means, for as the old philosopher answered one who jeered him because he could not gain the favor of one he made love to, "Friend, the hook will not stick in such soft cheese." (Montaigne, 1962, pp. 370–371)

Victor Hugo (1802–1885)
from *L'art d'être grand-père*

Hugo is telling his grandchildren that if they made him God, he would try to play the role as a nice grandfather would, doing away with Hell, among other things, as he does not really care to see "my children cook in a furnace."

> Ah! Do not elevate me to the rank of God!
> You see, I'd do all sorts of strange things.
> I would laugh, I would take pity on roses,
> On women, on victims, on the weak and the trembling;
> My rays would be as gentle as white hair.
> I'd have a watering pot vast enough to bring forth
> Millions of flowers, in every sphere, everywhere;
> And to extinguish that sinister hell down there.
> If ever I gave an order it would be clear;
> I'd conceal the deer from the dogs on his track.
> I'd never allow a tyrant to call
> Himself my scribe. But I'd say: Joy to all!
> My miracles would be these: —gentle people.
> No more wars. No plagues. No flood.
> Priests who believe. Judges who are just.
> I'd of course, being God, stay up in the clouds,
> As behooves my estate; but I wouldn't get angry,
> And I wouldn't sit straddling my cloud
> Because of a tot who didn't behave.
> When I'd offer you heaven, O son of Japhet,
> They'd see that I know what heaven is made of.
> I wouldn't announce that the webs of heaven
> Would some day let the stars fall right through their nets.
> 'Cause I'd be afraid if I ever said so
> To see Newton nudge Spinoza and give him a wink.
> I'd play Veuillot the incredible trick
> Of inviting Christ Jesus and Voltaire to lunch.
> And of having my best wine poured out, alas!,

By the son of Lazarus to the friend of Calas.
In my Eden (a garden with a broad gate) I'd set
A nice, mysterious little water-closet,
So that the Syllabus[Pius IX's Syllabus of Errors]
                              in Paradise would find a place.
I would say to kings: Kings you are abusers,
Go away. I would, with a wink in my eye,
Give the poor their due without telling Saint Peter,
And I'd sneakily make some holes in his basket,
Under the great gold pile called Peter's Pence.
I'd tell Father Dupanloup: A little less zeal!
You're trying to pile the Maid upon the Virgin.
That, Milord, is cumulative interest. Calm down.
A jehovah who finds that a people prostrate,
Is worth less than a man standing straight, head erect,
That's what I'd be. I'd have a pardon for the fault,
But I'd say: try to remain innocent.
And I'd ask of priests not incense,
But virtue. I'd be rational. In a word,
I'd be a good guy if I were the Good Lord.

                                        (Hugo, 1974, pp. 624–626)

Old Age

Children—and grandchildren—are the only palliative to feelings of despair in old age.

In old age,
All is discolored and deformed. Nothing's of interest.
To live? What good is time? To count? What is number?
A cold landscape in a somber fog,
That's what earth is. You have nothing before you than this
    slit of night,
Through whose window life enters, through whom memory
    leaves.
The first steps of a dark descending stair,
Appear, and one thinks, as dawn is ascending,
One witnesses in the wrinkled sky the birth of ancient
    morning.
A nest seems ironic; April is filled with rain.
Nature wears the face of a pale old hag.
The serene brightness of childhood alone
Is able to gild with a smile and a hope
This livid horizon which soon will be dark.

                                        (Hugo, 1974, p. 715)

Honoré de Balzac (1799–1850)
from *Père Goriot*

Père Goriot has amassed a modest fortune as a vermicelli merchant. After his wife's death, he retires to a seamy Parisian boarding house owned by Madame Vauquer, a widow who is much attracted by old Goriot's apparent prosperity. Madame Vauquer becomes progressively suspicious, however, when old Goriot begins to be visited by elegant "ladies." She does not know that they are Goriot's two daughters, the Comtesse de Restaud and the Baronne de Nucingen, who are constantly coming to ask their old father for money so as to maintain their lifestyle in the conservative and elegant Paris of the Restoration period. Madame Vauquer's suspicions turn to outright hostility when, over a three-year period, old Goriot moves upstairs in her boarding house to ever-cheaper rooms, from an elegant and spacious *premier étage* flat to a third-floor single room. Goriot, whom Balzac calls a "Christ of Paternity," will never tell anyone the real reason for his decline.

The thrifty frugality necessary to those who mean to make their way in the world had become an inveterate habit of life with M. Goriot. Soup, boiled beef, and a dish of vegetables had been, and always would be, the dinner he liked best, so Madame Vauquer found it very difficult to annoy a boarder whose tastes were so simple. He was proof against her malice, and in desperation she spoke to him and of him slightingly before the other lodgers, who began to amuse themselves at his expense, and so gratified her desire for revenge.

Towards the end of the first year, the widow's suspicions had reached such a pitch that she began to wonder how it was that a retired merchant with a secure income of seven or eight thousand livres, the owner of such magnificent plate and jewelry handsome enough for a kept mistress, should be living in her house. Why should he devote so small a proportion of his money to his expenses? Until the first year was nearly at an end, Goriot had dined out once or twice every week, but these occasions came less frequently, and at last he was scarcely absent from the dinner table twice a month. . . .

Unluckily, towards the end of the second year, M. Goriot's conduct gave some colour to the idle talk about him. He asked Mme. Vauquer to give him a room on the second floor, and to make a corresponding reduction in her charges. Apparently, such strict economy was called for, that he did without a fire all through the winter. Mme. Vauquer asked to be paid in advance, an arrangement to which M. Goriot consented, and thence forward she spoke of him as "old Goriot."

What had brought about this decline and fall? Conjecture was keen, but investigation was difficult. Old Goriot was not communicative; in the sham countess's phrase, he was a "curmudgeon." Empty-headed people who babble about their own affairs because they have nothing else to occupy them, naturally conclude that if people say nothing of their doings it is because they will not bear being talked about; so the highly respectable merchant became a scoundrel, and the late beau was an old rogue. Opinion fluctuated. Sometimes, according to Vautrin, who came about this time to live in the Maison Vauquer, old Goriot was a man who went on Change and dabbled (to use the sufficiently expressive language of the Stock Exchange) in stocks and shares after he had ruined himself by heavy speculation. Sometimes it was held that he was one of those petty gamblers who nightly play for small stakes until they win a few francs. . . .

There were yet other solutions; old Goriot was a skinflint, a shark of a moneylender, a man who lived by selling lottery tickets. He was by turns all the most mysterious brood of vice and shame and misery; yet, however vile his life might be, the feeling of revulsion which he aroused in others was not so strong that he must be banished from their society. . . .

Towards the end of the third year, old Goriot reduced his expenses still further; he went up to the third story, and now paid forty-five francs a month. He did without snuff, told his hairdresser that he no longer required his services, and gave up wearing powder. When Goriot appeared for the first time in this condition, an exclamation of astonishment broke from his hostess at the color of his hair—a dingy olive grey. He had grown sadder day by day under the influence of some hidden trouble; among all the faces round the table his was the most woe-begone. There was no longer any doubt. Goriot was an elderly libertine, whose eyes had only been preserved by the skill of the physician from the malign influence of the remedies necessitated by the state of his health. The disgusting colour of his hair was a result of his excesses and of the drugs which he had taken that he might continue his career. The poor old man's mental and physical condition afforded some grounds for the absurd rubbish talked about him. When his outfit was worn out, he replaced the fine linen by calico at fourteen sous the ell. His diamonds, his gold snuff-box, watch-chain and trinkets, disappeared one by one. He had left off wearing the cornflower-blue coat, and was sumptuously arrayed, summer as winter, in a coarse chestnut-brown coat, a plush waistcoat, and doeskin breeches. He grew thinner and thinner; his legs were shrunken, his cheeks, once so puffed out by contented bourgeois prosperity, were covered with wrinkles, and the outlines of the jawbones were distinctly visible; there were deep furrows on his forehead. In the fourth year of his residence, he was no longer like his former self. The hale vermicelli manufacturer, sixty-two years of age, who had looked scarce forty, the stout, comfortable, prosperous tradesman, with an almost bucolic air, and such a brisk demeanor that it did you good to look at him; the man with something boyish in his smile, had suddenly sunk into his dotage, and had become a feeble, vacillating septuagenarian. (Balzac, 1907, pp. 21–24)

Gustave Flaubert (1821–1880)
from *Madame Bovary*

It is hard to know who qualifies as "elderly" in Flaubert's masterpiece, since ages are so infrequently given; but two minor characters clearly stand out as typifying contrasting conditions of the elderly in rural mid-nineteenth-century France. One is Catherine Leroux, the prototype of the "simple-hearted" Fèlicité of the later *Three Tales*. She is, ironically, being decorated by a paternalistic bourgeoisie at a country fair for her "half century of servitude" on the same small Normandy farm. The other is the eminent Doctor Larivière, who arrives too late to save Emma Bovary from suicide. Described in an electrifying portrait as he enters Emma's home, Doctor Larivière seems to be the only character in the novel to elicit Flaubert's admiration. He is generally believed to be modeled after Flaubert's father, Doctor Achille Flaubert, whom Flaubert both admired and feared. In this passage, Catherine Leroux is awarded a silver medal for having worked on a single farm for fifty-four years.

"Catherine Nicaise Elizabeth Leroux, of Sassetot-la-Guerrière, for fifty-four years of service at the same farm, a silver medal—value, twenty-five francs!"

"Where is Catherine Leroux?" repeated the councilor.

She did not present herself; one could hear voices whispering. . . .

"Go up!"

"Don't be afraid!"

"Oh, how stupid she is!"

"Well, is she there?" cried Tuvache.

"Yes, here she is."

"Then let her come up!"

Then there came forward on the platform a little old woman with timid bearing, who seemed to shrink within her poor clothes. On her feet she wore heavy wooden clogs, and from her hips hung a large blue apron. Her pale face framed in a borderless cap was more wrinkled than a withered russet apple. And from the sleeves of her red jacket looked out two large hands with knotty joints; the dust of barns, the potash of washing the grease of wools had so encrusted, roughened, hardened these that they seemed dirty, although they had been rinsed in clear water; and by dint of long service they remained half open, as if to bear humble witness for themselves of so much suffering endured. Something of monastic rigidity dignified her face. Nothing of sadness or of emotion weakened the pale look. In her constant living with animals she had caught their dumbness and their calm. It was the first time that she found herself in the midst of so large a company, and inwardly scared by the flags, the drums, the gentlemen in frock coats, and the order of the councilor, she stood motionless, not knowing whether to advance or run away, nor why the crowd was pushing her and the jury were smiling at her. Thus stood before these radiant bourgeois this half century of servitude.

"Approach, venerable Catherine Nicaise Elizabeth Leroux!" said the councilor, who had taken the list of prize winners from the president; and, looking at the piece of paper and the old woman by turns, he repeated in a fatherly tone—"Approach! Approach!"

"Are you deaf?" said Tuvache, fidgeting in his armchair; and he began shouting in her ear, "Fifty-four years of service. A silver medal. Twenty-five francs! For you!"

Then, when she had her medal, she looked at it, and a smile of beatitude spread over her face; and as she walked away they could her her muttering—

"I'll give it to our curé up home, to say masses for me!"

"What fanaticism!" exclaimed the chemist, leaning across to the notary. (Flaubert, n.d., pp. 163–164)

Emile Zola (1840–1902)
from *Earth*

The setting is La Beauce, rich wheat-growing plainland of France, on the eve of the 1870 war. Fouan, a peasant proprietor grown too old to farm, divides his property, like King Lear, among his three children and goes to live with his youngest son, Buteau, his wife Lise, and their two children. For a while he derives some consolation from his grandchildren, but as he sinks into extreme old age, even they make him feel that he is an accessory and a burden, as he is not earning his keep.

He lost his last interest in life when his legs failed him. Soon he found walking so painful that he hardly stirred beyond the village. On good days he had three favourite places, the logs outside Clou's forge, the bridge over the Aigre, and a stone bench near the school. He tottered slowly from one to the other, taking an hour to cover a couple of hundred yards, dragging his wooden shoes as if they were heavy carts, waddling and twisted, with a shambling lurch of the hips. He often spent a whole afternoon of oblivion seated on a log, huddled up, just soaking in the sunshine. He sat inert in a state of torpor, though his eyes remained open. Passersby did not greet him; nowadays, he was merely a thing, not a man. Even his pipe was too much for him; he had stopped smoking because it weighed so heavily on his gums, apart from the labor of filling and lighting it. His one desire was never to move; for as soon as he stirred, he shivered with a chill even in the hot midday sun. His will and his authority had gone, and he was now in the last stages of decrepitude, an aged animal, completely abandoned, and miserable because of having once lived the life of a man. Yet he made no complaint, reared as he was on the understanding that a foundered horse, however well it was worked, must go to the slaughterer's as soon as it cannot earn its oats. An old man is quite useless and he costs money. He himself had longed for his own father's death. If, in turn, his children wanted him to die, he felt neither astonishment nor resentment. That was how things were.

Sometimes a neighbor exclaimed, "Well, well, so you're still alive?"

"Ah," he groaned in reply. "It's a damned long business, dying, and yet it isn't the will that's lacking."

He spoke truly, out of that stoicism of the peasant who accepts death, and wishes for it as soon as he has no land and the earth is calling him back. (Zola, 1967, pp. 353, 355–356)

from *Germinal*

Northern France under Napoleon III. The year is about 1863. Etienne Lantier, a young Frenchman from the South, is looking for work and stops in a mining town called Montsou. The first person he talks to is an elderly carman named Bonnemort who, like his father and grandfather before him, has spent his life in the coal pits; and like them, he is headed for an early grave.

The workman, after having emptied the trams, had seated himself on the earth . . . maintaining his savage silence; he had simply lifted his large, dim eyes to the carman, as if annoyed by so many words. The latter, indeed, did not usually talk at such length. The unknown man's face must have pleased him that he should have been taken by one of these itchings for confidence which sometimes make old people talk aloud even when alone.

"I belong to Montsou," he said, "I am called Bonnemort."

"Is it a nickname?" asked Etienne, astonished.

The old man made a grimace of satisfaction and pointed to the Voreux:

"Yes, yes; they have pulled me three times out of that, torn to pieces, once with all my hair scorched, once with my gizzard full of earth, and another time with my belly swollen with water, like a frog. And then, when they saw that nothing would kill me, they called me Bonnemort for a joke."

His cheerfulness increased, like the creaking of an illgreased pulley, and ended by degenerating into a terrible spasm of coughing. The fire basket now clearly lit up his large head, with its scanty white hair and flat, livid face, spotted with bluish patches. He was short, with an enormous neck, projecting calves and heels, and long arms, with massive hands falling to his knees. For the rest, like his horse, which stood immovable, without suffering from the wind, he seemed to be made of stone; he had no appearance of feeling either the cold or the gusts that whistled at his ears. When he coughed his throat was torn by a deep rasping; he spat at the foot of the basket and the earth was blackened.

Etienne looked at him and at the ground which he had thus stained.

"Have you been working long at the mine?"

Bonnemort flung open both arms.

"Long? I should think so. I was not eight when I went down into the Voreux and I am now fifty-eight. Reckon that up! I have been everything down there; at first trammer, then putter, when I had the strength to wheel, then pikeman for eighteen years. Then, because of my cursed legs, they put me into the earth cutting, to bank up and patch, until they had to bring me up, because the doctor said I should stay there for good. Then, after five years of that, they made me carman. Eh? That's fine—fifty years at the mine, forty-five down below!" . . .

"They tell me to rest," he went on, "but I'm not going to; I'm not such a fool. I can get the pension of one hundred and eighty francs. If I wished them good evening today they would give me a hundred and fifty at once. They are cunning, the beggars. . . ."

The rasping was again heard in his throat, followed by the black expectoration.

"Is it blood?" asked Etienne, at last venturing to question him.

Bonnemort slowly wiped his mouth with the back of his hand. "It's coal. I've got enough in my carcass to warm me till I die. And it's five years since I put a foot down below. I stored it up, it seems, without knowing it; it keeps you alive!" (Zola, 1972, pp. 5–6)

André Gide (1869–1951)
from *So Be It*

Gide died February 19, 1951, in his eighty-second year. *So Be It* [Ainsi soit-il] was written during the last months of his life. Like Montaigne, whom he admired greatly, Gide tried to avoid the clichés about old age and tried to be honest about the persistence of sexual desire.

It is a quite novel state that I am describing. I hardly know myself. Yes, I had been able to preserve in myself . . . until the approach of my eightieth year, a sort of curiosity, of almost frisky gaiety, which I described as best I could in my books, and which made me lunge forward toward everything that seemed worthy of love and admiration, in spite of disappointments. . . . The inhibition that I feel today does not come from the outside world, nor from other people, but from myself. I have for a long time maintained myself in a state of fervor through sympathy. When I travel I do so with a young companion; I then live by proxy. I marry his surprises, his joys. . . . I think I should still be capable of feeling a few myself; it is from myself that I am progressively becoming disinterested and detached.

Nevertheless, I remain extremely sensitive to the spectacle of adolescence. Moreover, I have taken care not to allow my desires to fall asleep. In this I have listened to the advice of Montaigne, who proved particularly wise in this matter; he knew, and I know, that wisdom is not to be found in renunciation or abstinence, and he took care not to let that secret source dry up, even going so far as to "encourage" himself toward pleasure, if I understand him correctly. . . . Nonetheless, my anorexia also derives, derives especially, from a "withdrawal of sap."

I am forced to admit that. Even at the age of eighty things like this are not easy to admit. King David was just about my age, no doubt, when

he used to invite the young girl Abishag to come and warm up his bed.
(Gide, 1954)

Alfred de Vigny (1797–1863)
from *Möise*

An aged and tired Moses, having nearly accomplished his mission, goes up to
Mount Nebo to ask God to let him die. The prayer is granted. The poem is
extraordinarily majestic.

> And standing before God, having taken his place,
> Through the dark cloud they came face to face.
> He said to the Lord: "Shall I not make an end?
> Shall I live forever powerful and alone?
> Let me, O Lord, sleep the sleep of the earth.
> What have I done to you to be your elect?
> I have led your people wherever you willed.
> Now they have reached the bourn of the promised land.
> Let someone else be the messenger between you and your folk;
> Let someone else tie the bit to the Israelian steed.
> I bequeath him my book and my rod of brass."
>   .   .   .   .   .
>
> "Why did you have to dry up my hopes;
> Why did you not keep me an ignorant man,
> Seeing as from Mount Horeb to Mount Nebo
> I was unable to discover my burial place?
> Alas! You have made me a sage among the wise.
> My finger has guided the crossings of a wandering people.
> I have rained fire upon the head of kings.
> A future in prostration will adore my laws,
> I open the most ancient of the tombs of men,
> Death finds in my words a prophetic voice."
>   .   .   .   .   .
>
> "I am very great, my feet are upon the nations.
> My hand makes and unmakes the generations.
> Alas! Lord, I am powerful and alone,
> Allow me to sleep of the sleep of the earth.
> Alas! I also know all the secrets of heaven,
> And you have lent me the strength of your eyes.
> I command the night to tear open her shrouds;
> With my mouth I have called upon each of the stars,
> And no sooner had I signaled to each in the sky,
> That each hastened forward and said: 'Here am I.'
> I lay both my hands on the forehead of clouds,
> To dry up in their bowels the sources of storms,

I engulf whole cities beneath moving sand;
I topple the mountains 'neath wings of the wind.
My tireless foot is stronger than space;
The waters of rivers draw up as I pass,
And the voice of the sea is silent at my voice.
When my people are in pain, or in need of laws,
I lift up my eyes, and Thy spirit comes down.
Then the earth trembles, and the sun hesitates,
Your angels regard me with envy and wonder,
And yet, O my Lord, I'm an unhappy man.
You have made me to age powerful and alone;
Allow me to sleep of the sleep of the earth."
                    . . . . .

"As soon as your breath inspired the shepherd,
Men said between them: 'He is a stranger to us.'
And they lowered their eyes before my fiery own,
For they happened to see there far more than my soul."

from *Möises III*

"I have seen love extinguished and friendships dry out;
Virgins have shrouded themselves and feared they would die.
Enshrouding myself then in a dark cloud,
I have walked before them sad and alone in my glory,
And I've said in my heart: 'What need I want now?'
My temple's too heavy to sleep on one's breast;
My hand instills fear in the hand that it touches.
There's a storm in my voice; there's a flash on my lips.
Far from being loved I make them all tremble.
When I open my arms, they fall on their knees.
I've lived out my life, Lord, powerful and alone;
Allow me to sleep of the sleep of the earth."
                    . . . . .

Now the people were waiting, and fearing his ire,
Prayed without looking to the angry God's mountain;
If they lifted their eyes, the black flanks of the cloud
Rolled and re-echoed the thunder of the storm;
And the fiery lightning, blinding their eyes,
Kept their heads lowered in rows as in chains.
Then the peak of the mountain shone—Moses was gone.
He was grieved for—walking toward the Promised Land;
Joshua came forward, pensive and pale,
For the hand of the Lord had made him His man.

                                        (Vigny, 1837)

REFERENCES

Balzac, H. de. (1907). *Old Goriot* (E. Marriage, Trans.). London: J. M. Dent & Sons.

Beauvoir, S. de. (1972). *The coming of age* (P. O'Brian, Trans.). New York: G. P. Putnam's Sons.

Corneille, P. (1957). *The chief plays of Corneille* (Introductory study by L. Lockert, Trans.). 2nd ed. Princeton, NJ: Princeton University Press.

Flaubert, G. (n.d.). *Madame Bovary* (M. Aveling, Trans.). New York: Grosset & Dunlap.

Gide, A. (1954). Ainsi soit-il. In *Journal, 1939–1949, Souvenirs*. Paris: Gallimard (Pleiade edition).

Hugo, V. (1974). L'art d'être grand-père, and Old age. In *Oeuvres poetiques III* (P. Albouy, Ed., P. Archambault, Trans.). Paris: Gallimard (Pleiade edition).

Montaigne, M. (1962). Upon some verses of Vergil. In *Essais II* (M. Rat, Ed., C. Gordon, Trans.). Paris: Garnier Frères.

Proust, M. (1981). *Remembrance of things past* (C. K. S. Moncrieff, T. Kilmartin, and A. Mayor, Trans.) (Vol. 3). New York: Random House.

Racine, J. (1957). *The best plays of Racine* (Introduction and notes by L. Lockert, Trans.). Princeton: Princeton University Press.

Racine, J. (1958). *Racine's midi-career tragedies* (Introduction by L. Lockert, Trans.). Princeton: Princeton University Press.

Ronsard, P. de. (1938). Pièces posthumes. *Oeuvres completes* (G. Cohen, Ed., P. Archambault, Trans.). Paris: Gallimard (Pleiade edition).

Sayers, D. (1969). *The song of Roland*. Harmondsworth: Penguin.

Vigny, A. de. (1837) *Möise. In livre mystique* (P. Archambault, Trans.). Paris: Vald. Rasmussen.

Villon, F. (1977). *The poems of François Villon* (Introduction by G. Kinnell, Trans.). Boston: Houghton Mifflin.

Zola, E. (1967). *Earth* (A. Lindsay, Trans.). London: Elek Books. (Original work published in 1923)

Zola, E. (1972). *Germinal* (H. Ellis, Trans.). London: Elek Books.

FURTHER READINGS

Aragon, L. (1967). *Le roman inachevé*. Paris: Gallimard.

Beauvoir, S. de. (1972). *Old age*. London: Deutsch, Weidenfeld & Nicholson.

Beauvoir, S. de. (1972). Tout compte fait. Paris: Gallimard. (The English translation of the work is entitled *All said and done* [New York: Putnam, 1972]).

Beauvoir, S. de. (1984). *Adieux: A farewell to Sartre*. New York: Pantheon.

Beckett, S. (1955). *Molloy, a novel*. Paris: Olympia Press.

Beckett, S. (1958). *Endgame, a play in one act*. New York: Grove Press.

Beckett, S. (1960). *Krapp's last tape, and other dramatic pieces*. New York: Grove Press.

Gide, A. (1951). *Journal, 1899–1939*. Paris: Gallimard.

Léautaud, P. (1968). *Journal littéraire*. Paris: Mercure de France.

Malraux, A. (1968). *Anti-memoirs*. New York: Holt, Rinehart, & Winston.

Malraux, A. (1977). *Lazarus*. New York: Holt, Rinehart, & Winston.

Mauriac, F. (1959). *Memoires interieurs*. Paris: Flammarion.

Mauriac, F. (1968). *The inner presence: Recollections of my spiritual life. Nouveaux memoires interieurs*. (H. Briffault, Trans.). Indianapolis: Bobbs-Merrill.

Sartre, J. (1964). *Words* (I. Clephane, Trans.). Harmondsworth: Penguin.

Valéry, P. (1972). *Occasions* (R. Shattuck and F. Brown, Trans.). Princeton: Princeton University Press.

5

Aging in German and Austrian Literature

Gerd K. Schneider

Many literary works of Austria, Germany, and Switzerland focus on the issue of old age. One of the oldest, best-known poems of old age, of which two verses are offered in the first of the selections, was written by Walter von der Vogelweide. This elegy, composed probably in 1227, is sometimes referred to as Walter's "Palinode" because he seems to retract in it most of the views he expressed in his earlier songs.

In the works of Johann Wolfgang von Goethe, numerous references to old people and old age can be found. This is especially true for his later years, as his remarks to his secretary Eckermann indicate. Goethe does not equate old age with perfection but considers it a period of life just as "defective" as youth, as illustrated in the "Old Age" selections. Old age, therefore, is not a "better" period of life, but just another one, providing man with a different perspective on life, shown in his journal entries.

The theme of the aging poet and the younger woman occurs frequently in Goethe's work, most notably in "Hatem" and the "Marienbad Elegy." In his later years, Goethe believed more and more in the immortality of the soul and of the individual. Immortality, however, was not granted to all persons—only to those whose lives had been filled with activity, as illustrated in the selection titled "Immortality," a personal belief also found in part 2 of *Faust*. The last words of the dying Faust offer striking testimony that activity and creativity do not have to dwindle with old age but can persist through all stages of life.

The same thought is expressed in the seminal essay "The Ages of Life" by Arthur Schopenhauer. Schopenhauer distinguishes four stages of life: childhood, youth, manhood, and old age. It is only in the last stage that the illusionary veil has been lifted, and one is able to see the world as it really is. In this contemplative state of old age, one can, according to Schopenhauer, achieve a measure of wisdom because one is no longer subject to passionate drives. This stage of life can, therefore, be considered superior to the preceding stages of manhood and youth.

Adalbert Stifter has portrayed the elderly in many of his works. His view on old age is closely connected to his personal philosophy as expressed in the foreword to his *Bunte steine* (Colored Stones, 1853), a collection of children's stories. In this foreword, he responds to the criticism that he only wrote about small and insignificant events and that he lacked the makings of a great writer. Stifter explains that he considered the "small" things in life, for instance the breeze of the wind, the trickling of the water, and the flittering of the stars, greater than the more obvious events, like volcanic eruptions and majestic thunderstorms. The latter are to him singular events that lack a lasting impact, while the former are indispensable for the continuity of life. Stifter believes that this "natural" law also works as a "moral" law in society: the so-called great events—anger, vengeance, and passion—are really small compared to the forces that guarantee the continuity of life—love and understanding between members of the family and between generations. He further believes that people should lead their lives so that "everyone should be esteemed and honored . . . everyone should be treated as someone precious, just as everyone is precious to all others. This law is present everywhere where man lies next to man and it is evident where people interact" (Stifter, 1963, vol. 4, p. 11).

Old people in Stifter's works usually reach a maturity that allows them to judge and value their lives more objectively. The balance does not necessarily need to be on the plus side, as we find in his narration *The Recluse* (1845). In this story, young Victor visits his misanthropic uncle, who had withdrawn from society to live on a small and isolated island with his servants. The recluse, reflecting on his life, concludes that his life has been wasted and that his passing away would be no great loss to those around him. His advice to young Victor is to travel now and then get married, because "a man surrounded in his old age by sons and grandsons often lives on for a thousand years." The narrative supports the recluse's judgment on his life as he thwarts the opportunity to gain Victor's love by holding him prisoner on the island. Stifter's closing words compare the old recluse, who refuses to come to his nephew's wedding, to a fruitless fig tree that is removed from the garden just as the old man is removed from man's memory.

Another, more positive model on old men can be found in Stifter's *Nachsommer* (Indian Summer) and *Die Mappe meines urgrossvaters* (Notebooks of My Great-Grandfather). The central figure of *Indian Summer* is the old Freiherr von Risach, who, after years of state service, has retired to the country, where he has created the idyllic place Asperhof. Risach has spent much time and effort to turn this estate into a model for others.

Here he constantly works the soil, looks after his bees, grafts his fruit trees, and surrounds the entire house with beautiful roses. The emphasis in the entire novel is on the organic principle: seeds are planted, germinate, grow, and bear fruit. Not restricted to nature, this principle extends also to human affairs. Risach and his aging companion Mathilde, whom he did not marry because of a tragic misunderstanding in their youth, serve as models for the two young people, Heinrich and Natalie. These two, however, do not repeat the mistakes of their educators; they prepare themselves for marriage by very slowly getting to know each other until their relationship finally blooms into a real, not just an Indian, summer.

Risach, in all of his activities, is constantly guided by the firm idea that he does not work only for himself, but also for future generations, since he sees himself as part of a *Geschlechterkette* (a chain of generations). His life is a perfect illustration of the old men to whom the seventy-five-year-old Jacob Grimm refers in his speech on old age before the Royal Academy of Sciences in Berlin in 1860:

In old age the feeling of health is intensified although vigor declines. This is not a contradiction because this decline is counteracted by a secret and happy drive which wants to secure and keep the life-affirming drive alive until the last moment. One can say further that in old men the feeling for nature is heightened. . . . With what devotion do old men look upon the bright stars which have existed thus from time immemorial . . . how well-founded is it that old men like to take over the invigorating care of the garden and apiculture; their protective and grafting care is not done for their own enjoyment but only for the coming generations which really are the first ones who can enjoy the shadow cast by the trees planted by them. (Grimm, 1964)

This same attitude pervades almost all of Stifter's works and is probably most noteworthy in the figure of the old Colonel from the *Notebooks of My Great-Grandfather*. The Colonel intends to start a plantation of fir trees with the physician Augustin, although he knows that the real benefits of this project will be enjoyed, not by the present generation, but by future ones.

Promoting intergenerational understanding through love and empathy can be found in the tale *The Old Grandfather and the Grandson,* which is contained in the Grimm collection of fairy tales. Here the message is clear: old people should not be isolated from society or the closest family, and it is a moral obligation to care for them if they cannot care for themselves. The importance of these tales should not be underestimated, because they have been read, and are still being read, by countless children whose attitudes toward the elderly are influenced by them.

The Viennese Arthur Schnitzler, a contemporary of Hugo von Hofmannsthal, is known for the psychological acuity with which he forms his characters. This is particularly the case in the figure of the Chevalier de Seingalt, known as Casanova in *Casanova's Homecoming* (1918). Casanova, feeling the advent of old age, wants to return to his native Venice, from which he was banished due to his adverse, liberal political views. While he is awaiting a pardon from the Doge, he meets Marcolina, a beautiful and highly intelligent woman with whom he falls in love. Marcolina, however, does not respond to his advances. He then makes a deal with the Lieutenant Lorenzi, Marcolina's lover, a man who in many respects is a younger replica of Casanova. In return for paying Lorenzi's gambling debts, Casanova earns the right to spend a night with Marcolina. During the night the aging adventurer, disguised as Lorenzi, enters her room and experiences a state of *unio mystica*: "Pleasure became worship." In the morning Marcolina finds out that she has been deceived, and in her eyes he reads "the word which to him was the most dreadful of all words, since it passed final judgement on him—old man." After he leaves her, he kills the Lieutenant, who is waiting for him, and continues with his journey to Venice, where he will spend the remaining days of his life as an informer to the police, thus betraying the very ideals in which he had believed in his youth. Schnitzler presents a study of the physical and psychological deterioration that may accompany old age in the figure of Casanova. This depiction of old age can be viewed as extremely negative, as Annan remarks in a recent review of the work: *"Casanova* is [not] short on sex, age, decay, and disgust, being about the humiliation of old age as suffered by the decrepit Italian adventurer" (Annan, 1983, p. 16).

A character whose experience of old age is reminiscent of Schopenhauer's views is Siddhartha in the novel of the same name by Hermann Hesse. Siddhartha, trying to find self-fulfillment, leaves home with his friend Govinda and spends three years with the ascetic Samanas. They then meet Gautama, the Buddha, and while Govinda stays with Buddha, Siddhartha goes into the world. Crossing a river, he comes to a large city where he meets the courtesan Kamalax and enters a phase of sensual pleasure, living a life of luxury. He finds, however, that this is just as disappointing as the ascetic life. He leaves again and, having come close to committing suicide, spends the rest of his life as a ferryman. Through the years he acquires the wisdom that time is just an illusion and that love is the underlying unity of all things. This insight comes to him in old age, and with this knowledge, he attains inner harmony and peace. This harmony is reflected in his smile, as the visiting Govinda realizes. Other views consistent with Hesse's ideas about old age and death are clearly illustrated in excerpts under those titles in the selections.

Another writer using themes related to old age in his works is Bertolt Brecht, who differs from Hesse in that he presents a more realistic picture of old people. In his "Ballad of the Old Woman" and in the short story

"The Unseemly Old Lady," Brecht renders two of the most life-affirming portraits of old women in all of literature. The ballad captures the typical concerns of a conventional old woman: making jam, taking pride in her clothing, caring for her teeth, worrying about her children, and putting all of these cares in God's hands. But it is apparent that the woman's true strength derives from a strong elemental will to live. In "The Unseemly Old Lady," the seventy-two-year-old woman had previously lived only for others, sacrificing herself and her dreams for the sake of her husband and her children, doing what was expected of her. However, following the death of her husband, she refuses to live according to the conventional expectations of her children and society. Instead, she forges a new life for herself; she does not give the house to her son, who has a large family, she makes new friends who are considered by her family members as unsuitable for an old lady, and she even goes out occasionally. Here Brecht shows us a vital old woman who has the courage to make a new beginning at the "end" of her life.

The selections for this chapter offer a general overview of Austrian, German, and Swiss writers who have portrayed the elderly in their works. Predominant themes are the aging poet lamenting the loss of his youth (Walter von der Vogelweide); productivity and activity in old age (Goethe, Stifter, Grimm); the relationship of older men to younger woman (Goethe, Schnitzler); acceptance of old people by society and the fostering of intergenerational understanding (Stifter); old age and wisdom (Schopenhauer, Hesse); and old age and prescriptive role behavior (Brecht). Brecht's portrayal of the "Unseemly Old Lady" is especially refreshing because he shows that it is possible for her, even at seventy-two, to start a new, unconventional life. This old woman brings to mind Nietzsche's three metamorphoses of the spirit, where one proceeds from the "Thou shalt" phase of the camel to the "I will" phase of the lion and, finally, to the child phase in which new values can be created and new attitudes can be formed.

SELECTIONS

Walter von der Vogelweide (ca. 1170–ca. 1230)
from *Elegy*

> Alas, where have they vanished, all the years I knew!
> Was all my life a vision, or can it be true?
> What'er I thought existed, was that reality?
> Since then methinks I've slept, though unbeknown to me.
> Now once again awake, in ignorance I stand
> Of all that was familiar as my either hand.
> The folk, and land where I from childhood's years was reared,
> Have grown to me as strange as falsehood e'er appeared.

And those who played with me are sluggish now and old;
The planted lands are waste, the trees cut down and sold.
Were not the river flowing as it used to flow,
In truth I think there were no limits to my woe.
I get a listless nod from men who knew me well;
When I recall the bygone days so full of glee,
Now just as lost as if I'd tried to punch the sea—Evermore,
    alas!

(Walter von der Vogelweide, 1968, pp. 159–160)

Johann Wolfgang von Goethe (1749–1832)
from *On Old Age*

We must not take the faults of our youth into our old age; for old age brings with it its own defects. (August 16, 1824) (Goethe, 1974, p. 18)

"From the letters I wrote at this period," said he, "I plainly see we have certain advantages and disadvantages at every time of life, as compared with earlier or later periods. In my fortieth year I was as clear and decided on some subjects as at present, and in many respects superior to my present self; yet now, in my eightieth, I possess advantages I should not like to exchange for those." (April 12, 1829) (Goethe, 1930, p. 327)

"People always fancy," said Goethe, laughing, "that we must become old to become wise; but, in truth, as years advance, it is hard to keep ourselves as wise as we were. Man becomes, indeed, in the different stages of life, a different being; but cannot say that he is a better one, and in certain matters he is as likely to be right in his twentieth as in his sixtieth year.

We see the world one way from a plain, another way from the heights of a promontory, another from the glacier fields of the primary mountains. We see, from one of these points, a larger piece of world than from the others; but that is all, and we cannot say that we see more truly from any one than from the rest. When a writer leaves monuments on the different steps of his life, it is chiefly important that he should have an innate foundation and good will; that he should, at each step, have seen and felt clearly, and that, without any secondary aims, he should have said distinctly and truly what has passed in his mind. Then will his writings, if they were right at the step where they originated, remain always right, however the writer may develop or alter himself in after times." (February 17, 1831) (Goethe, 1974, pp. 383–384)

Both are but one happiness; to be aware of the advantages of old age when one is young, and to preserve the advantages of youth when one is old. (Goethe, 1960, p. 542)

Elegy, from *Wanderer's Night Song II*

> Above every summit
> Is peace,
> On every treetop
> You perceive
> Scarcely a breeze;
> The birds in the woods are silent.
> Only wait, soon
> You will rest too.

> (Goethe, 1980, p. 89)

(Immortality)
from *The Wisdom of Goethe*

Man is entitled to believe in immortality; such belief is agreeable to his nature; and his instincts in this direction are confirmed by religious assurances. My belief in the immortality of the soul springs from the idea of activity; for when I persevere to the end in a course of restless activity, I have a sort of guarantee from Nature that, when the present form of my existence proves itself inadequate for the energizing of my spirit, she will provide another form more appropriate. When a man is seventy-five years old, he cannot avoid now and then thinking of death. This thought, when it comes, leaves me in a state of perfect peace, for I have the most assured conviction that our soul is of an essence absolutely indestructible; an essence that works on from eternity to eternity. It is like the sun, which to our earthly eyes sinks and sets, but in reality never sinks, but shines on unceasingly. (February 4, 1829) (Goethe, 1974, p. 74)

from *Faust*

> This is the highest wisdom that I own,
> The best that mankind ever knew:
> Freedom and life are earned by those alone
> Who conquer them each day anew.
> Surrounded by such danger, each one thrives,
> Childhood, manhood, and age lead active lives.

> (Goethe, 1961, p. 469)

Arthur Schopenhauer (1788–1860)
from *The Ages of Life*

Towards the close of life, much the same thing happens as at the end of a *bal masqué*—the masks are taken off. Then you can see who the people really are, with whom you have come into contact in your passage through the world. For by the end of life characters have come out in their true light, actions have borne fruit, achievements have been rightly appreciated, and all shams have fallen to pieces. For this, Time was in every case requisite.

But the most curious fact is that it is also only towards the close of life that a man really recognizes and understands his own true self, the aims and objects he has followed in life, more especially the kind of relation in which he has stood to other people and to the world. It will often happen that as a result of this knowledge, a man will have to assign himself a lower place than he formerly thought was his due. But there are exceptions to this rule, and it will occasionally be the case that he will take a higher position than he had before. This will be owing to the fact that he had no adequate notion of the *baseness* of the world, and that he set up a higher aim for himself than was followed by the rest of mankind.

The progress of life shows a man the stuff of which he is made.

It is customary to call youth the happy, and age the sad part of life. This would be true if it were the passions that made a man happy. Youth is swayed to and fro by them, and they give a great deal of pain and little pleasure. In age the passions cool and leave a man at rest, and then forthwith his mind takes a contemplative tone; the intellect is set free and attains the upper hand. And since, in itself, intellect is beyond the range of pain, a man feels happy just in so far as his intellect is the predominating part of him. (Schopenhauer, 1970, pp. 151–152)

Adalbert Stifter (1805–1868)
from *The Recluse*

"Oh, Victor, do you know what life is? Do you know what this thing is that is called old age?"

"How should I, Uncle, when I am still so young?"

"True, you don't know, and you can't know. Life is immeasurably long when one is still in one's youth. You always think there is plenty of time ahead of you and that you have only come a short way. And so you postpone things, you put this and that on one side, meaning to take it up again later. But when you try to take it up it is too late and you notice that you are old. So life seems unlimited when we are looking ahead into it, but when we reach the end and look back, it hardly seems to have spanned a few years. It is a field on which many fruits ripen that we never thought we had sowed. It's an enticing brightness of many colours, and we plunge into it, thinking it will surely last for ever—and old age is a moth in the dusk, an uncanny thing flitting round our ears. And so we stretch out our hands and cannot bear to leave, because we have missed so much. All the many different deeds of an old, old man may be heaped up high as a hill, but what good does it do him to stand at the top? I have done many things, all kinds of things, and they have brought me no reward. It all crumbles to nothingness in a moment—unless we have created an existence that will last us beyond the grave. A man surrounded in his old age by sons and grandsons and great grandsons often lives on for a thousand years. A life has been established, an existence which is diverse and yet all of the same kind, and when he has gone that life nevertheless continues just as before; indeed, no one even notices that one fragment of it has turned away and passed out of sight. At my death everything I have been, all that has made me myself, will perish forever. . . . This is why you must marry, Victor, and marry very young. . . . But for that matter you can do as you please. Enjoy what is yours in your own way. If you are wise, well and good; if you are a fool, you can spend your age regretting your life, as I have regretted mine. I have done many things that were good, I have enjoyed a great deal that life has to offer and rightly offers for our enjoyment—all this was good; but there are many things that I have left undone, and I came to regret them and brood over them later, when regretting and brooding were both useless. For life has flown past me before I could catch it. Since you are probably also my heir, I should like you to do better than I have done. Therefore my advice to you is this—and I say 'advice,' not condition, for one has no right to bind anyone; travel now for two or three years, then come back and get married. I have appointed a steward to manage your estate and to begin with you had better keep him on, for he will give you the right sort of guidance. This is how I see it; but you must do as you please." (Stifter, 1968, pp. 134–137)

The Brothers Grimm
Jacob (1785–1863) Wilhelm (1786–1859)
from *The Old Grandfather and the Grandson*

There was once a very old man whose eyes had grown dim, his ears deaf, and whose knees shook. When he sat at the table hardly able to hold his spoon he'd spill soup on the tablecloth, and a little would even run out of his mouth. This disgusted his son and his daughter-in-law, and so finally the old grandfather had to sit in a corner behind the stove. They gave him his food in an earthenware bowl and not even enough at that. He used to look sadly toward the table, and tears would come to his eyes. One day his trembling hands couldn't even hold the bowl, and it fell to the floor and broke to pieces. The young woman scolded, but he said nothing and merely sighed. For a few farthings she then bought him a wooden bowl, and he had to eat out of that. As they were sitting thus, his little four-year-old grandson was fitting some little boards together on the floor. "What are you doing there?" asked his father. "I'm making a trough for father and mother to eat out of when I'm grown up," answered the child.

The husband and wife looked at one another for a while, finally began to weep, and at once brought the old grandfather to the table. From then they always let him eat with them, and they didn't say anything even when he did spill a little. (Grimm and Grimm, 1960, p. 288)

Arthur Schnitzler (1862–1931)
from *Casanova's Homecoming*

At that instant he heard a gentle rattling, and knew it was made by the grating of Marcolina's window in opening. Then both wings of the window were drawn back, though the curtain still veiled the interior. Casanova remained motionless for a few seconds more, until the curtain was pulled aside by an unseen hand. Taking this as a sign, he swung himself over the sill into the room, and promptly closed window and grating behind him. The curtain had fallen across his shoulders, so that he had to push his way beneath it. Now he would have been in absolute darkness had there not been shining from the depths of the distance, incredibly far away, as if awakened by his own gaze, the faintest possible illumination to show him the way. No more than three paces forward, and eager arms enfolded him. Letting the sword slip from his hand, the cloak from his shoulders, he gave himself up to his bliss.

From Marcolina's sigh of surrender, from the tears of happiness which he kissed from her cheeks, for the ever-renewed warmth with which she received his caresses, he felt sure that she shared his rapture; and to him this rapture seemed more intense than he had ever experienced, seemed to possess a new and strange quality. Pleasure became worship; passion was transfused with an intense consciousness. Here at last was the reality which he had often falsely imagined himself to be on the point of attaining, and which had always eluded his grasp. He held in his arms a woman upon whom he could squander himself, with whom he could feel himself inexhaustible; the woman upon whose breast the moment of ultimate self-abandonment and of renewed desire seemed to coalesce into a single instant of hitherto unimagined spiritual ecstasy. Were not life and death, time and eternity, one upon these lips? Was he not a god? Were not youth and age merely a fable; visions of men's fancy? Were not home and exile, splendor and misery, renown and oblivion, senseless distinctions, fit only for the use of the uneasy, the lonely, the frustrate; had not the words become unmeaning to one who was Casanova, and who had found Marcolina?

·   ·   ·   ·   ·

Casanova sat up, his eyes riveted upon her. Neither was able to look away from the other. His expression was one of rage and shame; hers was one of shame and disgust. Casanova knew how she saw him, for he saw himself figured in imagination, just as he had seen himself yesterday in the bedroom mirror. A yellow, evil face, deeply lined, with thin lips and staring eyes—a face three times worse than that of yesterday, because of the excesses of the night, the ghastly dream of the morning, and the terrible awakening. And what he read in Marcolina's countenance was not what he would a thousand times rather have read there; it was not thief, libertine, villain. He read only something which crushed him to earth more ignominiously than could any terms of abuse; he read the word which to him was the most dreadful of all words, since it passed a final judgement upon him—old man. (Schnitzler, 1922, pp. 164–166, 172)

Hermann Hesse (1877–1962)
from *Siddhartha*

The two old men were silent for a long time. Then as Govinda was preparing to go, he said: "I thank you, Siddhartha, for telling me something of your thoughts. Some of them are strange thoughts. I cannot grasp them immediately. However, I thank you, and I wish you, many peaceful days."

Inwardly, however, he thought: Siddhartha is a strange man and he expresses strange thoughts. His ideas seem crazy. How different do the Illustrious One's doctrines sound! They are clear, straightforward, comprehensible; they contain nothing strange, wild or laughable. But Siddhartha's hands and feet, his eyes, his brow, his breathing, his smile, his greeting, his gait affect me differently from his thoughts. Never, since the time our Illustrious Gotama passed into Nirvana, have I ever met a man with the exception of Siddhartha about whom I felt: This is a holy man! His ideas may be strange, his words may sound foolish, but his glance and his hand, his skin and his hair, all radiate a purity, peace, serenity, gentleness and saintliness which I have never seen in any man since the recent death of our illustrious teacher.

While Govinda was thinking these thoughts and there was conflict in his heart he again bowed to Siddhartha, full of affection towards him. He bowed low before the quietly seated man.

"Siddhartha," he said, "we are now old men. We may never see each other again in this life. I can see, my dear friend, that you have found peace. I realize that I have not found it. Tell me one more word, my esteemed friend, tell me something that I can conceive, something I can understand! Give me something to help me on my way, Siddhartha. My path is often hard and dark."

Siddhartha was silent and looked at him with his calm, peaceful smile. Govinda looked steadily in his face, with anxiety, with longing. Suffering, continual seeking and continual failure were written in his look.

Siddhartha saw it and smiled.

"Bend near to me!" he whispered in Govinda's ear. "Come, still nearer, quite close! Kiss me on the forehead, Govinda. . . ." Govinda bowed low. Incontrollable tears trickled down his old face. He was overwhelmed by a feeling of great love, of the most humble veneration. He bowed low, right down to the ground, in front of the man sitting there motionless, whose smile reminded him of everything that he had loved in his life, or everything that had even been of value and holy in his life. (Hesse, 1971, pp. 148–149, 151–152)

from *On Old Age*

Old age is a stage in our lives, and like all other stages it has a face of its own, its own atmosphere and temperature, its own joys and miseries. We old white-haired folk, like all our younger human brothers, have a part to play that gives meaning to our lives, and even someone mortally ill and dying, who can hardly be reached in his own bed by a cry from this world, has his task, has something important and necessary to accomplish. Being old is just as beautiful and holy a task as being young, learning to die and dying are just as valuable functions as any other—assuming that they are carried out with reverence toward the meaning and holiness of all life. A man who hates being old and gray, who fears the nearness of death, is no more worthy a representative of his stage of life than a strong young person who hates and tries to escape his profession and his daily tasks.

To put it briefly, to fulfill the meaning of age and to perform its duty one must be reconciled with old age and everything it brings with it. One must say yes to it. Without this yea, without submission to what nature demands of us, the worth and meaning of our days—whether we are old or young—are lost and we betray life. (Hesse, 1975, pp. 269–271)

(Death)
from *Reflections*

Death agony, no less than childbirth, is a life process, and often one can mistake the one for the other.

After each death, life becomes more delicate and precious. The call of death is also a call of love. Death becomes sweet when we say yes to it, when we accept it as one of the great and eternal forms of life and transformation.

The rational man believes that the earth was given to man for his use. His most dreaded enemy is death, the thought that his life and activity are transient. He avoids thinking of death, and when the thought pursues him, he takes refuge in activity, he fights off death with redoubled striving: for possessions, for knowledge, for laws, for rational mastery of the world. His immortality is his belief in progress: he believes that as an active link in the endless chain of progress he will never entirely cease to be.

We should never repent of steps we have taken or of deaths we have died.

It seems to me that when a man's nature, education, and circumstances forbid him to commit suicide, he will be unable to do so, even if his imagination sometimes tempts him with this solution. When this is not the case and a man resolutely casts away a life that has become unbearable to him, he is, I believe, as much entitled to his suicide as others to a natural death. I have felt the death of some men who have made away with themselves to be more natural and meaningful than that of a good many who died a natural death.

A man dies so damned slowly, bit by bit; every tooth, muscle, and bone takes leave individually, as though we had been especially intimate with it.

Grief and lamentation are our first natural response to the loss of someone we loved. They help us through our first anguish; but they do not suffice to forge a bond between us and the dead.

On the primitive level, this is accomplished by the cult of the dead: sacrifices, decoration of the tomb, monuments, flowers. But at our level the sacrifice to the dead must take place in our own souls, through thoughts, through exacting memory, whereby we reconstruct the loved one within us. If we can do this, the dead live on by our side, their image is saved and helps to make our grief fruitful.

I need no weapon against death, because there is no death. What does exist is the fear of death. That can be cured. In the essentials of what they meant to us, the dead live on with us as long as we ourselves live. Sometimes we can speak to them and take counsel of them more readily than with the living. (Hesse, 1974, pp. 181–183)

Bertolt Brecht (1898–1956)
Ballad of the Old Woman

> Last Monday she got up about eleven
> They never thought she'd make it on her own
> She took her fever as a sign from heaven
> For months she'd been no more than skin and bone.
> For two whole days she'd vomited saliva
> And looked as white as snow when she got up
> Weeks back the priest had called to anoint and shrive her.
> Coffee, it seemed, was all she cared to sup.
> Once more, though, she'd evaded death's caresses
> The final rites had been mistimed a bit.
> She loved the walnut chest that held her dresses
> And could not bring herself to part from it.
> Old furniture is often worm-infested
> But still it's part of you. And so to speak
> She would have missed it. Well, may God protect it.

She made twelve pots of blackberry jam last week.
What's more, she's now made sure her teeth are working.
You eat much better if your teeth are right
You wear them in the morning when out walking
And keep them in old coffee cups at night.
Her children have remembered her existence
She's heard from them, and God will guard them.
Yes
She'll last the winter out with God's assistance
Nor is there much wrong with her old black dress.

(Brecht, 1976, pp. 92–93)

from *The Unseemly Old Lady*

When you come to think of it, she lived two lives in succession. The first one as daughter, wife and mother; the second simply as Mrs. B, an unattached person without the responsibilities and with modest but sufficient means. The first life lasted some seventy years; the second no more than two.

My father learnt that in the last six months she had permitted herself certain liberties unknown to normal people. Thus she might rise in summer at three in the morning and take walks in the deserted streets of the little town, which she had entirely to herself. And, it was generally alleged, when the priest called on her to keep the old woman company in her loneliness, she invited him to the cinema.

She was not at all lonely. A crowd of jolly people foregathered at the cobbler's, it appears, and there was much gossip. She always kept a bottle of her own red wine there and drank her little glassful whilst the others gossiped and inveighed against the town officials. This wine was reserved for her, though sometimes she provided stronger drink for the company.

She died quite suddenly on an autumn afternoon, in her bedroom, though not in bed but on an upright chair by the window. She had invited the "half-wit" to the cinema that evening, so the girl was with her when she died. She was seventy-four years old.

I have seen a photograph of her which was taken for the children and shows her laid out.

What you see is a tiny little face, very wrinkled, and a thin-lipped, wide mouth. Much that is small, but no smallness. She had savoured to the full the long years of servitude and the short years of freedom and consumed the bread of life to the last crumb. (Brecht, 1961, pp. 104–105)

REFERENCES

Annan, G. (1983, July 12). The return of La Ronde [Review of *Arthur Schnitzler: plays and stories*. *The New York Review of Books*, p. 16.

Brecht, B. (1961). The unseemly old lady. In *Tales from the calendar* (Y. Kapp and M. Hamburger, Trans.). London: Methuen.

Brecht, B. (1976). Ballad of the old woman. In *Poems* (J. Willet and R. Manheim, Eds.). London: Eyre Methuen.

Eckerman, J. P. (1958). *Gespräche mit Goethe in den letzten Jahren seines Lebens* (G. K. Schneider, Trans.). Berlin: Deutsche Buch-Gemeinschaft.

Goethe, J. W. (1930). *Conversations of Goethe with Eckermann*. New York: Dutton.

Goethe, J. W. (1957). Hatem. In *Poems of Goethe, a sequel to "Goethe the lyrist": New translation facing the originals and a list of musical settings* (E. H. Zeydel, Ed.). Chapel Hill: University of North Carolina Press.

Goethe, J. W. (1960). Maximen und Reflexionen. In *Werke in 15 Bänden* (G. K. Schneider, Trans.) (Vol. 12). Hamburg: Christian Wegner.

Goethe, J. W. (1961). *Faust: The original German and a new translation and introduction* (W. Kaufmann, Ed.). Garden City, NY: Doubleday.

Goethe, J. W. (1974). *The wisdom of Goethe* (J. S. Blackie, Ed.). New York: Folcroft Library Editions. (Reprinted from Charles Scribner's Sons, 1883.)

Goethe, J. W. (1980). Elegy, from Wanderer's Night Song II. In *The eternal feminine: Selected poems of Goethe* (O. K. Datene, Trans.). New York: Frederick Ungar.

Grimm, Jacob. (1964). Rede uber das Alter. In his *Reden und Abhandlungen. Kleinere Schriften* (vol. 6, pp. 188–210). Berlin: Ferdinand Dummlers.

Grimm, J. L., and Grimm, K. (1960). *German folk tales* (F. P. Magoun et al., Trans.). Carbondale: Southern Illinois University Press.

Hesse, H. (1971). *Siddhartha* (H. Rosner, Trans.). New York: Bantam.

Hesse, H. (1974). *Reflections* (V. Michels, Ed., R. Manheim, Trans.). New York: Farrar, Straus, & Giroux.

Hesse, H. (1975). On old age. In *My belief: Essays on life and art* (T. Ziolkowski, Ed., D. Lindley, Trans.). New York: Farrar, Straus, & Giroux.

Schnitzler, A. (1922). *Casanova's homecoming* (E. Paul and C. Paul, Trans.). New York: Thomas Seltzer.

Schopenhauer, A. (1970). The ages of life. In *Counsels and maxims* (T. B. Saunders, Trans.). St. Clair Shores, MI: Scholarly Press.

Stifter, A. (1963). *Gesammelte Werke in vierzehn Bänden* (K. Steffen, Ed., G. K. Schneider, Trans.). Basel and Stuttgart: Birkhauser.

Stifter, A. (1968). *The recluse* (D. Luke, Trans.). London: Jonathan Cape.

Vogelweide, W. v. d. (1968). Elegy (E. H. Zeydel, Trans). In G. F. Jones, *Walter von der Vogelweide*. New York: Twayne. (pp. 159–160).

FURTHER READING

Arnold, A. (1978). Näher mein Ich zu Dir: Die Problematik des Alterns, des Sterbens, und des Todes bei Max Frisch. In G. P. Knapp (Ed.), *Max Frisch: Aspekte des Prosawerks* (pp. 249–265). Las Vegas: Lang.

Bichsel, P. (1970). A table is a table. In *There is no such place as America* (M. Hamburger, Trans.) (pp. 15–25). New York: Delacorte Press.

Bienengräber, A. (1978). Altern und Alter in der Aussage von Wilhelm Busch. *Wilhelm-Busch-Jahrbuch: Mitteilungen der Wilhelm-Busch-Gesellschaft*, 41–44, 43–49.

Broch, H. (1955). Zerline, the old servant girl. In R. Pick (Ed.), *German stories and tales* (pp. 220–249). New York: Washington Square.

Frisch, M. (1980). *Man in the holocene* (G. Skelton, Trans.) New York: Harcourt Brace Jovanovich.

Grillparzer, F. (1967). *The poor fiddler* (A. Henderson and E. Henderson, Trans.) New York: Frederick Ungar.

Rilke, R. M. (1929). How old Timofei died laughing. In L. Melville & R. Hargreaves (Eds.), *Great German short stories* (pp. 380–386). New York: Boni & Liveright.

Schneider, G. (1983). Portrayal of the elderly in Stefan Zweig's novella "Vierundzwanzig Stunden aus dem Leben einer Frau." In M. Sonnenfeld (Ed.), *Stefan Zweig: The world of yesterday's humanist today: Proceedings of the Stefan Zweig symposium* (pp. 177–185). Albany: State University of New York.

Schneider, G. (1984). Das "sanfte Gesetz" und die Kontinuität der Geschlechter: Zur Darstellung der Senioren in Stifters Werk. In W. W. Moelleken (Ed.), *Dialectology, linguistics, literature: Festschrift für Carroll E. Reed* (pp. 249–266). Göppingen: Kümmerle.

Seidel, C. (1987). Alter[n]: Eine "zinsbare Kunst"? Betrachtungen zu *Agathon* mit einem Seitenblick auf die *Wahlverwandtschaften*. In U. Faulhaber et al. (Eds.), *Exile and Enlightenment: Studies in German and comparative literature in honor of Guy Stern* (pp. 105–113). Detroit: Wayne State University Press.

6

"No Joy":
Old Age in Russian Literature

Robert H. Stacy

In proverbs, more than in any other verbal devices, we find the various aspects of life and nature reflected in quintessentially pithy and often harshly realistic terms. But since man, more than any other animal, loves to adorn himself and his surroundings, even in the corpora of European proverbial wisdom the dour realism of life is frequently embellished. Thus the Russian proverb *starost ne radost* (old age is no joy), while succinctly presenting an essential truth, is itself adorned with assonance and syllabic symmetry. If "old age is no joy" is the essential reality, then everything else, beginning with the verbal adornment in our example and embracing all the possible topological variations (including the inverse: "old age is joy") and stylistic treatments, is literature. Amidst the variety, however, one can easily detect two polar extremes: senility as an abjectly forlorn and ugly condition and old age as a noble state of grace. Since literature, both in the East and the West, has been overwhelmingly a male affair, it is elderly women who are apt more often to fall into the former extreme as "crones," "witches," and "hags," and men into the latter as respected elders and Nestors.

Because Russian literature is an integral part of European literature, it shares the latter's prejudices and displays a full spectrum of those commonplaces involving old age that are so familiar in the West; certainly there is none of that gerontolatry that is a notable feature of Far Eastern, especially Chinese, culture. Of particular interest, however, is the Russian image of the *starets* or elder. Of Byzantine (Greek Orthodox) origin, the *starets* is a characteristic figure of Orthodox monasticism. An archetype was the fourth-century Saint Makarios, famed for his austere life and his wisdom and known as *paidariogeron* (childlike old man), an epithet reminding us of the *puer-senex* topos illustrated, for example, in the life of the Russian Saint Sergei of Radonezh (fourteenth century), who—without suffering from progeria—had been like an old man even as a child. This *paidariogeron* image of the elder appears again and again in Russian literature, perhaps the best example being that of Zosima in Dostoevsky's *The Brothers Karamazov.* Bearded elders live on, however, in secularized form, mouthing the ethics of Marxism-Leninism, as, for instance, stern senior officials of collective farms in numerous Soviet Russian novels.

Some old men in literature are clearly idealized personifications of what certain authors would like old men to be—healthy in mind and body and essentially pagan. Although Kazantzakis's Zorba the Greek has become an exemplary model in this category, an earlier version is the old Cossack Eroshka in Tolstoy's *The Cossacks* (1904). Eroshka, inspired by the author's own Rousseauan paganism (which eventually brought about his excommunication from the Russian Orthodox Church), holds that "God has made everything for man's joy" and rejects any orthodox religious tenets. His views are a constant revelation to the young but already-bored Olenin in this famous story (which Hugo von Hofmannsthal could never read without thinking of Homer). The figure of the "natural man" grown old but still rejecting the established system and its beliefs appears again in the character of Spiridon in Nobel Prize Laureate Alexander Solzhenitsyn's *The First Circle,* a character who maintains his natural goodness amidst the ravages of Stalinism. Tolstoy, who reached the age of eighty-two, is a good example of opsimathy or "late learning." Like Solon, he could say, "I grow old always learning something new." Tolstoy bravely attempted to learn Greek in his old age so that he might read his beloved Homer in the original; but he never managed to gain any lasting facility. Toward the end of his life he wrote *Fables and Fairy Tales,* and one thinks of Longinus, who remarked in speaking of Homer that "when a great genius is falling into decline, it is characteristic of his old age that he should be fond of fables."

Speaking of Cossacks, we might mention that Nobel Prize Laureate Mikhail Sholokhov in his novel *And Quiet Flows the Don* (1928–1940) gives a new twist to the theme of old age by having the old Cossack Pantaleimon resist seduction by his randy daughter-in-law in a barn. The scene is an unusual one, with considerable naturalistic detail; one does not find in Sholokhov or elsewhere in Russian literature the reverse situation, an old woman resisting seduction by a son-in-law. Evidently male writers consider such a scene repulsive and not at all provocative. On the other hand, European literature, including Russian, can provide numerous examples of children as objects of lechery and seduction by old men, especially in the works of Dickens and Dostoevsky. But can one recall, even in pornography, a single instance of seduction by an old woman? Old women in literature, even when portrayed by men as witches, are quite devoid of sexuality. Perhaps the closest we come is in the obscenities and double entendres of characters such as La Celestina or the Nurse in *Romeo and Juliet.*

In Russian literature, as in the other European literatures, old women tend for the most part to be either pitiful, abused creatures or notoriously garrulous gossips (note the Greek phrase *hythlos graon,* "old wives' tales"). Stylistically, they provide writers with excellent opportunities for idiolect techniques. Indeed, in real-life nonmongrelized cultures, old women are of special linguistic interest, preserving as they often do a purer and more archaic language than their male counterparts. Still, the more or less unvarying portrayal of old women in literature becomes boring and maudlin, even in the case of the long-suffering Matryona in Solzhenitsyn's 1963 work, *Matryona's House.* But a good deal of verbal artifice is bromidic, and only that artist captures our attention again and again who can either use his imagination to good effect or render competently in words both the sadness and the delights of actual reality. The enigmatic Nikolai Gogol presents numerous absurd caricatures of old men and women. Sergei Aksakov in his semifictional *Family Chronicle,* originally published in 1856, provides a touching yet comical picture of his own grandfather, a strict disciplinarian but with a sense of humor, being hoodwinked by his serfs. In Turgenev's well-known novel, *Fathers and Sons,* six years later, one of the saddest events that can occur in the lives of old people—the prior death of an only child—is sensitively described. The modern Soviet writer Georgii Sadovnikov, in a short story entitled "Vadik, the Old Man," tells about an old man who briefly escapes the surveillance of his children and grandchildren and wanders out into the city. He recalls his past life from time to time and tries to talk with people, but they ignore him. He watches a young woman in a phone booth and tries to give her a plastic fan he has found, but she angrily walks away. Vadik finally stands in front of a store window and sadly sees what other people see in the reflection: a bald skull, networks of wrinkles, and a potbelly.

Old people, especially men, have appeared frequently in dramatic works ever since Greco-Roman times. The old men in Aristophanes are hilarious, and the *senex* is a conventional figure in Roman comedy. But aside from such major characters as Shakespeare's Lear, they are most often minor and comic figures, *laudatores temporis acti,* and the butts of coarse humor. An excellent example in Russian literature is the pathetic old butler Firs (the name is the Russian form of the Greek *thyrsos*) in Chekhov's *The Cherry Orchard,* first performed in 1903. He grumbles and mutters to himself throughout the play, laments the passing of the old ways, and is finally forgotten as the former owners of the auctioned-off estate move out. He is ridiculed by the other servants, and one character in the play suggests that Firs should long ago have "croaked,"

Death, pictured either as the liberation of the soul or as mere termination of life, has always been an important theme in Western poetry. There is no such preoccupation with death in, for example, Chinese poetry; but old age, a kind of limbo between youth and vibrant maturity on the one hand and death on the other, has not been an attractive theme for poets in the West. (Again, the reverse is true in Chinese literature.) As writers in the West have been attracted by death but not by the process of dying,[1] so some attention has been paid to old age as an abstract concept but not to the process of growing old. One might paraphrase Montaigne and say, "Ce n'est pas la vieillesse qui m'effraie, mais le vieillir." Russian poetry, too, while avoiding almost completely the theme of senescence, offers a few examples of the treatment of old age itself and its pleasures and tribulations. Perhaps the best example out of the nineteenth century is the poem "Last Love" by Fedor Tiutchev (1973, p. 91), which begins:

> How much more superstitiously
> And fondly we love in declining years.
> Shine on, shine on, farewell light
> Of this last love, this light of sunset!

The poem draws upon the emotions, intense and tragic, stemming from the poet's own Goethean liaison, late in life, with his daughter's French governess.[2] Another exemplary poem is by the contemporary Leningrad poet, Alexander Kushner, and is simply entitled "Starik" ("The Old Man"):

> What is so still
> As an old man staring
> At a bird through his final
> Hospital window?
>
>   (Kushner, 1972, p. 190)

Asking if the old man were a clerk, domino fan, or tinker, the poet notes that it really does not matter for even the old man has forgotten: all he has now is his window.

   In science fiction involving advanced societies of the future or in some other corner of the universe, old age—unless it be simply ignored—is handled generally in one of two ways: either old age as a "disease" has been done away with, or old people themselves have been eliminated by various techniques of euthanasia. Soviet science fiction follows this pattern, and, because of the mandatory politicization, is even more boring than such writing in the West. On a significantly higher level than science fiction, however, are the major twentieth-century dystopian novels, a Russian exemplar of which is Evgenii Zamiatin's novel *We* of 1924, the acknowledged model for Orwell's *1984*. Here, in the highly disciplined and automated United State of the distant future, old age is chillingly absent; but the narrator, a space engineer who is attracted by the Mephis (the name of a small band attempting in vain to overthrow the rule of the Benefactor), meets an old woman, along with other mementoes of the past, outside the glass dome of the city. Here, in the wild, where wrinkles are once more a pleasant sight to see, the dropouts are returning to essential humanity.

Old age in literature is one thing; old age in real life is quite another. The joy, the foibles, the maliciousness, the suffering, and even the wisdom of old people are, between the covers of a book, illusion. But in life, senile eccentricities and irascibility in particular produce family discord, while on a governmental scale, the archconservatism that seems to be an almost natural concomitant of age (how refreshing it is to encounter an old radical!) and that is usually associated with greed and religious hypocrisy produces the stultifying and illiberal effects we see in certain states today. Of all the contradictions between the aspirations of the early revolutionaries in Russia and the present elaborate and corrupt Soviet bureaucracy, none stands out quite so vividly as the picture we see from time to time of the members of the party and government gerontocracy arrayed before the ancient walls of the Kremlin.

The concept of entropy, whether we are talking about cosmic systems, governments, people, or literatures—understood in our case more perhaps as metaphor than as thermodynamic theory—is particularly relevant. The Soviet Union, for example, under primarily Russian influence, is a notoriously closed system, and in such systems, we are told, the effects of the law of entropy are strikingly facilitated and aggravated; thus Andrei Siniavsky showed in *On Socialist Realism* (Tertz, 1965) how Soviet Russian literature has already settled down into a rigid, dogmatic, pseudoclassical form, having more affinities with the eighteenth century than with either the nineteenth or twentieth centuries. And Zamiatin (who left Stalin's Russia in 1931) in his famous *On Literature, Revolution, and Entropy* sings the virtues of heresies and continuous revolution in both thought and politics as the only real antidotes against entropy. The effects of entropy tend to be maximalized also in our personal lives as we grow old, do less and less, and begin to shut ourselves off, not necessarily from the world (which for the most part is bad), but from "the best that has been said or thought." There is one slight consolation, however, amidst the desolation: heresies are not limited to the young, and at least some of the great heretics of the past managed to reach old age before they were destroyed.

SELECTIONS

Ivan Turgenev (1818–1883)
from *Fathers and Sons*

One of the saddest events in the life of old people is the prior death of a son or daughter. The hero in this novel, the young radical "nihilist," Eugene Bazarov, planned on becoming a physician, but died after being infected during an autopsy. His old parents visit his grave.

Like most of our graveyards, it looks dismal: weeds have long overgrown the ditches around it, the drab wooden crosses sag and rot beneath their once freshly painted gables; the tombstones are all askew, as though some-one were pushing them from below; two or three scanty fir trees barely afford some meager shade; sheep wander at will over the graves. . . . But in their midst stands a grave untouched by any human being, untrampled by any animal: only the birds at dawn perch and sing on it. An iron railing fences it in; two fir trees have been planted there, one at each end; in that grave Eugene Bazarov lies buried. Often from a nearby village a tottering old couple, man and wife, make their way here. Supporting each other, they walk with heavy steps; on reaching the railing, they fall down upon their knees, and long and bitterly they weep, and long and yearningly they gaze at the mute tombstone beneath which their son is lying; exchanging a brief word, they brush the dust from the stone, set a branch of a fir tree right, and then resume their prayers, unable to tear themselves away from this spot where they feel themselves so close to their son and their mem-ories of him. . . . Can it be that their prayers, their tears, will remain unanswered? Can it be that love, sacred and devoted love, is not omni-potent? On, no! However passionate, sinful and rebellious the heart wrapped away in that grave, the flowers that blossom there peep at us tranquilly with innocent eyes: they speak to us not only of all-embracing peace, of the vast repose of "indifferent" nature; they tell us also of everlasting rec-onciliation and life without end. (Turgenev, 1961), pp. 206–207)

Sergei Aksakov (1791–1859)
from *Family Chronicle*

This is a semifictional novel based largely on family memoirs. In this passage, the author describes a trick played on his grandfather, Stepan, by some serfs. While the old man is a strict disciplinarian, he also has a sense of humor, as illustrated in his dealing with thirsty serfs who devise a plan to get some of their master's cold beer.

Just at the entrance to my grandfather's room, his dressing gown and night-cap lay on a chair, and it was a quite simple matter to stretch one's hand through the half-opened door and secure them. Having done so, Tanait-schenok proceeded to array himself in his master's costume, and seated himself outside on the balcony; while Masan hurried down to the cellar with the beer jug, woke up the old housekeeper . . . and imperatively demanded iced beer for the master. As the old woman demurred, saying that it was impossible that the master should be awake so early in the afternoon, Masan begged her to step outside, which she did—and having duly observed his friend Tanaitschenok perched aloft, disguised in my

grandfather's cap and bed-gown, she filled the jug with beer without further ado, added some lumps of ice, and gave it to Masan, who ran off
with his booty. The beer was shared in all brotherly love, and the night
clothes carefully replaced on the chair. . . . A good hour elapsed before
the master awoke. He sprang up in a yet gayer mood than in the early
morning, and his first words were: "Cold beer!" . . . Consternation reigned!
Tanaitschenok hastened once more to the cellar-dame who instantly guessed
what had become of the first jug of beer. She said nothing, however, but
refilled the vessel, and brought it herself to the balcony where, this time,
the real master, crowned with his night-cap, was sitting. In a very few
words she described the trick played upon her; while Masan and Tanait-
schenok, trembling with fear, threw themselves at their master's feet. And
what did my grandfather do? He roared with laughter, sent for his wife
and daughters, and related the servants' ruse to them amid fresh bursts of
merriment. (Aksakov, 1961, pp. 29-30)

Mikhail Sholokhov (1905–1984)
from *And Quiet Flows the Don*

An epic account of the impact of the Revolution and the Civil War on the Don
Cossacks, the book affords numerous "naturalistic" passages. This particular passage might be entitled, "Old Age Resisting Seduction."

He went back to the winnowing machine, asking: "What's the matter?"
    "Here, Father, here's something . . . Come and look," she said, bend-
ing sideways and stealthily glancing across the old man's shoulder at the
open door. He went right up to her. Suddenly she flung out her arms,
and embracing his neck and interlocking her fingers, she stepped back,
dragging him after her and whispering:
    "Here, Father . . . Here . . . It's softer . . ."
    "What's the matter with you?" Pantaleimon asked in alarm. Wriggling
his head from side to side, he tried to free himself of her arms; but she
drew his head more strongly towards her own face, breathing hotly in his
beard and laughing and whispering.
    "Let me go, you bitch!" The old man struggled, feeling his daughter-
in-law's straining belly right against him. Pressing still closer, she fell
backward and drew him down on top of herself.
    "The devil! She's gone silly! Damn you! Let me go!" he sputtered.
    "Don't you want to?" Daria panted. Opening her hands, she shoved the
old man in the chest. "Or perhaps you can't? Then don't judge me, do
you hear?"
    Jumping to her feet, she hurriedly adjusted her skirt, brushed the chaff
off her back, and shouted into the frenzied old man's face:
    "What did you beat me for the other day? Am I an old woman? Weren't
you the same when you were young? My husband . . . I haven't seen

him for year! And what am I to do, lie with a dog? A fig for you, one-leg! Here, take this!" She made an indecent gesture and, her eyebrows working, went towards the door. At the door, she once more carefully examined her clothes, brushed the dust from her jacket and kerchief, and said without looking back at Pantaleimon:

"I can't do without it. I need a Cossack, and if you don't want to . . . I'll find one for myself, and you keep your mouth shut!"

With a furtive, hurried gait she went to the door of the threshing-floor and disappeared without a glance back, while Pantaleimon remained standing by the winnowing machine, chewing his beard and staring guiltily and disconcertedly around the chaff-shed. "Perhaps she's right after all. Maybe I should have sinned with her?" he thought in his perplexity, flabbergasted by what had happened to him. (Sholokhov, 1966, p. 322)

Georgii Sadovnikov (b. 1933)
from *Vadik, the Old Man*

An old man escapes the surveillance of his children and grandchildren one morning and wanders out into the city. He recalls his actions here as a young man, and scenes of the past are mixed with those of the present. He attempts to get involved and speak with others, but they ignore him. He then stops in front of a telephone booth to watch a girl talking with someone on the phone.

The girl saw him and made a sorrowful grimace. She raised her little finger—she was asking for a minute to continue her conversation.

"Go ahead, go ahead. I don't need the telephone." Vadik began to stir. He hit himself in the chest and energetically began to wave his hands.

The girl pressed herself to the telephone receiver and her lips moved soundlessly as if she were in an aquarium.

A presentiment urged him on; he lowered his eyes to the base of the booth and saw a folded fan of yellow plastic. He bent over with a quickness that was unusual for him and raised the lady's trinket. The fan whirred in his hands with an electric crackle and its blades formed a Japanese landscape. Something in this simple thing touched Vadik's heart. . . . Finally she hung up. For a while she just stood in the transparent box, coming to her senses. Afterwards she opened the door and fluttered out, pale from happiness. In reality she turned out to be plain, with a flat nose and sparse eyelashes.

"Please," said Vadik. Succumbing to the desire to make her happy, he tendered the folded fan to her.

The girl looked at the fan not understanding anything.

"A fan," whispered Vadik, laughing at her protracted return to the real world.

"A fan?" she asked, and suddenly said with unexpected hoarseness, "So what, give it to your wife, dad"; and having tilted up her sharp little chin, she made her way past Vadik.

"But allow me! This . . . this is a fan! It's your fan!" he called after her.

His embarrassment softened the angry girl, and she turned around and said reproachfully: "Why do you say that? This fan isn't mine. Nobody carries them anymore."

"Indeed . . . indeed," recollected Vadik. "Fans are not in style. My late wife, Nina, yes, she had a fan twenty years ago . . ."

Dejected, he wandered back downtown and stopped opposite the first shop window. He looked at his own reflection, trying to see himself with the eyes of the girl. He saw a bald skull with a pitiful fringe of gray hair, and a network of wrinkles surrounding his eyes, soft sloping shoulders, and a pot belly. (Sadovnikov, 1977, pp. 74, 75, 76)

Fedor Tiutchev (1803–1873)
Last Love

Most love poetry has been written by young men, but one can find, here and there in the major literatures, love poems by men in their late years. Probably the best example in Russian is this poem by Fedor Tiutchev.

> How much more superstitiously
> And fondly we love in declining years.
> Shine on, shine on, farewell light
> Of this last love, this light of sunset!
>
> The shadows have spread across the sky
> And only westward does radiance wander.
> Linger, linger, evening-day,
> Lengthen, lengthen, O enchantment.
> Let blood run thin in veins, our fondness
>
> Does not run thin within our hearts.
> O you, O you, O my last love!
> You are my bliss and my despair.

(Tiutchev, 1973, p. 91)

Alexander Kushner (b. 1936)
The Old Man

> What is so still
> As an old man staring
> At a bird through his final
> Hospital window?
> . . . Seeing the bushes
> Against a kiosk,
> Wearing the hospital

Striped pyjamas.
Was he a clerk?
A builder or what?
Whatever, already
He has forgot.
A domino fan?
Stereo tinker?
This window the last
Toy he has got.

(Kushner, 1972, p. 190)

NOTES

1. A most notable exception would of course be Tolstoy's almost offensively clinical *The Death of Ivan Ilych*.

2. For an interesting illustrated study of relationships of old women and young men (and vice versa) in art, see Alison Stewart, *Unequal Lovers: A Study of Unequal Couples in Northern Art* (New York: Abaris, 1977).

REFERENCES

Aksakov, S. (1961). *The Family chronicle* (M. C. Beverley, Trans.). New York: Dutton.

Chekov, A. (1977). *The cherry orchard*. New York: Grove Press.

Dostoevsky, F. (1968). *The brothers Karamazov*. New York: Barnes & Noble.

Gogol, N. (n.d.). *Family chronicle*. In *Evenings near the village of Dikanka*. Moscow: Foreign Languages Publishing House.

Kushner, A. (1972). The old man. In S. Mossie (Ed.) and P. Roche (Trans.), *The living mirror: Five young poets from Leningrad* (p. 190). Garden City, NY: Doubleday.

Orwell, G. (1949). *1984*. New York: Harcourt, Brace.

Sadovnikov, G. (1977). Vadik, the old man. In Vytas Dukas (Trans.), *Twelve contemporary Russian stories*. Cranbury, NJ: Associated University Press.

Shakespeare, W. (1954). *Romeo and Juliet*. New Haven: Yale University Press.

Sholokhov, M. (1966). *And quiet flows the Don* (S. Garry, Trans.). New York: Vintage.

Solzhenitsyn, A. (1963). *Matryona's house*. Columbia: University of South Carolina Press.

Solzhenitsyn, A. (1968). *The first circle*. New York: Harper & Row.

Tertz, A. (A. Siniavsky). (1965). *On socialist realism*. New York: Vintage.

Tiutchev, F. I. (1973). Last love. In *Poems and political letters of F. I. Tiutchev* (J. Zeldin, Trans.) (p. 91). Nashville: University of Tennessee Press.

Tolstoy, L. (1904). *The Cossacks: A novel of the Caucasus*. In L. Wiener, *A landed proprietor*. New York: Colonial Press.

Turgenev, I. (1961). *Fathers and sons* (G. Rearvey, Trans.). New York: Signet.

Zamiatin, E. (1924). *We*. New York: Dutton.

Zamiatin, E. (1967). *On literature, revolution and entropy*. In I. Howe (Ed.), Literary modernism. New York: Fawcett.

FURTHER READING

Brown, E. J. (1982). *Russian literature since the revolution* (rev. ed.). Cambridge: Harvard University Press.

Hingley, R. (1977). *Russian writers and society, 1825–1904* (2nd rev. ed.). New York: World University Library (Random House).

Mirsky, D. S. (1958). *A history of Russian literature*. New York: Vintage (Random House).

Pomorska, K. (1971). *Fifty years of Russian prose*. Cambridge: Massachusetts Institute of Technology Press.

Slonim, M. (1962). *From Chekov to the revolution: Russian literature, 1900–1917*. New York: Galaxy (Oxford University Press).

7

Aging as Cultural Reflection in Hispanic American Literature

Myron I. Lichtblau

Hispanic American literature today is rich, rewarding, aesthetically sensitive, socially committed, and, for the first time, included in the mainstream of world letters. Until very recently, this literature of the Americas has been neglected, forgotten, disparaged, misunderstood, and, perhaps worst of all, not even given the chance to be understood. It is not difficult to explain this belated recognition, for Hispanic American writers in the past thirty years have shown unusual creativity, skill, and artistry and have endowed their works with a profound social and psychological significance.

The treatment of the elderly or of old age in Hispanic American literature does not readily come to mind nor seem a particularly important or relevant theme. Other themes are usually thought of first and are more closely associated with that literature, such as themes of social consciousness, national identity, dictatorship and oppression, the church, the exploitation of the Indian, untamed nature, Yankee "imperialism," and the downtrodden masses. But on closer examination, concepts of old age can be found manifested in many important works, although such themes are generally meshed with others in the text and do not become the fulcrum of action. Aging is neither a consistent nor a recurring theme; it does not have a clearly defined literary pattern, yet it is certainly worthy of attention and literary appreciation.

As a reflection of society and culture, Hispanic American literature has always sought its own identity, with a further need to present the reality of the American scene. It has tried to define the civilization that developed from an Indian heritage, from conquest by the Spaniard in search of "God, glory, and gold," from the independence movement that severed its political bonds to the mother country, from the ensuing periods of political instability and anarchy, from the influx of immigrant groups, and finally from the impact of foreign cultures and governments. In literature, artistic and aesthetic values were perhaps too frequently undermined by political and social concerns. At its worst, Hispanic American literature down through the 1880s was openly derivative but rarely imitative of European models; at its best, it adapted and molded European literary movements to its own needs, aspirations, and purposes and constantly sought to portray the distinctiveness of the American scene.

In many respects, the roles old people play in Hispanic American literature, although stereotypic at times, set up either contrastive situations or situations that help define traits or modes of behavior of the other characters. Thus the old chieftain Colocolo in Alonso de Ercilla's epic poem on the Spanish conquest of Chile, *The Araucanian* (1569), is seen as the grand patriarch of the tribe, as the sage, and as the esteemed military leader whose death is mourned not so much as a passing but as the loss of a vital member of the group. Ercilla extols the valor and fierce pride of the Araucanian Indians and collectively makes them the real hero of his poem. One of the means of glorifying their valor and humanity is to have the reader feel the presence of the old man and appreciate his virtues. On one occasion, near the beginning of the work, we learn of heated arguments over the selection of a leader. Resentments and ill feeling are inflamed even more by the heavy drinking that customarily takes place at these meetings. As the conflict threatens to divide the Araucanian nation, Colocolo arises and addresses the assemblage in words that urge conciliation, self-control, and, above all, oneness of purpose. The chieftain feels that the several candidates are equal and says that the new leader should be the one who can bear a huge log on his shoulders for the longest time. The scenes between Colocolo and his men are also interesting for their dramatic effect, for they contrast the impetuousness and sheer physical force of the soldiers with the composed demeanor, moral reflection, and wise judgment of the older man.

As an inspiration to Hispanic American youth, the Uruguayan José Enrique Rodó wrote *Ariel* in 1903, a long political and philosophical treatise of great stylistic beauty. In reality, the essay is the farewell speech of an aging, venerable university professor on the point of retirement, who exhorts his students to live a more spiritual, less utilitarian life than that which prevails in the United States, which he sees as the "Colossus of the North." The professor advocates an intellectual aristocracy to counteract the increasing menace of North American power, although at the same time he recognizes the virtues of democracy. That Rodó chose as his spokesman an elderly sage and not a rebellious, impetuous youth is significant in many ways. Since Hispanic America in the 1900s was a group of young nations, vulnerable, inexperienced in self-government, and at times wildly unrealistic, it needed the restraining and conciliatory hand of an elder statesman who saw the needs of his people from a lifelong perspective of struggle and compromise and was not rash in his judgments. The elderly scholar also recognizes the necessary limitations of his contemporary society and urges future generations to uphold traditional values and carry on with renewed vigor and purpose where he has left off.

One of the outstanding dramas in Hispanic American literature is *Down the Gully* (1905) by the Uruguayan Florencio Sánchez. The protagonist is Don Zoilo, a proud old gaucho who sees his comfortable world destroyed by the onrush of modern society bringing new ideas to the pampa and new ideologies to his children. The play effectively portrays the moral decadence of a gaucho family, as Don Zoilo successively loses his property, his sense of honor, the respect and affection of his friends and acquaintances, and the love of his ungrateful daughters. The disrespect and sense of worthlessness Zoilo feels is no better illustrated than in the scene between the gaucho and a career sergeant who has run away with one of his daughters. Now that Zoilo is a broken man, the officer refuses to grant him the courtesy of addressing him as "don," a simple title of respect reserved for those held in high esteem. Don Zoilo is a patriarchal figure, once revered for his spirit of independence and liberty. His words and actions, although those of an anguished man, reveal a noble resignation and sense of self-esteem. At the same time, his predators, his betrayers, and his hostile family bestow the shabbiest, if not cruelest, treatment on the old man. The rewards of old age in *Down the Gully* are abuse and victimization. The gaucho, who throughout his life has fought against the imposition of rules and regulations by the central authority in Buenos Aires, endures the ultimate enemy in his old age, a fateful series of circumstances leading to a tragic conclusion. The encroachment of radical ideas and the ingratitude and maliciousness of his own children eventually overwhelm him, and he succumbs.

The Oxcart (1963) by René Marqués is an odyssey of a rural Puerto Rican family from their small farm to a poor neighborhood in San Juan and finally to New York City. Each change of residence weakens the moral and economic fabric of Doña Gabriela's family until a tragic accident prompts them to abandon their search for fulfillment in an alien environment and return to their plot of land. In the first act of this play, as preparations are being made to move to San Juan, the grandfather Don Chago steadfastly refuses to go along with the family not only because change is difficult for him but because leaving his land would be tantamount to betraying the essence of his life for a spurious hope of greater economic security. Don Chago stands alone, defying his children and grandchildren, whose attitude toward him is one of respectful tolerance. His role in *The Oxcart* is an ideological rather than a dramatic one. The fact that Don Chago remains on the farm is symbolic of Puerto Rico's cherished traditional values, while the family's contemplated return to the land symbolizes the grandfather's ultimate victory.

The destruction of traditional values of Chilean society becomes the central theme in many of José Donoso's celebrated novels. In *This Sunday,* the scene is grandmother's house, where, in an interesting technique of temporal and structural dislocation, various members of the family analyze each other as well as the grandparents, children, and grandson. What emerges is that the so-called staid middle class is really a class of frustrated, lonely men and women in a world devoid of lasting and spiritual values. In Donoso's *Coronation,* a ninety-four-year-old widow, Elisa Grey, holds on desperately to her declining mentality and disintegrating world. Estela, employed to look after the old woman, helps her criminal friend Mario break into the house. Elisa is generally portrayed as crotchety and unpleasant, but in a grotesque scene on her birthday she is crowned queen, a symbolic act suggesting perhaps that the old continue to reign in tradition although in nothing else.

In 1967, the Colombian Gabriel García Márquez published *One Hundred Years of Solitude,* the extraordinarily successful novel that earned him the Nobel Prize. In a masterful blend of realism and fantasy, the work follows the Buendía family across seven generations, until the last member commits suicide. The beginnings of the Buendía family coincide with the mythological founding of the fabulous city of Macondo; the end corresponds to the city's ultimate destruction in a terrible flood. The novel is so framed that no one character dominates the action, but the one who comes closest to being the protagonist is perhaps Ursula, the matriarch of the Buendía family, who lives beyond one hundred years and is able to predict the exact day and time of her death. Ursula is the impetus and energy behind the family's actions, even in her old age. Completely moral, honest, and firm in her convictions, she bestows loving care on all her offspring and descendants and guides them in their ways and beliefs. Even more to her credit, she does not turn away her bastard grandchildren. An inconsolable widow, she hides her blindness to avoid compassion. *One Hundred Years of Solitude* is a timeless novel, and, on one occasion, Ursula philosophically says, "It's as if time were turning about, and we returned to the beginning." When Ursula finally dies, Macondo loses its strength and soon afterward also perishes. Symbolically, Ursula represents the legendary greatness of all womanhood, and in her old age is seen the maturity of Hispanic America.

The clash between the old and the new, between tradition and progress, between conservative forces and more dynamic liberal forces, between the oligarchy and the new middle class, has been as dramatic and pronounced in Hispanic American countries as in other areas of the world. In the novel *Aura* (1965) by the Mexican Carlos Fuentes, an old widow, Señora Consuelo, invites a young historian to narrate the military exploits of her long-deceased husband. Fuentes's story is a fantasy, for shortly after Felipe Montero enters the home on his assignment, he finds himself face to face with a rejuvenated old lady transformed into a beautiful girl named Aura. In the duality—old lady/Aura—Fuentes may want us to believe that there are really two different women, that Aura really exists and that Montero is reacting to her alone. Navares suggests (Brushwood, 1966) that the Señora represents old, worn-out, traditional customs and ideologies and that Aura is the hope of a new, reborn Mexico. Implicit in this interpretation is the idea that in order for Mexico to progress and prosper, it must first rid itself of outmoded traditions and attitudes. It must build itself up out of the ashes of its destroyed past. In order for Aura to exist, the old lady must be destroyed. Or perhaps through another interpretation of the novel, the old and the new can exist side by side, can co-exist in harmony because one needs the other, because old values and traditions are just as important as the new values that may develop. The Señora's closing words of the novel reveal one of its basic themes: "Felipe, Aura will return, together we shall bring her back. Let me regain my strength and I shall have her return."

We could continue describing the role of the aged in Hispanic American literature in many more works in many more countries. The examples multiply; the instances of the elderly being portrayed in drama or fiction or poetry show an infinite variety of forms and styles. Some tentative conclusions do emerge: writers have been somewhat conscious of the aged as a special group; the treatment of the aged is both traditional and stereotypic as well as innovative; and the peculiar social and psychological problems of the aged have been subsumed by the intense preoccupation of writers over society's ills in general.

SELECTIONS

Alonso de Ercilla (1533–1594)
from *The Araucanian*

The Araucanian is an epic poem written by a Spanish soldier who took part in Spain's efforts to conquer the heroic Indians of Chile. In this passage, the aged and venerated chieftain Colocolo urges his people to reconcile their differences and fight as one nation to defeat the common foe.

> Why should we now for marks of glory jar?
> Why wish to spread our martial name afar?
>   Crushed as we are by Fortune's cruel stroke,
> and bent beneath an ignominious yoke,
>   ill can our minds such noble pride maintain,
> while the fierce Spaniard holds our galling chain.

Your generous fury here ye vainly show;
ah! rather pour it on the embattled foe.

(Hayley, 1968, p. 47)

René Marques (1919–1981)
from *The Oxcart*

Puerto Rican play. Don Chago, the grandfather, chooses to remain on his land rather than move to urban San Juan with the rest of the family.

Juanita: But gramps, you seem like a young boy!

Don Chago: That's right. The world is upside down. They say that we old folks seem like boys, but the fact is that the boys of today seem like old good-for-nothings. . . .

Doña Gabriela: Times change, father. Today boys are more concerned about things than we were. And they have ambition.

Don Chago: Inconformity is what they have. Before, the man worked and the woman got married. And nobody complained. . . .

Don Chago: You're only repeating what you hear all over. The radio says the same thing, and the newspapers, and the school teachers, and the politicians of the capital.

Doña Gabriela: And what does all that have to do with shame?

Don Chago: Well, the fact is that everybody preaches the almighty dollar. Even to have shame today one needs to have money. Before, one could be poor and still have dignity. You know why? Because the poor believed in something. Some believed in God, others believed in the land, others believed in men. Nowadays they don't let us believe in anything. Today they teach their children to believe only in money—and in what they call science. They say all our germs can be seen in this thing they call a microscope. And everything good they promise us is in this piece of green paper they call a dollar. But they say nothing about the heart. No one remembers the heart. And the heart dries up like an old bean. Ay, my daughter, no one can have dignity or shame with the heart dried up like a bean! . . .

Luis: (With subtle irony). You bet, gramps, now we know that everything was done better in your time.

Don Chago: It was a good time, my boy. There were fewer people, that's true, but people were better. Life was long and we didn't hurry to live it. What wasn't finished today was finished tomorrow. The important thing wasn't when it was finished; it was that it was well done. Today everything is done in a hurry; and for this reason it's so bad. And everything is done without real feeling. And so it hurts to do it. Before, each person, no matter how poor he was, had his little piece of land, his pride, his dignity. Today, there isn't enough room for so many people. And there's no place for pride. And there's no heart for dignity.

(Marques, 1974, pp. 16–18, 33)

Florencio Sánchez (1875–1910)
from *Down the Gully*

This selection is representative of a Uruguayan drama. Zoilo Carbajal is a proud old gaucho who loses everything he ever held dear—his land, his children's respect, and his material possessions. A cruel sergeant even denies him his one title of respect—don. Desperate, Zoilo contemplates suicide.

Sergeant: Come along peaceably. If you resist, it'll just make things worse.
Martiniana: That's right. It's better to go willingly.
Zoilo: Shut up, you! Are you sure there isn't some mistake? You know who I am, don't you? Don Zoilo Carbajal, the citizen don Zoilo Carbajal.
Sergeant: Yes, sir, begging your pardon, sir, but that's what you used to be. Now you're just "Old man Zoilo." That's what they all call you.
Zoilo: "Old man Zoilo?"
Sergeant: Yes, my friend. When a man goes broke, folks don't bother with surnames.
Zoilo: I wouldn't kill myself for their sakes. It would be for my own.
Aniceto: No, boss. Calm yourself! What would you gain by getting reckless?
Zoilo: . . . People find a good, healthy, honest, industrious worker, and they rob him of everything he has, including his money, saved up by the sweat of his brow, the love of his family, his only consolation; they take away his honor, which is his reliquary. Damn it, they lose him his good name, deprive him of all consideration and respect, they push him about, trample on him, beat him. And when that poor fellow, that old Zoilo, tired, worn out, good-for-nothing, hopeless, crazy with shame and suffering—when once he decides to put an end to such a filthy life, everybody runs to stop him. "Don't kill yourself! Life is good!" Good for what?

(Sanchez, 1961, pp. 153, 165–166)

José Donoso (b. 1924)
from *This Sunday*

The narrator vividly describes his grandmother in several revealing scenes from this Chilean novel.

"You don't have anything else to do."
    It wasn't true. My grandmother had a lot to do, with her shantytown and her poor people. We often saw some toothless woman carrying a set

of twins who screamed continuously in her arms. She would ring the doorbell and ask to speak with my grandmother. We knew that all week long my grandmother drove her little car from one place to another on errands for her poor people. But, in spite of her preoccupations, she would always take the trouble to look for some completely useless present to give us on Christmas or on our saint's day.

· · · · ·

Saturdays and Sundays, at least, were entirely ours, and she responded to any call or exigency. Even though she might be shut up with a woman's committee in the piano room, she would leave them until we no longer needed her.

· · · · ·

When I saw her again, it was hard to recognize my grandmother: a little old lady who scarcely spoke.

   Sometimes they took us to see her or encouraged us to do it on our own. I would find her in bed, with her eyes fixed on the ceiling. . . . No matter how much one might call to her or tell her things she wouldn't say a word. Later she began to smile a bit, but only a little, as if she lacked the strength and the faith to move her lips more than that. . . . She lasted a long time that way, silent, smiling, terribly sad—ten years in which she kept getting sadder and more fragile.

· · · · ·

And when she dresses . . . Chepa doesn't have any conception of modesty. Like now, for example. Would it be so hard for her to shut the door while she's putting on her girdle?

                                        (Donoso, 1967, pp. 76, 79, 173, 64)

from *Coronation*

Through narrative and dialogue of another novel, there emerges a vivid picture of the changes that occur in grandmother's personality.

Rosario and Lourdes were the only people who could put up with Misia Elisa [the grandmother], and even they avoided going into her room more than they had to during one of her bad spells. Strictly speaking, they were no longer servants, for Grandfather Abalos had left them both handsome legacies on condition that they remain with his wife till her death. This stipulation had proved unnecessary, as things turned out: both of them would have stayed on anyway, legacy or no legacy. Their whole world consisted of the corpse of a family, and its traditions, represented by Misia Elisa.

· · · · ·

Perhaps having someone young near her might help to alleviate his grandmother's anguish, that smoldering hate, that diabolical force which drove her to spit obscene, gutter insults at everyone. Luckily the poor woman was not always in such a state. There were spans of hours, days, even weeks when the manic frenzy and exaltation were replaced by serenity and peace. But these intervals of calm seemed a pitiful consolation when Andres thought of his grandmother as she had once been. She had been so gracious then, so quiet and so clever. The whole house breathed serenity in those days: everything she touched seemed to take on a new significance and harmony. And she had been so beautiful! Her Anglo-Saxon blood showed in the fairness of her skin and hair, in the almost excessive refinement of her features, and also in a certain suggestion of a captive bird, which became more and more accentuated with the years until at last senility obliterated all traces of individuality from her face, leaving only the ridge of an arrogant nose and a certain peculiar fixity in her mad, staring eyes. The affliction from which she suffered had crept up on her over the years, so many years that his memories of a perfect, irreproachable grandmother went far back to Andres's early youth. He had been seventeen when he first noticed . . . a symptom of the malady that was finally to destroy her reason.

"What's the matter, Grandma? Don't you feel well?"

She sighed and covered her face with her hands.

"Can I get you something?"

"No, thank you, dear. Go help Ramon."

"No. Something's wrong . . ."

There was a short but ominous silence. Then, turning her blue gaze on Andres, she cried:

"All they ever think about is humiliating me! I can't imagine what they get out of it . . ."

Is my grandma mad?

Cerebral arteriosclerosis, according to the doctors. It started very early. She is still more manic than lunatic, but it will go on getting worse. Everything she has kept hidden all these years, out of fear or shame or insecurity, erupts into her life once the conscious censor is relaxed, and peoples it with these fantasmal presences.

(Donoso, 1965, pp. 12–13, 15, 19)

Gabriel García Márquez (b. 1928)
from *One Hundred Years of Solitude*

Ursula, who lives more than one hundred years, is the matriarch of the mythical Buendía family in these selections from a Colombian novel. Even in old age she continues to be a strong and dominant figure.

Although she was already a hundred years old and on the point of going blind from cataracts, she still had her physical dynamism, her integrity of character, and her mental balance intact. No one would be better able than she to shape the virtuous man who would restore the prestige of the fam-

ily, a man who would never have heard talk of war, fighting cocks, bad
women, or wild undertakings, four calamities that, according to what Ursula thought, had determined the downfall of their line.

    That woman has been your ruination, Ursula would shout at her great-
grandson when she saw him coming into the house like a sleepwalker.
She's got you so bewitched that one of these days I'm going to see you
twisting around with colic and with a toad in your belly.

· · · · ·

The years nowadays don't pass the way the old ones used to, she would
say, feeling that everyday reality was slipping through her hands. In the
past, she thought, children took a long time to grow up.

· · · · ·

The truth was that Ursula resisted growing old even when she had already
lost count of her age and she was a bother on all sides as she tried to
meddle in everything and as she annoyed strangers with her questions as
to whether they had left a plaster Saint Joseph to be kept until the rains
were over during the days of the war. No one knew exactly when she had
begun to lose her sight. Even in her later years, when she could no longer
get out of bed, it seemed that she was simply defeated by decrepitude, but
no one discovered that she was blind. She had noticed it before the birth
of José Arcadio. At first she thought it was a matter of a passing debility
and she secretly took marrow syrup and put honey in her eyes, but quite
soon she began to realize that she was irrevocably sinking into the darkness. . . . She did not tell anyone about it because it would have been a
public recognition of her uselessness. Even though the trembling of her
hands was more and more noticeable and the weight of her feet was too
much for her, her small figure was never seen in so many places at the
same time. She was almost as diligent as when she had the whole weight
of the house on her shoulders. Nevertheless, in the impenetrable solitude
of decrepitude, she had such clairvoyance as she examined the most insignificant happenings in the family that for the first time she saw clearly the
truths that her busy life in former times had prevented her from seeing.

· · · · ·

It was then that it occurred to her that her clumsiness was not the first
victory of decrepitude and darkness but a sentence passed by time.

· · · · ·

Ursula cried in lamentation when she discovered that for more than three
years she had been a plaything for the children.

· · · · ·

She finally mixed up the past with the present in such a way that in the
two or three waves of lucidity that she had before she died, no one knew
for certain whether she was speaking about what she felt or what she
remembered. Little by little she was shrinking, turning into a fetus. . . .

One Palm Sunday they went into the bedroom while Fernanda was in church and carried Ursula out by the neck and ankles.

Poor great-great-grandmother, Amaranta Ursula said. She died of old age.

Ursula was startled.

I'm alive! she said.

You can see, Amaranta Ursula said, suppressing her laughter, that she's not even breathing.

I'm talking! Ursula shouted.

She can't even talk, Aureliano said. She died like a little cricket.

Then Ursula gave into the evident. My God, she exclaimed in a low voice. So this is what it's like to be dead.

(García Márquez, 1970, pp. 195, 251–252, 253–254, 256, 339, 347–348)

Carlos Fuentes (b. 1928)
from *Aura*

In this Mexican novella of fantasy, Señora Consuelo and her niece Aura are blended into one person, as old age and youth symbolically vie for supremacy.

You move aside so that the light from the candles and the reflections from the silver and crystal show you the silk coif that must cover a head of very white hair, and that frames a face so old it's almost childlike.

. . . . .

When you look at her again you see that her eyes have opened very wide, and that they're clear, liquid, enormous, almost the same color are the yellowish whites around them, so that only the black dots of the pupils mar that clarity. It's lost a moment later in the heavy folds of her lowered eyelids, as if she wanted to protect that glance which is now hiding at the back of its dry cave.

. . . . .

She's thin, even emaciated, like a medieval sculpture; her legs are like two sticks, and they're inflamed with erysipelas.

. . . . .

Excuse me. . . . excuse me, Señor Montero. Old ladies have nothing left but . . . the pleasures of devotion. . . . Give me my handkerchief, please.

. . . . .

Ah, yes . . . it's just that I'm so accustomed to the darkness. To my right. . . . Keep going till you come to the trunk. They've walled us in, Señor Montero. They've built up all around us and blocked off the light. They've tried to force me to sell, but I'll die first. This house is full of memories for us. They won't take me out of here till I'm dead!

. . . . .

As you undress you think of the old lady's distorted notions, the value she attributes to these memoirs.

· · · · ·

This time Señora Llorente is at the head of the table, wrapped in her shawl and nightgown and coif, hunching over her plate. . . . As you watch her eating her soup you try to figure out her age. There's a time after which it's impossible to detect the passing of the years, and Señora Consuelo crossed that frontier a long time ago.

Now you know why Aura is living in this house: to perpetuate the illusion of youth and beauty in that poor, crazed old lady. Aura, kept here like a mirror, like one more icon on that votive wall with its clustered offerings, preserved hearts, imagined saints and demons.

· · · · ·

[The silvery moonlight] falls on Aura's eroded face, as brittle and yellowed as the memoirs, as creased with wrinkles as the photographs. You stop kissing those fleshless lips, those toothless gums: the ray of moonlight shows you the naked body of the old lady, of Señora Consuelo, limp, spent, tiny, ancient, trembling because you touch her.

(Fuentes, 1965, pp. 10, 13, 25, 26, 27, 30, 34, 35, 46, 74)

REFERENCES

Donoso, J. (1965). *Coronation* (J. Goodwin, Trans.). New York: Knopf.

Donoso, J. (1967). *This Sunday* (L. O. Freeman, Trans.). New York: Knopf.

Fuentes, C. (1965). *Aura* (Lysander Kemp, Trans.). New York: Farrar, Straus, & Giroux.

García Marquez, G. (1970). *One hundred years of solitude* (G. Rabassa, Trans.). New York: Harper & Row.

Hayley, W. (1968). *Essay on epic poetry; in five epistles.* In John E. Englekirk et al. (Eds.), *An anthology of Spanish American literature.* New York: Appleton-Century-Crofts. (Original work published in London in 1792.)

Marques, R. (1963). *La carreta (The oxcart)* (M. I. Lichtblau, Trans. of selection). Río Piedras, Puerto Rico: Editorial Cultural.

Navares, S. R. (1964). Una obra maestra. *La Cultura en México. Siempre* (Suppl. 127), p. 19. Cited in J. S. Brushwood. (1966). *México in its novel.* (pp. 39–40). Austin: University of Texas Press.

Rodó, J. E. (1988) *Ariel.* (M. Peden, Trans.). Austin: University of Texas Press.

Sánchez, F. (1961). *Down the gully.* In *Representative plays of Florencio Sanchez* (W. K. Jones, Trans.) (pp. 122–167). Washington: General Secretariat of the Organization of American States.

FURTHER READING

Anderson Imbert, E. (1963). *Spanish American literature: A history* (J. V. Falconieri, Trans.). Detroit: Wayne State University Press.

Aponte Bolivar, M. (1978). *El anciano en la sociedad venezolana*. Caracas: Universidad Central de Venezuela.

Ellis, J. A. (1975). *Latin America: Its peoples and institutions* (2nd ed.) New York: Macmillan.

Franco, J. (1967). *The modern culture of Latin America: Society and the artist*. New York: Praeger.

Franco, J. (1969). *An introduction to Spanish-American literature*. London: Cambridge University Press.

Halper, S. A., and Sterling, J. R. (Eds.). (1975). *Latin America: The dynamics of social change*. New York: St. Martin's Press.

Henriquez Urena, P. (1966). *A concise history of Latin American culture* (G. Chase, Trans.). New York: Praeger.

Mira y Lopez, E. (1961). *Hacia una vejez joven: Psicologia y psicoterapia de la ancianidad*. Buenos Aires: Kapelusz Editores.

Nash, J. (Ed.). (1977). *Ideology and social change in Latin America*. New York: Gordon.

Palmore, E. (Ed.). (1980). *International handbook on aging: Contemporary developments and research*. Westport, CT: Greenwood Press. (Sections on Latin American countries: Chile, pp. 60–74; Mexico, pp. 270–277; Uruguay, pp. 455–466.)

Shafer, R. J. (1978). *A history of Latin America*. Lexington, MA: D. C. Heath

Silvert, K. H. (1966). *The conflict society: Reaction and revolution in Latin America*. New York: American Universities Field Staff.

Talice, R. V. (1979). *Vejentud, humano tesoro*. Movtevideo: Master Fer.

Wolf, E. R., and Hansen, E. C. (1972). *The human condition in Latin America*. New York: Oxford University Press.

8

Old Age in Arabic Literature

Roger Allen

The specialist in Arabic literature will often be asked to discuss different aspects of his subject within the context of the comparative study of world literatures in the West. The topics of such discussions will normally center around such areas as commitment, the role of the writer, literature and society, the Third World, and so on. Much contemporary writing in the Arab world contains within it, in one way or another, a considerable concern with issues of politics and society. While that is, of course, a generalization of large proportions, it seems to me to be a reasonable one. The truly lyrical voice is a rarer phenomenon, at least within the frame of reference of the readings that I have undertaken.

With this in mind, the request to select some works on the subject of old age gave me some pause. For in addition to the impressions already given, most literary-historical studies of modern Arabic literature have talked in terms of a "renaissance" (the Arabic word is *nahda*) or, in some cases, of more than one. "Adolescence" and "maturity" are regularly used in talking about the various stages in the development of belles-lettres in the Arab world. Many Arab critics have described the development of their literature during the course of this century as a process of catching up, and within such a framework, the emergence of new talent and fresh ideas is a source of constant concern.

Yet many Arab writers also indulge in retrospect, no more so than at those times when the actions and values of contemporary society are questioned and challenged. The period following the 1967 War with Israel, for example, led to a profound and durable concern with the ancient heritage *(turaath)*, which in turn led Arabo-Islamic culture in a search for an entity called *asaala*, the best translation for which might be "authenticity" or "closeness to one's historical roots." Thus, if the first part of the modern renaissance involved in some way a process of catching up, that would seem to have been achieved. We now appear to be witnessing a period in the development of Arabic literature in which an established local tradition is finding innovations from within as well as without, a process that may sometimes involve a rediscovery of the treasures of the past.

It has to be admitted that this "young" tradition has not concerned itself to any large degree with old age as a subject. Yet the selections included herewith are representative of the larger tradition in that they provide a cross section of the Arab world and also of different periods, schools, and philosophies. Poetry has been, in terms of quantity, the most prevalent form of expression within the earlier Arabic literary tradition, but that is no longer the case. Thus the use of six poets and one prose writer is not a reflection of "the larger picture" today, although it may serve as a reflection of my earlier comment about the lyrical element.

The contemporary tradition of literature in the Arab world is, then, as varied as the peoples of that vast region. While there are a number of writers in each genre within every country of the region, there is little doubt that critical opinion throughout the Arab world is united in dubbing Najib Mahfuz as its most eminent writer of fiction. Indeed, he will be recognized, no doubt, beyond the Arab world as a result of his 1988 Nobel Prize for literature. I have described him elsewhere as the writer whose name personifies the Arabic novel's achievement of genuine maturity (1982), and while it is probably true that the novel is the genre in which his mastery is most evident, his short stories also give us interesting insights into his political and social views. The short story included here, "An Old Photograph," chooses a theme of quest through retrospect that might indeed have served as the core of a longer and more elaborate work. Our third-person journalist-narrator seeks out some of his former school friends on the basis of a class photograph. Some things in the story are constants—the lapse of time, the changes in society, and the onset of old age—but, as is often the case with Mahfuz's writings, it is in the variety that much of the import is to be found. Mahfuz is not slow to pass social comment here, as is made clear by the linkages between the poor among his acquaintances (Muhammad Abd al-Salam and Fayiqa, Amm Salama's daughter) and the rich (al-Mawardi and Hamid Zahran). The great scholar of the group, al-Urfali, is summed up in a notable sentence: "A noble monasticism, a continuing struggle, eight children and mysticism!" Within this series of cameo retrospects, the reader may thus discover many of the author's thoughts on social transformation in his homeland.

Modern Arabic poetry has been treated in a variety of ways: by literary "school," political opinion, country of origin, and so on. A major change in form began to prevail in the period following World War II when many Arab poets decided to rid themselves of the trammels of traditional metrical prescriptions in favor of freer forms, be it "free verse" or the prose poem. This subdivision allows us to separate Abd al-Rahman Shukri and 'Abu al-Qasim al-Shabbi from the other four poets. In fact, both these writers—Shukri from Egypt and al-Shabbi from Tunisia—belong firmly within the Romantic period of modern Arabic poetry, as the poems included here make abundantly clear. Life was short for al-Shabbi, and the illness from which he suffered and the awareness of the imminence of death gradually impinged more and more on his poetic output. Shukri did not have to share al-Shabbi's dire concerns, but the fatalistic attitude evident in the poems included reflects a pessimistic tendency. This pessimism is very much an echo of one of the great poets of the early classical period, Abu 'Ala al-Ma'arri, as, for example, in these lines:

> Leisurely through life's long gloom
> I have journeyed to my tomb.
>
> (Nicholson, 1969, p. 64)

Shukri himself may have regarded the vicious treatment that he received at the hands of two of his poetic contemporaries and fellow countrymen as reason enough for his request for mercy "in my life," although he would not, of course, be the only Romantic poet to express such sentiments.

Turning to the more modern poets, we again encounter congruity and variety. Two poets, the Iraqi Buland al-Haydari and Yusuf al-Khal, the Christian Lebanese, write poems on the major theme of this collection in which a first-person speaker discusses the subject within the context of seasons of the year; if the singular voice and the more direct presence of al-Haydari's poem give a greater sense of immediacy, al-Khal's more universal utterance, forcefully aided by metaphor, is effective on a different level.

Adunis is the pen name of the Arab world's most famous poet, Ali Ahmad Sa'id, Syrian born, now living in Lebanon. With his calls for a renewal of language as the central purpose of poetic writing, he is the undoubted figurehead of the more radical elements in contemporary Arabic poetry and poetics (being himself the editor of the journal *Mawaqif,* published in Beirut). The poem included here, "The Days," is typical of much of his poetic output: brief and perhaps initially opaque, but gradually revealing through its unfamiliar juxtapositions a host of ideas and impressions for the cognizant reader.

The death of Khalil Hawi during the Israeli invasion of Lebanon in June 1982 was to many Middle Eastern intellectuals a personification of the terrible problems of that country. In fact, it might also be said that much of his poetry had been giving graphic evidence of his awareness of those problems and others as well for some time. The extract included here is taken from a longer poem, "The Genie of the Shore." Some critics have taken issue with the violence of Hawi's imagery, but cannot one say that the events in Lebanon in recent years, not to mention Hawi's ultimate commitment of his own life in his grief over the fate of his homeland, represent cogent evidence in support of his dark vision?

The contemporary Arab world thus presents aspects of old age as varied in theme and technique as the vast area encompassed within that term and the many religions and people who populate it. The thought of the inevitability of old age prompts feelings and images that reflect the local and share in the universal, thus presenting a suitable exemplar of the literature from which they are drawn.

SELECTIONS

Abd al-Rahman Shukri (1886–1958)
Welcome

>Welcome to the decrees of fate
>   for the arbiter merits greetings and respect.
>Pass to me all the cups of life!
>   joy and misfortune, honor and disgrace.
>If I must live . . . life can be endured;
>If I must die . . . there is no retreat from death.
>
>   (Shukri, 1974, p. 133)

Life

>Life is but a continual dying,
>   goodness and pleasures are but borrowed.
>Would that I were like the flower whose life is but a summer;
>   then I would face before the afflictions of winter.
>To life with its pleasures, from me, one greeting;
>   but ah, a thousand to peace-giving death!
>Who will convey my greeting unto the dead?
>   Peace be upon them . . . nay, upon me:
>For in their graves they have no need of mercy
>   as I do in my life.
>
>   (Shukri, 1974, p. 133)

Yusuf al-Khal (b. 1917)
Old Age

>We wipe the chill wave from our faces
>And tell ourselves the story of spring:
>How the breeze smiles,
>The birds sing,

The trees dance;
How the seed stretches its roots in the soil
And bears fruit.
We tell ourselves the story of autumn,
When the shadows are bowed
And evening lengthens,
Then suddenly a star appears,
Or a moon shines,
And when the fence falls,
The fields stretch out naked,
As far as the eye can see.
We tell ourselves the story of summer,
Which comes to us on the wings
Of a warm melody,
Or the leap of a joyous swallow,
While we gather the crop,
Or recall the halt of a cloud,
Here and there in the distance.
We wipe the chill wave from our faces
And tell ourselves the seasons' story.
But the wave sinks deep in our veins and vanishes.
We think it vanishes,
Yet, suddenly, it appears—
Here, in a hair turned white,
There, in a lip turned dry.

(al-Khal, 1974, pp. 53–55)

Adunis, pen name of Ali Ahmad Sa'id (b. 1930)
The Days

My eyes are tired, tired of days,
Tired regardless of days.
Still, must I drill
Through wall after wall
Of days to seek another day?
Is there? Is there another day?

(Sa'id, 1971, p. 3)

Khalil Hawi (1925–1982)
A Mad Old Woman

The lightning flashes of the night capered
And decked in flames the corners of the cave:
Fever and chills, darkness and flames and haze.
And when I stirred from the oppressive spell

I was enamored of the glistening scar
Branded upon my brow in scarlet hue,
And blazing out of my excessive joy
At seeing people gripped in fear.
Indeed, I cook the flesh of babes at night
And in the moonlight, when the rubies bloom,
My white locks change their color, and the grooves
In my sad face are rubbed and levelled smooth.
Transfiguration day is soon at hand,
When I shake off the ancient tree of rages,
The hardened shell of old imprisoned flesh
And then exultant on the road I shout:
I am the apple of the fertile wild,
A dark-skinned girl from wayward gypsy tents,
The morning finds its heart within my breast
And from its lustre borrows all its light.
Then with the dawn I revel in my masks,
Avoid the curses, mock the human race.
In vain they seek my true identity,
A beldame searching dumps for orange peels.

(Hawi, 1981, p. 103)

Najib Mahfuz (b. 1911)
An Old Photograph

It was a sudden flash of inspiration, but it seemed to put an end to his predicament. It came to him as he was looking at an old school photograph. As a journalist, he had to look for something new to write about every day, and for some time he had been at a loss. Then came this sudden flash of inspiration. The photograph had been hanging there in exactly the same spot in the sitting room for over thirty years; it had said nothing, given no inspiration, and in fact, it had hardly even been noticed. But now its time to talk had come; at least it seemed that way. He eagerly focused all his attention on the picture which was so old that it looked faded. It was a photograph of the final year in the Arts section of al-Giza Secondary School in the year 1928. How would it be if he wrote a study for the newspaper of the people behind those youthful faces: school and life, 1928 and 1960? In principle, it was a fine idea. The question was: could he get hold of all the necessary facts which would be needed as a basis for such an unusual study? Many years had passed, and he had not looked at the photograph even once! Many things in it had disappeared for good: those tarbushes[1] they were wearing on their heads, for example, and the British and French teachers! Merely by looking at each face he could tell whose it was, even if he could not quite remember the name and had no idea what had happened to them all ever since. None of them had anything to do with him now, not even that exciting young fellow who had lived in the same building with him for a long time.

He started looking at the faces, beginning with the top row. He passed over two faces which did not mean anything to him, but then his eyes fell on one of the heroes of the soccer team who had died right in the middle of a game between al-Giza and another school. What an unforgettable incident that had been, and there was the victim, a young lad with gleaming eyes, self-reliant, his mouth pursed into something akin to a smile. And today he was just bones buried in the ground. He carried on, shifting from one face to the next, until he stopped at a thin, elongated face. It reminded him of the occasion when his friend had stood on the steps by the school secretary's office delivering an inflammatory speech in which he called on the students to strike in protest against the Declaration of the 26th of February 1942 during the Second World War.[2] Standing right next to him was a face with a distinguished look about it, stamped with all the marks of elegance and good family. He soon recalled the family name; it was Mawardi. He put it down in his notebook feeling sure that he would have no trouble tracking it down, quite apart from the fact that the person in question had been a leading figure in politics ten years earlier. This man would be a key element in his research project.

Now there was the personification of scholastic achievement with all its accompanying magic: first in his class, first in every class, first in the school, al-Urfali. His brilliance at school and his odd name had both made sure that the name stuck in his memory. He had been an important figure in the Law College, and then he had been appointed a public prosecutor in the days when such an appointment was an important event. He could be tracked down easily by consulting the Ministry of Justice. He would be the second key element in his study; al-Urfali after al-Mawardi. Yet another face sprung at him from the photograph; this one with a bloody reminder. They had had a fight in the school yard, but he could not remember who had caused it. The faces went past in stony silence till he came to the exciting face of his old neighbor, Hamid Zahran, the director of the Step Pyramid Company. He gave a cold smile. This was the young man of the age indeed! He could still remember how he had left the al-Giza Secondary School when he had contracted cholera. He had joined the staff of the War Ministry with a satisfactory rating. They had stayed in touch until he himself had left Abu Khawdha Lane ten years ago when he had found an opening in journalism. He had heard how Hamid had resigned from the government service to work as secretary for the Step Pyramid Company and eventually he learned that he had been made the company director with a salary of five hundred Egyptian pounds a month. What an amazing series of events, not only because of their crazy impetuosity but also since he was basically stupid. At any rate, he too would be an important and significant element in the study. He began to hope that the whole thing would prove unusual. He decided to rely on his own analysis and inventiveness rather than on what his unknown heroes had to say, since the unusual aspect of the whole thing was not so much the people themselves as their social significance. Whatever happened, he decided not to write up his report until he had gathered together all the materials.

He began by asking for a meeting with Abbas al-Mawardi on his country estate in Qalyub, having discovered from the al-Mawardi office in al-Azhar Square that that was where he was living. At the appointed hour he found himself walking along the path surrounded on both sides by pots of roses. He was heading for the salamik[3] with the house behind him, a wonderful two-storied mansion surrounded by a garden of many acres full of mango, orange and lemon trees, vine bowers, and countless squares, triangles and circles of flowers, vegetables and rivulets. And there he was standing like a demon in the midst of all this greenery which stretched away to the horizon; he seemed to be enveloped in an aura of silence, calmness and conformity. You could see people in the distance bending over at work but they looked lost in the midst of this expanse of plants and sky. Abbas al-Mawardi came striding towards him in a loose-fitting garment; his face looked full and blooming while his oval-shaped head was covered with a thick mop of shiny hair. He had grown both taller and broader, and that gave him the appearance of a statue covered by a cloth before it is to be unveiled. His smile of welcome was accompanied by a certain sense of surprise and caution. "Hello, Professor Husayn Mansur!" he said, "Welcome to my home!"

They shook hands and sat down.

"I've been following your journalistic endeavors with great admiration," he went on. "It always reminds me of our friendship at school, even though we haven't met since we both left al-Giza Secondary School."

"We did meet again once, briefly," Husayn reminded his host with a smile. "It was in Parliament in 1950 or '51."

"Really?" the other asked with raised eyebrows. For a moment they both gave way to memories of school days, but then Husayn came round to the real purpose for his visit.

"Wouldn't it be better to leave me to my own devices here, just as I am?" Abbas asked hopefully.

"I don't think so," Husayn replied with enthusiasm. "This study might well be the first stage in following up on an entire generation. I won't publish a single word before referring back to you; I promise you that. I may be able to dispense with names altogether . . ."

He did not object, but neither did he sound enthusiastic. His expression showed no particular reaction until Husayn Mansur asked anxiously about what had happened to him. Did this situation and the memories it aroused cause him any sadness? For, however rich he might be now, he had most certainly been a millionaire in the past. In those days he had been a key political figure. By virtue of his status he had won in the elections on the question of credibility, and rumors had him nominated for a position in the ministry late in 1950.

"I'm living out here all the time now," he replied, "and so I've sent my university-age son to live with his aunt in Cairo. I only rarely leave the estate . . ."

His features began to relax, and he started talking freely. He told me he worked in his own fields using the very latest agricultural machinery and was particularly interested in raising cattle and poultry. For his leisure time he had provided himself with a large library, and he liked riding horses both as a hobby and for exercise. There he was squatting in his own tiny kingdom where he could dispense with the entire world. His only wish was to spend the rest of his life within its boundaries without ever having to leave.

Husayn asked him about the peasants.

"I'm a peasant too!" he replied, "and so was my father. I have no trouble dealing with them. They're good folk!"

Husayn started asking questions again. "Didn't you put your name forward for the National Union?" he enquired, subtly changing the subject.

"Many people suggested that to me," he replied, "but I'm happy as I am."

Husayn tried to imagine what this life must be like, combining elements of nature and civilization, made enjoyable by all sorts of good things, and yet enveloped in isolation and aloofness; consolation here came in the form of worldly and intellectual pleasures, strolling in the light of the moon and indulging in the delights of the American bar and the local drug ring.

"And what about old friends?"

"Who? My close friends come to stay here at the weekend; the others I know nothing about . . ."

He absolutely refused to say a single word about public affairs, and so Husayn did not push him.

"Don't you ever long to go to the cinema for example?" he asked.

"I have my own private projection room. There's nothing I go without!"

Husayn showed him the old school photograph in case he might know someone on it. Al-Mawardi took it with a smile and then pointed at one of the faces. "Ali Sulayman," he said. "He was hit by a bullet during Sidqi's time.[4] For that he was appointed to the diplomatic service after his graduation. Eventually he was thrown out during the purge which followed the 1952 Revolution . . ."

Husayn pointed to Hamid Zahran's face, but Abbas shook his head.

"Hamid Zahran," Husayn told him, "company director with a monthly salary of five hundred pounds!"

"Really?" he asked with his eyebrows, although he did not actually say a word. His eyes shone with an expression which showed a combination of bewilderment and anxiety. And with that the conversation came to an end.

Husayn headed for the Ministry of Justice and discovered where the top boy in the school, Professor Ibrahim al-Urfali, the felony court justice, now worked. He waited for him in front of the court building. Eventually the judge emerged followed by a clerk who started calling for a taxi. Husayn moved towards him with a smile. The justice stared at him in amazement and then recognized who he was. They shook hands. When Husayn broached the subject of his project, the justice invited him to have lunch with him. The taxi took them both to his house on Mahir Street. They went into a decent looking house, although the overall appearance was really quite ordinary, something which came as a surprise to Husayn Mansur. However, when his eyes fell on eight boys whose ages followed closely on one another, all of them sitting around the table with them, he was surprised no longer.

"Your journalistic activities are truly spectacular," his host said.

Husayn thanked him. He looked at the justice's thin body and tired, gleaming eyes. How he had relished the magical glory of this man's academic brilliance at school! But now, no one outside of judicial circles even knew his name. Husayn now began to ask for some more details for his project.

"My job has nothing to do with the press!" al-Urfali replied quickly. "When I was in charge of the public prosecutor's office during the investigation of a particularly notorious case, the press tried to push me into the limelight, but I refused. To a judge fame means nothing. The accused are either innocent and need to be protected, or else they're guilty and should not be turned into a publicity stunt!"

"Don't worry about names being published," Husayn assured him, "I'm doing a study on school and life, that's all. If you like, I can allude to your name with just a letter. I may even be able to do without it altogether . . ."

"That would be the best thing. But what do you want to know exactly?

As they sat there by themselves sipping coffee in the salon, Husayn gave him the sort of encouraging look which journalists keep at the ready. All they could hear of the boys was an occasional buzz through the closed door.

"I want to record your thoughts about our generation and this one," said Husayn. "What are the most important cases you've judged; what's your philosophy of life and work. That kind of thing . . ."

Abbas started expressing his opinions slowly and with a certain diffidence. He was prejudiced, in favor of the past generation as individuals, but in favor of this one, philosophically speaking. He seemed to like his job and enjoyed it even though he was continually pressed with work as a result. Then he told me with relish about some of the cases he had encountered.

"You were always the first in everything!" Husayn said.

"I was first in the baccalauriat[5] for the whole area . . ."

Husayn thought for a moment. "You seem oddly at ease," he commented, "in spite of everything!"

"In spite of what?"

"Being someone who can condemn his fellow men to death . . ."

Abbas interrupted him emphatically. "I'm still quite content," he said, "I don't know the meaning of the word 'worry' . . ."

"This inner peace you have is really unusual!"

Abbas laughed loudly. "You can think of me as a Sufi if you like!" he said.

Husayn's astonishment showed in his eyes and he immediately tried to probe deeper. But his friend seemed to regret what he had let slip fairly quickly and refused to say another word on the subject.

"You seem to work very hard."

"Yes, our entire life seems to vanish beneath piles of case dossiers."

It was clear that he was working incredibly hard just as he had done as a student. A noble monasticism, a continuing struggle, eight children and mysticism!

"Even so, civil servants all think that the cadre of judges must be a life of sheer paradise!"

"We've got paradise!" he replied with a smile.

Husayn showed him the school picture and he looked at it with interest. Husayn pointed to Hamid Zahran. "Do you remember that student?" he asked.

"No . . ."

"Hamid Zahran. He failed the baccalauriat. He's a company director now making five hundred pounds a month!"

He looked at the picture as though it were a flying saucer or something.

"My, my, I didn't think news like that would shake up a Sufi!" Husayn joked.

They both burst into laughter. He asked al-Urfali whom among his school colleagues he could recognize. He looked along the rows of students and put his finger on a face in the second row.

"Muhammad Abd al-Salam," he said, "a clerk in the public prosecutor's office. He worked with me when I was first in the service at Abu Tij, but I've no information on him now . . ."

Husayn had to travel to al-Minya to find Muhammad Abd al-Salam in his latest place of work. He looked at least ten years older than he actually was. His generally ragged appearance, the white disheveled hair on his head and the two missing front teeth were reminiscent of ruined buildings. The man did not remember him or even believe what he was being told until he was shown the old photograph. Then they both sat down together in a shoddy reception room inside an old apartment full of children.

"I don't recognize anyone in this photograph," Muhammad said. "I've been in the service for a long time, moving from one place to another . . ."

Husayn felt a painful sensation pricking at him inside, a feeling of profound sorrow and respect for this man. He asked him about his rank.

"I've been in the fifth grade for a year," he replied. "Write that down, Professor. It would be wonderful if you could publish my picture along with my children, six girls and four boys. What do you think? Isn't it possible that God has sent you here to serve as my relief after so much hardship?"

Husayn wished him well. But then he brought him back to the conversation about his memories from his job. He asked him to write out a detailed family budget for a year to serve as an example. Then he pointed to the picture of Hamid Zahran.

"That former colleague of ours is making five hundred pounds a month!" he said.

The other man was so astonished that his face seemed to get even paler than it already was. "What's his job?" he asked.

"Factory director."

"But even a minister doesn't make half that amount!"

"That's one thing, and this is another . . ."

"But how does he spend it all?" he asked in bewilderment. "On what kinds of things?"

Husayn gave a smile but did not try to answer.

"What kind of certificate did he get?"

"A pass!"

"Good grief! You're kidding . . ."

"No, I'm not. Certificates are not basis for making judgements."

"So on what basis *do* you make them then? Just explain to me how a man can have such good luck. Look at him, standing there in the photograph in the same row as I am. Tell me, how can he have reached such a salary scale?"

"There's something called good luck . . ." Husayn replied amiably.

The other man shook his head sadly. "There's no job in the entire country which is worth that amount of money," he said with confidence. "Otherwise, why haven't we reached the moon?"

Husayn gave a laugh. "At any rate," he said, "you're better off than millions of others . . ."

"Millions!" his friend protested. "Yes, I know that, but it's Hamid Zahran who's the problem . . ."

Husayn had no difficulty in arranging a meeting with his old neighbor, Hamid Zahran. As the company itself was not a good place for them to meet, Hamid invited Husayn to his home in Doqqi. Husayn looked in wonder at the villa surrounded by willow trees. It soon reminded him of Abbas al-Mawardi's mansion on his estate in Qalyub: the superb building itself, the spacious garden and the heady perfume of status. He wondered how his old neighbor would look to him now. All he could remember about him was that he was thin and had a pale complexion, that he laughed vacuously, and looked half-starved. That kind of image certainly did not fit with this exciting villa. God have mercy on the march of time, Hamid! Just think of the days when you used to try a whole variety of ruses to borrow a shilling without ever giving it back; if only we had not been kept apart by time, you would have seen from close up the way these human earthquakes happen!

"Hello, Husayn!" he said. "Where have you been all this time, my dear fellow?"

He was fully dressed, as are most important men at home. The salon looked dazzling with all its lights and mirrors. Hamid himself no longer looked as young as he once had; life seemed to have taken its toll from him.

"I protest," Hamid said in mock indignation, "at such a self-interested visit as this! You should have regarded this house as your own home long ago. You didn't even send me the proper congratulations when they were due!"

Husayn paused for a moment in some confusion. "I can't come up with any mitigating excuses," he said. "I therefore beg to be forgiven . . ."

Hamid laughed in satisfaction. As they chatted about their memories of the past, they forgot about quite a long space of time. Then Husayn got down to his business. He avoided asking the kinds of questions which might suggest either insinuations or sarcasm, and confined himself to his great success and how he had achieved it so easily. He questioned him about his policy with regard to the company, his views on his own generation, and so on . . .

"I had a good working relationship with the previous director even before he was appointed as director. He chose me to be his secretary and then his office director. His choice of me was based on former experience."

"Former experience, eh? What that really meant was that you had opened up your house as a gambling club for your directors, a gaming club and a drug den as well. It's quite obvious that you made clever use of opportunities when they arose!"

"While I was serving in his office, I studied every detail connected with the job, large and small, very carefully, and got to know all the important people who had any dealings with the company . . . .

"That was my own director who nominated me for the post when he left to go abroad.

"A fine choice it was, too! Tell me, what policy have you set for the future?"

He began to talk about the subject with great confidence. Husayn copied down essentials of what he was saying, watching him from close-by all the while; he made a note of his gestures and the times when he sat motionless. When the questions were over, Zahran got up.

"Wait here a moment," he said, turning towards the interior of the house. "I'll introduce my wife to you."

Ah! Fayiqa! The girl who used to live nearby! How had life treated her, he wondered. Zahran had married her when he still was a student; he was then living close to the home of her father, Amm Salama, the trolley driver. How would she look in the setting of this palatial villa!?

Hamid Zahran came back bringing a girl in her twenties, dazzlingly beautiful with a face which seemed to have borrowed the very best characteristics from both the East and the West. Good Heavens! Was this a new wife?

They were introduced and then proceeded to talk to each other in English most of the time. Zahran was laughing, and his own pride seemed to shout its happiness from his very facial expression. But where was Fayiqa, Husayn wondered? Had she died, or had he divorced her?

He decided that the picture would not be complete until he had made sure of that one detail. He went immediately to al-Kirmani Alley in Bab al-Shariyya and reached Amm Salama's old house. At the very beginning of the Alley he found out from the local drycleaner that Amm Salama had died years earlier and his daughter Fayiqa had opened a cigarette and sweet store on the ground floor. With pounding heart he approached the house, making sure that she did not see him until he had taken a look at her. Yes, there she was, sitting behind a table with only her face and neck visible. She was smoking a cigarette. Her face made her look a good ten years older than she really was, just like Muhammad Abd al-Salam, the public prosecutor's clerk in al-Minya. She seemed distracted and gloomy, as though she had resigned herself to her fate. Husayn remembered now that she had been a very model of patience, vivacity and optimism. He felt a very decent and worthwhile emotion inside him reach out to her in pity and respect . . .

He left al-Kirmani Alley feeling downhearted and disgusted at the foul smell. He started thinking about the materials he had collected for his study and making a preliminary analysis. "I wonder," he asked himself, "what kind of sense we'll be able to squeeze out of this old photograph!"
(Mahfuz, 1981, pp. 91–99)

Buland al-Haydari (b. 1926)
Old Age

Another winter,
And here am I,
By the side of the stove,
Dreaming that a woman might dream of me,
That I might bury in her breast
A secret she would not mock;
Dreaming that in my fading years
I might spring forth as light,
And she would say:
This light is mine;
Let no woman draw near it.
  Here by the side of the stove,
  Another winter,
  And here am I,
  Spinning my dreams and fearing them,
  Afraid her eyes would mock
  My bald, idiotic head,
  My greying, aged soul,
  Afraid her feet would kick
  My love,
  And here, by the side of the stove,
  I would be lightly mocked by woman.
Alone,
Without love, or dreams, or a woman,
And tomorrow I shall die of the cold within,
Here, by the side of the stove.

(al-Haydari, 1974, pp. 129–131)

Abu al-Qasim al-Shabbi (1909–1934)
In the Shadow of the Valley of Death

We walk, as all round walks on creation . . . yet, to what
    goal?
With the birds we sing to the sun; as the spring plays on its
    flute;
We read out to Death the tale of Life . . . yet, how ends that
    tale?
Thus I spoke to the winds, and thus they answered: ask of
    Being itself how it began.
Covered over in mist, in bitter weariness cried out my soul:
    Whither shall I go?

I said: walk on with life; it replied: what reaped I as I walked
before?
Collapsed like a parched and withered plant I cried: Where, o
heart, is my rake?
Bring it, that I may trace my grave in the dark silence, bury
myself,
Bring it, for darkness is dense around me, and the mists of
sorrow are settled on high.
Dawn fills the goblets of passion, yet they shatter in my hands;
Proud youth has fled into the past, and left on my lips a la-
ment.
Come, o heart! We are two strangers who made of life an art
of sorrow;
We have fed long on life, sung long with youth.
And now with night go barefooted over the rocky paths—and
bleed.
We are satiated with dust, our thirst quenched with tears,
Left and right we have scattered dreams, love, pain and sor-
row,
And then? I, remote from the joy of the world and its song,
In the darkness of death bury the days of my life, cannot even
mourn their passing,
And the flowers of life, in grievous, troubling silence, fall at
my feet.
The magic of life is dry: come, o my weeping heart, let us now
try death.
Come!

(al-Shabbi, 1974, p. 137)

Khalil Mutran (1872–1949)
A Rose That Died

O questing birds, what seek you in your wanderings?
    They made answer:
We are the hopes of youth; and here our beloved
    lived and suffered.
She was the rose in our garden, reigning
    justly with the submission of all therein.
Yet all too soon we saw her fall from her throne,
    then disappear.
And so you see us ever searching for some trace of her,
    or flocking where once she was wont to be.

(Mutran, 1974, p. 41)

NOTES

1. Tarbush: the red headwear (fez) worn by civil servants in Egypt in the pre-Revolutionary period and also worn by schoolboys; very similar to the British schoolboys' cap.

2. 26th of February Declaration: a politial decision taken during World War II whereby the British installed the Egyptian government of their liking backed up by a military force.

3. Salamik: a garden house or gazebo to serve as a place of relaxation on large estates.

4. Sidqi: the regime of Isma il Sidqi in the early 1930s is a byword for a tyrannical rule in modern Egyptian history. During that period, the constitution of the country was suspended.

5. Baccalauriat: the certificate granted to students upon successful completion of secondary education.

REFERENCES

Allen, R. (1982). *The Arabic novel: An historical and critical introduction.* Syracuse: Syracuse University Press.

Hawi, K. (1981, Spring/Summer). A mad old woman. *Nimrod, 24*(2), 103.

al-Haydari, B. (1974). Old age. In M. A. Khouri and H. Algar (Eds. and Trans.), *An Anthology of modern Arabic poetry* (pp. 129–131). Berkeley: University of California Press.

al-Khal, Y. (1974). Old age. In M. A. Khouri and H. Algar (Eds. and Trans.), *An Anthology of modern Arabic poetry* (pp. 53–55). Berkeley: University of California Press.

Mahfuz, N. (1981, Spring/Summer). An old photograph (R. Allen. Trans.). *Nimrod, 24*(2), 91–99.

Mahfuz, N. (1973). The man on the thirty-fifth floor. In A. Abadir and R. Allen (Trans.), *God's world: An anthology of short stories.* Minneapolis, MN: Bibliotheca Islamica.

Mutran, K. (1974). A rose that died. In M. A. Khouri and H. Algar (Eds. and Trans.), *An anthology of modern Arabic poetry* (p. 41). Berkeley: University of California Press.

Nicholson, R. A. (Ed.) (1969). *Studies in Islamic poetry.* Cambridge: Cambridge University Press.

Saʿid, Ali Ahmad [Adunis, pseud.] (1971). The days. In *The blood of Adonis* (S. Hazo, Trans.) (p. 3). Pittsburgh: University of Pittsburgh Press.

al-Shabbi, A. a-Q. (1974). In the valley of the shadow of death. In M. A. Khouri and H. Algar (Eds. and Trans.), *An Anthology of modern Arabic poetry* (p. 137). Berkeley: University of California Press.

Shukri, A. a-R. (1974). Welcome and Life. In M. A. Khouri and H. Algar (Eds. and Trans.), *An anthology of modern Arabic poetry* (p. 133). Berkeley: University of California Press.

FURTHER READING

Mahfuz, N. (1973). Passers-by. In *God's world* (R. Allen and A. Abadir, Trans.) (pp. 115–126). Minneapolis: Bibliotheca Islamica.

Sayigh, T. (1976). A national hymn. In I. J. Boullata (Ed. and Trans.), *Modern Arab poets, 1950–1975* (pp. 135–136). Washington: Three Continents Press.

9

"Withered Blossoms": Aging in Japanese Literature

Virginia Skord

Westerners often assume that Japanese attitudes toward aging are firmly rooted in principles of respect, reverence, and deference toward the aged, and that the Japanese individual contemplating the onset of old age is assured of a secure and comfortable place within society. One may point to Respect for the Aged Day *(Keirō no hi)*, a national holiday honoring elderly citizens, or to the relative absence of nursing homes or retirement colonies due to a long-standing presumption that elderly parents will remain in the family home in the care of their adult offspring. "Silver" seats, specially reserved for the elderly or infirm, are standard features on all public transportation vehicles, and one is not presumed a master of any art (including the delicate art of business management) until middle age at least. All these and a plethora of other examples that might be cited appear to indicate a fundamentally positive attitude toward aging resting on a deeply ingrained respect for the elderly and acknowledgment of the values of mature wisdom. Yet aging is such an intrinsic and emotionally charged element of human experience that it is not surprising to uncover in Japanese literature deeply ambivalent attitudes that, although expressed in themes and forms particular to Japanese culture, nonetheless span cultural barriers to express easily recognized human sentiments. Attitudes toward aging seem to be universally ambivalent: we note with distress signs of our own advancing years, realizing all the while that death is the sole alternative to slow decline. Old age is seen as both a blessing and a curse, a time of renewal and decay, of hard-won wisdom and derisible senility: a twilight zone of existence with no clear demarcation between the vitality of youth and the darkness of death. Gestation is to life as old age is to death.

Japanese ambivalence toward aging may be compared to two natural metaphors: the plum and the cherry blossoms. The plum blossom, its delicate petals sprouting from gnarled, twisted old limbs, has traditionally been regarded as the first flower of the new year and a symbol of renewed vitality. The short-lived cherry blossom, on the other hand, has frequently served as a symbol of the ephemerality of life: its bloom lasts for only a few days before it gracefully gives way, scattering in the spring winds. The image of a withered cherry blossom stubbornly clinging to the branch is highly distasteful according to traditional Japanese aesthetics. Japanese literary expression has long vacillated between attributing to the elderly the vitality of the plum or the frailty of the cherry blossom past its prime. To be sure, other natural metaphors have been invoked to describe old age. In medieval Buddhist "maps" depicting the stages of human life, maturity is often represented by the pine, late middle age by autumnal maple leaves, and old age by bare snow-covered trees in a wintry landscape. But the divergent Japanese cultural attitudes regarding the plum and cherry blossoms best reflect the similar bifurcation of opinion regarding the elderly and old aged: a still-vital, life-affirming state, a miserable reminder of death and decay, or, in more sophisticated literary formulations, a complex combination of both. This ambivalence may be traced to the often mutually contradictory but coexistent religious values of Shinto and Buddhism. Generally speaking, Shinto is concerned with the celebration of life and fecundity; Buddhism with the annihilation of the self and negation of bodily pleasure. Yet it would be an oversimplification to see Shinto attitudes as positive and Buddhist as negative relative to aging, for while Shinto shuns death and decay, Buddhism holds that old age and death can present opportunities to realize the ephemerality of all existence.

There is evidence that the ancient courts of Nara and Heian Japan (ca. 700–1159 A.D.) conferred special honors upon their senior members. Forty was considered the threshold of old age; one's fortieth year, and every subsequent ten years, marked a cause for special celebration. Indeed, the imperial court practiced the custom of presenting a "dove cane" *(hatozue)* to octogenarian nobility until early in this century. The *Tales of Ise* (ca. 900 A.D.) contains several passages referring to such occasions. The excerpted passage is a particularly moving address from an older nobleman to one who has turned forty, in which cherry petals serve as a metaphor for the enjoyment of life, which softens the painful impact of old age. The poem is typical of congratulatory poems in early anthologies in its delicately expressed acknowledgment of the inevitability of aging and of the continuing possibilities for happiness in later life.

In the *Tale of Genji* (ca. 1000 A.D.), the preeminent masterpiece of Japanese prose narrative, we find another, more complex view of aging. In this novel, as in Buddhist orthodoxy in general, we can see the Buddhist ideal of nonattachment take an interesting twist relative to old age. Since the self should be as a wisp of smoke, liable to ready dispersal by the ever-changing currents of fate, extreme longevity can indicate that one has not relinquished attachment to this world. The *Tale of Genji* gives few portraits of the old that are not gloomy or disparaging. Indeed, most of the characters either die at an early age or enter religious seclusion, which is presented as the only way to grow old gracefully. Retirement from the world denies the physical self and its desires, severs formal relations with society, and anticipates the final oblivion of self that occurs at death. There is no place here for the rage of Dylan Thomas, only a bittersweet acceptance of decline and the futility of struggle. The hero, Prince Genji, is depicted only until he reaches the apex of his worldly power and is poised at the brink of decline. The final chapter in which he appears (the novel continues for another fourteen chapters) shows Genji looking back on his life, his moments of glory, and the women he has known and loved; the succeeding chapter summarily informs the reader that Genji is dead. This fictional paragon of courtly elegance and beauty never appears as an old man; rather, like the ideal cherry blossom, he expires in his prime.

A major theme of the *Tale of Genji* concerns the feelings of parents for their offspring. Aging parents are continually caught between the instinctive desire to protect their children and promote their success and the necessity to break from the world. This dilemma is underscored in the figure of the old priest of Akashi, who in spite of having taken religious vows still actively maneuvers to install his daughter as consort of the illustrious Prince Genji. It is only when the child born of that union in turns gives birth to an imperial prince that the priest finally is able to reject the world and enter the mountains alone, to die shortly thereafter. This priest's machinations receive unfavorable commentary within the text: the narrator implies that the old should keep to themselves and fade away as quickly and as quietly as possible.

This same sentiment is voiced rather cruelly in Sei Shōnagon's *Pillow Book,* where the undeniable physical presence of the elderly seems to irk the author no end. She sees the elderly as ugly, tedious beings who defy social convention by indulging in creature comforts. That an old man warming his hands at the brazier may genuinely feel the cold more acutely than his juniors does not occur to his observer. She even views changed sleeping patterns as an unwarranted impingement upon the sensibilities of others. If they must grow old, the author seems to say, must they be so very obvious about it? Writing some two centuries after Sei Shōnagon, the monk Kenkō echoes that lady's sentiments about the aged less frivolously, but certainly with a similar opinion of the behavior appropriate to the elderly. Kenkō assumes that when one passes the age of forty, ugliness and decrepitude inevitably follow, and that this shameful state is best avoided by gracefully expiring beforehand. Neither he nor others of this school of gerontological thought ever overtly endorse suicide as an alternative, but Kenkō does suggest that one who finds himself prone to aging should retire to live in seclusion as soon as possible. Sexual activity indicates a concern with the mortal body and physical gratification unbecoming to one who should be contemplating the brevity and evanescence of life. Kenkō equates the elderly with the undistinguished and poor and says that such folk should refrain from presuming intimacy with their "betters."

In both Japan and the West, the physical ravages of age have traditionally been thought of as particularly cruel to women, whose fortunes often depend upon youth and beauty. The image of the aged beauty reduced to miserable circumstances occurs frequently in Japanese literature. Tradition has it that after her backer fell from imperial favor, Sei Shōnagon married, was widowed, became a nun, and lived out the remainder of her days in poverty and wretchedness. Ōno no Komachi, a poet famed for her beauty and sensuality, mourns the passage of youth in the poem included here. The metaphor of the blossom operates relative to youth and sensuality, both diminished by the steady flow of time that she is powerless to halt. The nō play *Komachi at Sekidera* concerns an aged woman who is revealed to be the famed poet herself. In the play, she relives her past glory, dancing with abandon, yet although her spirit is still young, her body is uncooperative, and she weeps in despair. Past and present, vitality and decay, genius and waning creativity, spontaneity and deliberation are all juxtaposed in this celebration of life and art. Rather than present old age in a facile, one-dimensional fashion, this moving text suggests that the delicate interplay of vital forces operates even in the elderly, hampered only by physical limitation. In the passage included here, Komachi expresses the pleasure she takes in life even as death approaches, and in composing poetry even though her creative vision has waned.

Perhaps the generous treatment afforded Komachi is due to her having voluntarily left society to live in a shabby hut; a literary portrait of a bustling old Komachi very much involved with the world might well have been considerably less compassionate. Although there do exist many folktales of kind or resourceful old women, literature in general had been particularly harsh to older women, who are most often depicted either as calculating shrews or withered old crones, bereft of value as soon as they lose their youthful allure. In the ribald tales of the seventeenth-century novelist Saikaku, the still-potent aging hero of *The Life of an Amorous Man* sails off to an island of women after he has exhausted the female talent of the mainland, while the equally sexually active heroine of *The Life of an Amorous Woman* ends her life as a procuress for prostitutes and later in an isolated hut, recounting adventures of her youth to a pair of curious young men.

The medieval short story "Old Lady Tokiwa" presents a fascinating if depressing portrait of an old woman who continually interrupts her Buddhist devotions with plaintive requests for food and drink. Shunned by her disgusted family and racked with physical pain, she grows increasingly lonely and her prayers less and less focused until at last she dies. That she finally manages to achieve salvation at the moment of expiration provides scant consolation to the reader of this disturbing text. If, as "Old Lady Tokiwa" suggests, old women were often seen as easily distractable beings oriented to the mundane, elderly men, on the other hand, were largely seen in positive terms. The twelfth-century peripatetic poet-priest Saigyō established an image of wisdom and devotion that endured for centuries and inspired generations of poets, including the well-known Bashō in the seventeenth century. Saigyō's spare, contemplative verse evokes a vision of old age as a time of cool reflection and matter-of-fact acceptance of one's own mortality.

One of the central paradigmatic images of a popular medieval war chronicle, *The Tales of the Heike,* is that of the premature death of a young aristocratic warrior accomplished in both literary and martial arts. The noble death in battle of the youthful brave hero evoked an enormous degree of pathos, an effect derived from the juxtaposition of youth and death. The samurai has traditionally been identified with the cherry blossom: both are at their peak of manhood and glory before uncomplainingly meeting a swift and sudden end. The old are closer to natural death, and their demise, even unjustly or violently, does not provoke the same reaction. Ideally, there would be no elderly warriors in the Japanese martial aesthetic. Seen in this light, the excerpted passage is particularly moving. A fallen warrior has been identified as Sanemori, a man well advanced in years; he has dyed his hair black in order to appear younger and thereby avoid ridicule.

Lest we take this dismal picture of aging as axiomatic in Japanese culture, it is necessary to turn again to more positive depictions of the elderly. The monk Ryōkan invokes ancient legends in his injunction to esteem and cherish the wisdom and experience that come with age. The nō play *Takasago,* a celebratory piece extolling the virtues of past reigns and invoking future prosperity, features an old man and woman who are identified with ancient twin pine trees. Like the trees, the couple is aged, yet ageless, still strong and vigorous. In the latter half of the play, the old man, rejuvenated as the young pine god, dances in celebration of eternal renewal. Here age and youth are inseparable; the seeds of one are contained in the other. Fallen needles are replaced by fresh new verdure, produced and sustained by the vitality of the old pine.

The motif of the benevolent, wise old man or woman often appears in folktales in which their devotion, sincerity, or meritorious conduct is rewarded with earthly prosperity. Of the popular Seven Gods of Fortune *(Shichifukujin),* five are normally represented as aged men. One well-known legend, originating in China, but incorporated into Japanese folklore, tells of an imperial edict ordering that anyone over the age of forty be put to death. Rather than comply with this harsh decree, one particularly filial man conceals his aged father from the authorities, and when the country is threatened, the father's sage advice saves it from disaster. In contrast, however, the legendary Obasute mountain, where it is said the old were left to perish, is a monument to the grisly truth that the elderly were also seen as useless mouths to feed out of scanty resources.

Turning to modern literature, we find a generally pessimistic view of aging. "The Hateful Age," a short story by Niwa Fumio, concerns a family's attempts to cope with the senile grandmother. It explores the lamentable predicament in which so many families find themselves, saddled with the burden of having to care for a person no longer able to care for himself or herself, no longer loved, who finds no joy in living, yet lives on. Social expectations require that these families care for their aged relatives, yet much of modern society has discarded traditional reverence for the elderly, seeing them as an unwelcome drain upon their resources. Like the medieval "Old Lady Tokiwa," "The Hateful Age" is extreme in its brutal and physical depiction of a senile grandmother, no more than a wasted bag of flesh greedily demanding to be fed, who destroys the lives of her resentful family members with her insatiable wants and compulsive habits. The reader is never given a glimpse into the mind of this old woman, but is placed squarely on the side of the family as he witnesses a vision of objectified, despised senility devoid of humanity.

Other modern writing expresses the experience of age from the point of view of the aged subject. Both Kawabata Yasunari and Tanizaki Junichirō explored aging in depth. Written in the authors' later years, the excerpts included here poignantly evoke the pathos, hopelessness, and passion of the elderly. The passage from *The Sound of the Mountain* presents a portrait of an aged couple, their feelings for each other deadened by years of familiarity. *The House of the Sleeping Beauties,* a fascinating exploration of youth, old age, and sexuality, concerns an elderly man who frequents a house catering to old men who wish to sleep with young women, yet who are unable to consummate the sexual act. The young women are not to be touched in any unseemly way; they serve only as reminders of the old men's lost infancy. The sexuality of the old as seen in modern Japanese literature is passive yet obsessive: the elderly are withered blossoms whose yearning for lost vitality leads them to seek fulfillment in bizarre and pathetic ways. Although impotent and dying, Tanizaki's mad old man pursues his voluptuous daughter-in-law, manipulating her and in turn becoming manipulated by her. Impatient with his uncooperative flesh, he sees his body as a hideous mask preventing him from exercising his still-insatiable sexual urges.

It seems fitting that the last excerpt should be a passage from *The Decay of the Angel,* the final book of Mishima Yukio's tetralogy, *The Sea of Fertility,* delivered to his publisher just hours before the author killed himself at the age of forty-five. Mishima turned his own life and death into self-conscious enactments of his complicated and often misunderstood ideology in which, like the cherry blossom falling at its peak of beauty, death was intensely meaningful as the ultimate affirmation of life. Rather than face the anathema of the slow decline of old age, he chose to die at the prime of life and the peak of his career. In the passage included here, he suggests that life is death, that the fabric of existence is woven of the warp of vitality and the woof of decay. Perhaps it is through this tragic yet mature and profound vision with which Mishima himself failed to come to terms that we can best understand and accept old age. The flower that is youth implies the withered flower that is old age, yet the dried blossom is no less a flower because it is withered. Aging is life itself.

SELECTIONS

Anonymous
from *Tales of Ise*

There was once a personage known as the Minister of State from Horikawa. On the day of a banquet celebrating the minister's fortieth birthday, held at the Ninth Ward House, an elderly Middle Captain composed this poem:

> Scatter in clouds,
> Cherry Blossoms,
> That you may hide the path
> By which old age
> Is said to approach.

(McCullough, 1968, p. 137)

Sei Shōnagon (ca. 1000)
from *The Pillow Book of Sei Shōnagon*

An elderly person warms the palms of his hands over a brazier and stretches out the wrinkles. No young man would dream of behaving in such a fashion; old people can really be quite shameless. I have seen some dreary old creatures actually resting their feet on the brazier and rubbing them against the edge while they speak.

• • • • •

An elderly couple who have several grown-up children, and who may even have some grandchildren, are taking a nap in the daytime. The children who see them in this state are overcome by a forlorn feeling, and for other people it is all very depressing. (Sei Shōnagon, pp. 24–25)

Kenkō (ca. 1283–1350)
from *The Tsurezuregusa of Kenkō*

We cannot live forever in this world; why should we wait for ugliness to overtake us? The longer man lives, the more shame he endures. To die, at the latest, before one reaches forty, is the least unattractive. Once a man passes that age, he desires (with no sense of shame over his appearance) to mingle in the company of others. In his sunset years, he dotes on his grandchildren, and prays for long life so that he may see them prosper. His preoccupation with worldly desires grows ever deeper, and gradually he loses all sensitivity to the beauty of things, a lamentable state of affairs.

•   •   •   •   •

If a man over forty occasionally has a secret love affair, what can be done about it? But if he openly discusses it, or jokes about his relations with women or the private affairs of other people, it is unbecoming at his age and ugly.

In general, nothing is more unpleasant to hear or see than an old man mingling with a group of young people and relating such stories in the hope of ingratiating himself; or an undistinguished person addressing a man of reputation as if they were intimates; or a poor man, fond of feasting, going to extravagant lengths to entertain his guests. (Kenkō, 1967, pp. 8, 94)

Ōno no Komachi (mid-ninth century A.D.)
Untitled

> The color of these flowers
> No longer has allure, and I am left
>   To ponder unavailingly
> The desire that my beauty once aroused
> Before it fell in this long rain of time.
>
> (Brower & Miner, 1961, p. 217)

attributed to Zeami (ca. 1364–1443)
from *Komachi at Sekidera*

Old woman: The temple bell of Sekidera
Chorus: Tolls the vanity of all creation—
   To ancient ears a needless lesson.
   A mountain wind blows down Osaka's slope
   To mourn the certainty of death;
   Its message still eludes me.
   Yet, when blossoms scatter and leaves fall,
   Still in this hut I find my pleasure:
   Grinding ink, I dip my brush and write.
   My words are all dry, like seaweed on the shore.
   Touching, they once said, but lacking strength—
   My poems lacked strength because they were a woman's.
   Now when I have grown decrepit

My poems are weaker still. Their life is spent.
How wretched it is to be old!

(Brazell, 1970, p. 79)

Anonymous (ca. sixteenth century)
from *Old Lady Tokiwa*

The old woman realized the truth of the Amida Buddha's vow to save all sentient beings who desired salvation. "Just watch me, Amida," she announced. As soon as she had washed and gargled to purify herself, she faced west and bowed low. "Oh Amida Buddha of the West! Please send me to the Western Paradise and grant me good karma!"

She continued to pray as the night wore on. "How miserable I am! I'd like a little water, Amida. Warm or cold—either will do, but just give me some. And while you're at it, may I go to paradise right away? Oh, Amida Buddha! Aren't you there? Or are you just not paying attention? Isn't my voice reaching you? I'm praying for my very own salvation, not for others, and if I hear that you've ignored me and sent others to paradise, I'll be angry with you for a long, long time! Make sure that doesn't happen!"

Her children heard her prayers, and rather than sympathize with her plight, were both amused and disgusted. "Listen to her at her prayers!" they said to each other. "She thinks that she won't find a place in paradise unless she shouts. What a din she's raising! That typical shrill whine of the aged has been going on night after night!" No one encouraged her; all ordered her to stop. (Skord, 1987, p. 313–314)

Saigyō (1118–1190)
Untitled

> While noticing how time
> Has bent my body's silhouette
>   Cast in the moonlight . . .
> Away off in the distance the moon
> Sank closer to the world's rim.

(Saigyō, 1977, p. 71)

Anonymous
from *The Tales of the Heike*

Mitsumori galloped over to General Yoshinaka. "I have just killed an odd foe. He might have been a retainer, but he was wearing a brocade battle robe; he might have been a general, but there were no forces following him. I pressed him to declare himself, but he refused. Judging from his accent, he must have been from the eastern provinces."

"Ahah!" replied Yoshinaka. "It must be Sanemori. But if so, I saw him once in Kozuke when I was young, and his hair was streaked with grey at the time. Now surely it must have turned white, but oddly enough the hair and beard on this head are black. Call Kanemitsu—he has known him for a long time and would recognize him."

Kanemitsu took one look at the head. "What a pity!" he cried. "This is the head of Sanemori."

"But he must have been more than seventy! Certainly he must have turned white! What do you make of this black hair?" asked Yoshinaka.

Tears streaming down his face, Kanemitsu replied: "This is so sad that it makes me weep. . . . Sanemori used to tell me that if he went into battle after the age of sixty, he would dye his hair so as to look younger. He feared that he would be ridiculed as an old war horse, for it would be unseemly to do battle with younger men. Truly he has dyed his hair black. Wash the head and see."

After the head was washed, they saw that indeed the hair had turned white. (Takagi et al., 1980, pp. 80–81)

Ryōkan (1758–1831)
from *The Zen Poems of Ryokan*

> A tale too sacred
> to tell with my own tongue
> A legend too true
> To relate in mortal speech:
> Once upon a time,
> A sovereign in high heaven
> Detected at night
> A silver hair upon his head,
> And early at dawn
> Called a minister of state,
> And directed him
> To fetch a pair of clippers
> Glowing in silver
> And to cut his silver hair
> And to put it within
> A big chest of silver sheen,
> And the sovereign
> At his death ceded the gift
> To his successor,
> And he in turn at his death
> Left it as a boon.
> Thus, always from son to son,
> Endlessly in line,
> I heard it was handed down,

The silver hair above price.
  Respect it in awe,
The silver hair on your head.
  Divine in its birth,
It has deigned to honour you
In your extreme advanced age.
  Do not despise it.
It could well come a herald
  From the underworld,
To call you out to darkness
The silver hair on your head.
  Not for a moment
Hold it in worldly contempt.
  Now if not before
Learn to adore it in your heart
The silver hair on your head.
  Of all the riches
That I can find in this world
  Nothing can equal
In price, no matter how dear,
The silver hair on your head.

(Ryōkan, 1981, pp. 155–156)

Kawabata Yasunari (1899–1972)
from *The Sound of the Mountain*

Yasuko was a good sleeper. Sometimes, in the middle of the night, Shingo would be tempted to blame her snoring for having awakened him. She had snored, it seemed, as a girl of fifteen or sixteen, and her parents had been at great pains to correct the habit; it had stopped when she married. Then, when she passed fifty, it had begun again.

When she [Yasuko] snored, Shingo would twist her nose in an effort to stop her. If the twisting had no effect, he would take her by the throat and shake her. On nights when he was not in good spirits he would be repelled by the sight of the aged flesh with which he had lived for so long.

Tonight he was not in good spirits. Turning on the light, he looked at her profile and took her by the throat. She was a little sweaty.

Only when she snored did he reach out to touch her. The fact seemed to him infinitely saddening.

He took up a magazine lying at his pillow. Then, the room being sultry, he got up, opened a shutter, and sat down beside it.

The moon was bright. (Kawabata, 1970, pp. 6–7)

from *The House of the Sleeping Beauties*

The ugly senility of the sad men who came to this house was not many years away for Eguchi himself. The immeasurable expanse of sex, its boundless depth—what part of it had Eguchi known in his sixty-seven years? And around the old men, new flesh, young flesh, beautiful flesh was forever being born. Were not the longing of the sad old men for the unfinished dream, the regret for days lost without ever being had, concealed in the secret of this house? Eguchi had thought before that girls who did not awaken were ageless freedom for old men. Asleep and unspeaking, they spoke as the old men wished. (Kawabata, 1969, pp. 40–41)

Tanizaki Junichirō (1886–1965)
from *Diary of a Mad Old Man*

I know very well that I am an ugly, wrinkled old man. When I look in the mirror at bedtime after taking out my false teeth, the face I see is really weird. I don't have a tooth of my own in either jaw. I hardly even have gums. If I clamp my mouth shut, my lips flatten together and my nose hangs down to my chin. It astonishes me to think that this is my own face. Not even monkeys have such hideous faces. How could anyone with a face like this ever hope to appeal to a woman? Still, there is a certain advantage in the fact that it puts people off guard, convinces them that you are an old man who knows he can't claim that sort of favor. But although I am neither entitled nor able to exploit my advantage, I can be near a beautiful woman without arousing suspicion. And to make up for my own inability, I can get her involved with a handsome man, plunge the whole house into turmoil, and take pleasure in *that*. (Tanizaki, 1965, p. 18)

Mishima Yukio (1925–1970)
from *The Decay of the Angel*

If the cause of decay was illness, then the fundamental cause of that, the flesh, was illness too. The essence of flesh was decay. It had its spot in time to give evidence of destruction and decay.

Why did people first become aware of that fact only as old age came on? Why, when it buzzed faintly past the ear in the brief noontide of the flesh, did they note it only to forget it? Why did the healthy young athlete, in the shower after his exertions, watching the drops of water hit his shining flesh like hail, not see that the high tide of life itself was the cruelest of ills, a dark, amber-colored lump?

For Honda now, life was senescence, senescence was life. It was wrong that these two synonyms should forever be libeling each other. Only now,

eighty-one years after he fell into this world, did Honda know the per-
verse essential at the heart of every pleasure? (Mishima, 1974, p. 210)

REFERENCES

Brazell, K. (Trans.). (1970). *Komachi at Sekidera*. In D. Keene (Ed.), *Twenty plays
of the No theatre* (pp. 65–80). New York: Columbia University Press.

Brower, R., & Miner, E. (1961). *Japanesee court poetry*. Stanford, CA: Stanford
University Press.

Kawabata, Y. (1969). *The house of the sleeping beauties* (E. G. Seidensticker, Trans.).
New York: Kodansha International.

Kawabata, Y. (1970). *The sound of the mountain* (E. G. Seidensticker, Trans.). New
York: Knopf.

Kenkō. (1967). *Essays in idleness: the tsurezurengusa of Kenko* (D. Keene, Trans.).
New York: Columbia University Press.

McCullough, H. (Trans.). (1968). *Tales of Ise: Lyrical episodes from tenth-century
Japan*. Stanford, CA: Stanford University Press.

Mishima, Y. (1974). *The decay of the angel* (E. G. Seidensticker, Trans.). New
York: Knopf.

Murasaki Shikibu. (1976). *The tale of Genji* (E. G. Seidensticker, Trans.) New
York: Knopf.

Niwa, F. (1967). The hateful age (I. Morris, Trans.). In I. Morris (Ed.), *Modern
Japanese short stories: an anthology* (pp. 320–348). Tokyo and Rutland, VT:
Charles E. Tuttle.

Ryōkan. (1981). *The zen poems of Ryokan* (N. Yuasa, Trans.). Princeton: Princeton
University Press.

Saigyō. (1977). *Mirror for the moon* (W. R. LaFleur, Trans.). New York: New
Directions.

Sei Shōnagon. (1967). *The pillow book of Sei Shōnagon* (I. Morris, Trans.). New
York: Columbia University Press.

Skord, V. (1987). *The comic consciousness in medieval Japanese narrative: Otogi-zoshi
of commoners*. Unpublished doctoral dissertation, Cornell University.

Takagi, I., et al. (Eds.). (1980). *Heike monogatari* (V. Skord, Trans.). Nihon koten
bungaku taikei, vol. 33. Tokyo: Iwanami shoten.

Tanizaki, J. (1965). *Diary of a mad old man* (H. Hibbitt, Trans.). New York: Knopf.

FURTHER READING

Inoue, Y. (1983). *Chronicle of my mother* (J. O. Moy, Trans.). New York: Kodansha International.

Palmore, E., & Daisaku, M. (1985). *The honorable elders revisited*. Durham, NC:
Duke University Press.

Plath, D. (1972). Japan: The after years. In D. Cowgill & L. Holmes (Eds.), *Aging
and modernization* (pp. 133–150). New York: Appleton-Century-Crofts.

Tsukimura, R. (1983). *Life, death, and age in modern Japanese fiction*. Toronto: University of Toronto–New York University Joint Centre on Modern East
Asia.

10

The Honored Aged in Chinese Literature

Edward Gunn

Among the oldest surviving texts of Chinese writing, *The Book of Rites (Li chi)* contains references to the aged within its elaborate ideal system of etiquette. It was the *Confucian Analects (Lun yü)* of the fifth century B.C., however, which became the central document for educated Chinese, laying down the ethical basis for the doctrine of filial piety reflected in the etiquette. The *Analects* are a collection of dialogues between the sage Confucius (K'ung-tzu) and his disciples at a time when China was divided into separate kingdoms whose rulers employed men such as Confucius to be advisors on maintaining or enlarging their states. Confucius saw himself as the upholder of the best of what were already traditions in Chinese society, including the sincere practice of rituals and customs calling for consideration and respect for the elderly, particularly one's own parents.

The reason that political advisors of the Confucian school of thought stressed the concept of filial piety lies in their vision of the centrality of the ethic of consideration for the aged as fundamental to the concept of the state. This is suggested in a passage of the *Analects* portraying the attitude of a disciple of Confucius toward a recluse, in which the disciple compares the relationship of old and young to that of sovereign and minister of state. Perhaps no other principal Confucian text presents such a concept more cogently than does *The Great Learning (Ta hsüeh)*.

The portrait of the aged in early Chinese writing is not confined to the laconic suggestiveness of the *Analects* or the rhetorical rhythms of *The Great Learning*. After Confucius himself, the sage most widely read and revered in traditional China was Mencius (Meng-tzu), who continued and developed the principles and theories of Confucius as an advisor to rulers and a teacher to those who would be advisors. His discourse with rulers was compiled in *The Works of Mencius (Meng-tzu)* in the third century B.C. Here the fondness for codifying doctrines and policies of all kinds in China, a practice that has survived into the present, and the resulting profusion of such codes are evident in the "three things" and "five things" that are unfilial. Among the three things that are considered unfilial, the sin of having no children by which to honor one's ancestors and continue the family line has always had such profound impact that the other two of the three sins have been relegated to parenthetical notes. These two are to agree to immoral behavior by one's parents in order to flatter them, and to neglect their poverty and infirmity by refusing to take an official post and the income that goes with it. These point toward conflicts of values and complexities of human nature that were taken up by other writers. Further, what is evident in the passages from Mencius and several well-known anecdotes in historical texts is the frequent indifference of society to the aged that made the constant reiteration of the ethic of filial piety an imperative.

If the failings of the actual social practice did not go unrecorded in early literature, neither did the imperfections of the aged themselves. While for a sage such as Confucius, aging might mean the ultimate attainment of wisdom and morality, the Chinese were well aware that for many this was not the case. In the discussions of filial piety, which prompted so many early descriptions of aging and the aged, important refinements to ethics arose out of consideration of those among the elderly who were less than exemplars of righteousness. Confucius himself pointed out the duty of the young to offer "righteous remonstrance" to their elders when they erred, enjoining the young to maintain an attitude of reverence even when abused by their elders for giving such admonishment (*Confucian Analects* 6.18). *The Classic of Filial Piety (Hsiao ching)*, the oldest extant text of which dates to the eighth century A.D., though the work is considered much older, argued that a son faced with the unethical conduct of his father must no more refrain from remonstrating with his father than a just and loyal minister would with a ruler who showed poor judgment. The ancient historical document *Tso chuan* offers a touching illustration of how a son resolves the quandary of honoring his father's wishes while upholding a larger ethical imperative. This tale of an otherwise minor historical figure, Wei K'o, also presents what may be the earliest extant mention of the dark side of aging as a psychological process, as seen in the portrait of Wei K'o's father.

Sober portraits of aging were at times offset by those that might delight and amaze. The effort to popularize for the young the ethic of filial piety resulted in such anecdotes as the legendary Lao' Lai-tzu in *The Twenty-four Examples of Filial Piety (Er-shih-szu hsiao,* ?fourteenth century A.D.). Like the other exemplars in the series, Lao' Lai-tzu carries his piety to extremes by obeying the injunction to remain a child to his parents even when he himself at seventy has achieved venerable status. Yet through the anecdote we have an actual portrayal of an elderly person and not simply mention of an elderly person as a figure in an ethical scheme devoted primarily to prescriptions for the behavior of the young that characterizes much of the traditional literature on aging.

If Confucian texts generally avoided actual descriptions of aging in preference to discussing the ethics of attitudes toward the aged, there was in the Chinese tradition another widespread current of literature that indulged in the Taoist fantasy of avoiding aging altogether. No selection of literature on aging would be complete without some representation of this facet of the culture, the popular Taoist conceptions that captured many an imagination with their alchemy, dietary prescriptions, and physical and sexual regimens, all designed not to bring men into harmony with an ideal society, but to attain an existential transcendence. P'eng Tsu appears as the original Chinese Methuselah in a long line of Taoist immortals whose careers were summed up in the fanciful *Biographies of Immortals* as well as portrayed in many paintings.

The actual pursuit of immortality, as well as its legendary achievement, being limited to a relative few, the experience of aging and the image of the aged for most Chinese has been captured in various proverbs and figures of speech. These give ample testimony to the fact that popular perceptions of attitudes toward aging and the aged were not restricted to the ethical considerations of philosophers and historians. Quite the contrary, these sayings are by turns irreverent, light-hearted, and commonsensical, often at the expense of the aged.

The testimonies of the aged themselves, their own reflections on their condition, have most often appeared in poetry. Ruled by formal and thematic conventions as it was, traditional Chinese poetry still produced a considerable variety of voices, as suggested in the selections included here. Viewed by Chinese at times as a major villain and at times as a great hero, Ts'ao Ts'ao was a significant figure in both the art of war and of poetry. His metaphor of an old warhorse who has endured a lifetime of war became a favorite emblem in later poetry on aging. One of the few famous women writers in traditional China, Li Ch'ing-chao left behind a series of poems describing her life as the widow of a civil servant, as well as her glamorous youth in the capital city of Ch'ang-an. Civil servants themselves comprised the most numerous group of poets prior to the twentieth century, and they had a good deal to say about growing old. The "Autumn Meditations" and "Lament for Lu Yin" by Meng Chiao are among the grimmest examples of conventional poetic themes, their difficulty the mark of a poet known for his iconoclastic style. Tu Fu, on the other hand, has been much more widely imitated, regarded for centuries as a major contender for the status of China's greatest poet. In this selection from his *The Autumn Wastes* Tu Fu looks back on his failure to achieve high rank as an official (with his portrait hung in the Unicorn Hall of the Imperial Palace) and wonders about his children, who have taken up the fashion of inserting foreign (Central Asiatic) words into their poetry after the example of an influential poet-official of the day. In another poem, Tu Fu takes up the image of the "old horse," this time adding a more complex image of himself as a "withered pedant" between the metaphysical forces of heaven *(Ch'ien)* and earth *(K'un)*, symbols of ultimate universal order in the divination system of the *Book of Changes (I ching)*. Such cosmic vision and seriousness of reflection were also shared by another profound poet and zealous statesman, Han Yü. Here, however, he is represented in an uncharacteristically light mood as he begins a cycle of five poems titled "The Pond in a Bowl."

Occasionally journals also provide an intimate sharing of the experience of aging, none more so than the *Journal* of Wu Yü-pi. For Chinese seeking self-improvement and moral cultivation, the personal example provided by pious and earnest men such as Wu Yü-pi could be as inspiring as the more abstract ethical texts of Confucian philosophy themselves. Through this man's journal we have also a glimpse into the way such purposefulness in youth and middle age was also expressed in old age. To Wu himself the era in which he lived was not one that permitted men to achieve with grace and ease a moral stature equivalent to that of the ancients in their more idyllic world, and his fretful modesty and determination stayed with him to the end of his life, sparked with moments of great joy and a growing detachment from his own ego.

Many observers of Chinese society have supported the view that the individual in Chinese society is first and foremost to be seen as the member of a family. Ts'ao Hsüeh-ch'in's *Dream of the Red Chamber (Hung-lou meng)*, also known as *The Story of the Stone (Shih-t'ou chi)*, is an eighteenth-century novel that focused on this theme with such richness of observation that it remains one of the central works of Chinese imaginative literature. The recurrent passages describing the Matriarch of this very large, very elite family, Grandmother Chia, are the most vivid descriptions of a woman aging. As the supreme authority in a household containing hundreds of servants and dozens of relatives, the Matriarch is attended and assisted— and always humored—by the younger women of the family, related by marriage to the Chia family or still residing in the family compound as unwed granddaughters. The passage included here, abridged and slightly edited, from chapter 54, though without any dramatic action, suggests slightly the wealth of allusions, implications, and innuendos that flow through the novel.

The twentieth century brought with it in the 1910s and 1920s a violent reaction, emotionally and intellectually, against Confucian traditions, including automatic respect for the elderly, among the young and educated, who saw the tradition as irrational, inhuman, and incapable of preserving the nation and society in the face of foreign and modern challenges. The popular novel *Family (Chia)* by Pa Chin (Li Fei-kan) took youthful readers by storm in 1931, offering scenes of youthful defiance and elderly despotism that were common to their imagination. Here two separate passages have been spliced together to portray the elderly Patriarch of the family as seen through the eyes of a grandson and in his own mind.

Family is neither rhetorically nor conceptually the finest work of this century. Yet it undeniably testifies to the uncertain status of the aged as it documents the rise of a youth culture, giving social form to the tensions of the younger generation, moved at once to honor and care for their elders and to instruct and triumph over them. These are themes that have endured through the turbulent, complex course of revolutions that have shaped Chinese societies in this century.

SELECTIONS

Confucius (fifth century B.C.)
from *Confucian Analects*

Filial piety and fraternal submission—are they not the root of all benevolent actions?

The Master said, "A youth, when at home, should be filial, and, abroad, respectful to his elders."

The Master said, "At fifteen, I had my mind bent of learning. At thirty, I stood firm. At forty, I had no doubts. At fifty, I knew the decrees of Heaven. At sixty, my ear was an obedient organ for the reception of truth. At seventy, I could follow what my heart desired, without transgressing what was right."

Mang I asked what filial piety was. The Master said, "It is not being disobedient."

Tsze-lu asked what filial piety was. The Master said, "The filial piety of nowadays means the support of one's parents. But dogs and horses are likewise able to do something in the way of support;—without reverence what is there to distinguish the one support given from the other?"

Mang Wu asked what filial piety was. The Master said, "Parents are anxious lest their children should be sick."

Tsze-lu, following the Master, happened to fall behind, when he met an old man, carrying across his shoulder on a staff a basket of weeds. Tsze-lu asked him, "Have you seen my master, sir?" The old man replied, "Your four limbs are unaccustomed to toil; you cannot distinguish the five kinds of grain:—who is your master?" With this, he planted his staff in the ground and proceeded to weed. Tsze-lu joined his hands across his breast, and stood before him. The old man kept Tsze-lu to pass the night in his house, killed a fowl, prepared millet, and feasted him. He also introduced him to his two sons. Next day, Tsze-lu went on his way, and reported his adventures. The Master said, "He is a recluse," and sent Tsze-lu back to see him again, but when he got to the place, the old man was gone. Tsze-lu then said to the family, "Not to take office is not righteous. If the relations between old and young may not be neglected, how is it that he sets aside the duties that should be observed between sovereign and minister? Wishing to maintain his personal purity, he allows that great relation to come to confusion. A superior man takes office, and performs the righteous duties belonging to it. As to the failure of right principles to make progress, he is aware of that—but will not therefore shrink from his righteous service." (Confucius, 1933)

Learned Sages (Ancient China)
from *The Great Learning*

When the sovereign behaves to his aged, as the aged should be behaved to, the people become filial; when the sovereign behaves to his elders, as the elders should be behaved to, the people learn brotherly submission; when the sovereign treats compassionately the young and helpless, the people do the same. Thus the ruler has a principle with which, as with a measuring square, he may regulate his conduct. (*The Great Learning*, 1933)

Mencius (third century B.C.)
from *The Works of Mencius*

Mencius said, "There are three things which are unfilial, and to have no posterity is the greatest of them."

. . . . .

There are five things which are said in the common practice of the age to be unfilial. The first is laziness in the use of one's limbs, without attending to the nourishment of his parents. The second is gambling and chess playing, and being fond of wine, without attending to the nourishment of his parents. The third is being fond of goods and money, and selfishly attached to his wife and children, without attending to the nourishment of his parents. The fourth is following the desires of one's ears and eyes, so as to bring his parents to disgrace. The fifth is being fond of bravery, fighting and quarreling so as to endanger his parents.

. . . . .

Let mulberry trees be planted about the homesteads with their five *mow*, and persons of fifty years may be clothed with silk. In keeping fowls, pigs, dogs, and swine, let not their times of breeding be neglected, and persons of seventy may eat flesh. Let there not be taken away the time that is proper for the cultivation of the farm with its hundred *mow*, and the family of several mouths that is supported by it shall not suffer from hunger. Let careful attention be paid to education in schools, including in it especially the filial and fraternal duties, and gray-haired men will not be seen upon the roads, carrying burdens on their backs or on their heads. It never has been that the ruler of a state where such results were seen . . . did not attain to the imperial dignity. (Mencius, 1933, Bk. 4, Pt. 1, chap. 26, 1; Bk. 4, Pt. 2, chap. 30, 2; Bk. 1, Pt. 2, chap. 3, 4)

Author Unknown (eighth century A.D.)
from *The Classic of Filial Piety*

The father who had a son that would not remonstrate with him would sink into the gulf of unrighteous deeds. Therefore when a case of unrighteous conduct is concerned, a son must by no means keep from remonstrating with his father, nor a minister from remonstrating with his ruler. Hence, since remonstrance is required in the case of unrighteous conduct, how can simple obedience to the orders of a father be accounted filial piety? (*The Classic of Filial Piety*, 1933, pp. 64–65)

Tso-ch'iu Ming (fifth century B.C.)
from *Tso-chuan*

According to the *Tso-chuan*, Wei K'o of the state of Chin was the son of Wei Wu-tzu. Wei Wu-tzu had a favorite concubine who had borne him no children. Falling ill, he gave orders to his son, saying, "After I am gone, see that she is provided with a husband." When his illness grew more severe, however, he said, "Make certain that she is put to death and buried with me!" At length, when he died, his son Wei K'o arranged for the concubine to be married, saying, "When the illness was severe, my father's mind became deranged. I abide by the orders he gave when his mind was still clear." Later, when an army from Ch'in invaded Chin (594 B.C.), Wei K'o defeated it at Fu-shih and captured Tu Hui, a warrior of Ch'in noted for his great strength. While the battle was still in progress, Wei K'o saw an old man tying the grasses together in such a way as to block Tu Hui's way. Tu Hui stumbled over the grasses and fell to the ground, thus making it possible for Wei K'o to capture him. That night the old man appeared to Wei K'o in a dream and said, "I am the father of the woman you gave away in marriage. You followed the orders which your honored father gave when he was still in his right mind. I have done this to repay you." (Tso-ch'iu, 1979, p. 104)

Anonymous (?fourteenth century A.D.)
from *The Twenty-four Examples of Filial Piety*

The very filial Lao' Lai-tzu was born in the state of Ch'u at the time of the Chou dynasty [1122–255 B.C.]. He provided lavishly for his father and mother. Although he was seventy years of age, he would not concede that he was old. Clad in multi-colored clothes, he played children's games and danced in front of his parents. He also would carry water into their front hall, and then pretend to be childishly awkward and fall to the ground, in this way amusing his parents and making them happy. (*The Twenty-four Examples,* 1933)

Anonymous (sixteenth century)
from *Biographies of Immortals*

The Taoist immortal P'eng Tsu (his real name was Ch'ien K'eng) was the great-grandson of the Emperor Chuan Hsu, who reigned from 2513–2435 B.C. P'eng Tsu was still in his prime when the Yin dynasty fell to the Chou dynasty—over seven hundred years later! He enjoyed leading a quiet life and devoted himself solely to cultivation of his spirit and nourishment of his life force. When King Mu of the Chou dynasty [reigned 1001–946 B.C.] heard of P'eng Tsu he awarded him a post as a minister in his administration. But P'eng Tsu feigned illness and declined to serve in the government. Now P'eng Tsu consumed some special Taoist recipes, such as crystals, powdered mother-of-pearl, and reindeer antlers. Moreover he was extremely adept at Yoga breathing exercises and a technique of sexual intercourse whereby Taoists nurtured and conserved their essence by not ejaculating upon climax. So the fresh-faced young palace concubines frequented his residence in their covered carriages to learn "the Way" from P'eng Tsu. Then they taught what they had learned to King Mu so that he could experiment with these techniques. When P'eng Tsu learned of this he disappeared, no one knows where. . . . But some say he survived forty-nine wives and fifty-four children; others that he had ninety wives and left two sons who gave their names to a mountain range in Fukien province. (*Biographies of Immortals,* n.d.)

Lin Yutang (1895–1976)
from *Proverbs and Sayings*

Wisdom does not depend on age; a man of a hundred may be full of empty talk.

A parent who is long sick in bed is often ignored by even the most filial of sons.

Eat until you are old; learn until you are old.

If the father and mother are not lenient, it will be difficult to bring about a filial course on the part of children.

Like an old lady's tooth,—loose.

Like an old lady wearing spectacles,—all for show.

Like an old lady's food,—good.

Like an old lady attending a funeral,—coming on behind.

Like an old lady trying to bite with her teeth,—forgetting she has none.

The old villager having never seen cherries: what small apricots.

The old villager never having seen a peacock: what a big-tailed hawk!

Like the old villager taking snuff,—a violent fit of weeping.

At seventy-three and eighty-four, if the King of Hades does not summon a man he will die by himself.

People of seventy you should not keep over night; and do not invite a person of eighty to sit down.

The strength of the aged is like spring cold, or heat after harvest. (Lin, 1914, pp. 230, 269, 272–273, 303)

Ts'ao Ts'ao (155–220)
from *Ts'ao Ts'ao*. **Ballad**

> Old warhorse leans at trough,
> Ambitious to travel a thousand li.
> Heroic warrior in twilight years,
> Brave heart not yet exhausted.

(n.d.)

Li Ch'ing-chao (1084–?1151)
from *Tz'u verse*

> Long placid evening
>
>   my diversions few
> I vacantly dreaming of Ch'ang-an
> how the road
>
>   goes up
>   to the old capital
> Please tell them: spring
>   is fine
>   this year

Flower glow   set each other off
moon shadow
Pleasant to take   wine
                          food
        without picking and choosing
Excellent wine
                          a tart plum
Just right for my mood
Tipsy
            I put a flower in my hair
              O flower! Flower!
              don't make fun of me
Have pity!
              Spring
              like all men living
                        will soon
                        grow old

Sunset
            molten bronze
evening clouds
                        marbled white jade
      Where is he?
A mist of light
                  stains the willows
Plum blowing
                  A flute's wail
    Spring reveries
    how much you know!
New Year's Eve
                  the merrymaking festival
Serene weather—   wind
                        no   in its wake?
                        rain
Friends come   to invite me out
                              horses
                                    traveling carts
                  wine-drinking friends
I thank these
                  poem-making companions
At the capital   joyful days
In my room   much
                  time to myself
I recall   another New Year's Eve
how I put on   the green-feather headdress

narrow snow-white sash   worked
                                                     with gold thread
Headdress and sash
                                to vie with any beauty
I   haggard now
                     wind-tangled locks
                     hair
                                frosted white
                                at the temple
Too diffident   to venture among flowers
                            under the window screen
I loiter
eavesdropping   on the talk
                          and laughter
                          of others.

                                                     (Li, 1965, pp. 359–361)

Meng Chiao (751–814)
Autumn Meditations

Old and sick, many strange broodings,
Dawn and evening, the heart's not the same.
Autumn insects weep for the declining cycle.
I cannot unravel their tangled echoes.
Autumn grass frail as hair.
A pure fragrance adorning sparse cassia blooms.
Yet how can this late fragrance last long?—
The speeding sunlight also darkens easily.
In vain I'm ashamed of my studies as a youth.
To what can I apply my wisdom in these twilight years?
I displayed my talent and it was slandered,
Then, early the wisdom within me deepened.
Fending off that depth, not fending off eminence,
Was the attitude the ancients warned against.

                                                     (Meng, 1975, p. 163)

Lament for Lu Yin

Poets are usually pure, rugged,
Die from hunger, cling to desolate mountains.
Since this white cloud had no master,
When it flew off, its mind was free from care.
After long sickness, a corpse on a bed,
The servant boy too weak to manage the funeral.
Your old books, all gnawed by famished rats,

Lie strewn and scattered in your single room.
As you go off to the land of new ghosts,
I look on your features white as old jade.
I am ashamed that, when you enter the earth,
No one calls after you, to hold you back.
All the springs lament for you in vain.
As the day lengthens, murmuring waters mourn.

(Meng, 1975, p. 185)

Tu Fu (712–770)
from *The Autumn Wastes*

My ambition, to be pictured in Unicorn Hall:
But my years decline where the ducks and herons troop.
On the great river autumn is soon in spate,
In the empty gorge the night is full of noises.
The by-paths hide in a thousand piling stones:
The sail has come to a stop, one streak of cloud.
My children too have learned a barbarous tongue,
Though it's not so sure they will rise to high command.

(Tu, 1965, p. 42)

from *Yangtse and Han*

By Yangtse and Han, a stranger who thinks of home,
One withered pedant between the Ch'ien and K'un.
Under as far a sky as that streak of cloud,
The moon in the endless night no more alone.
In sunset hale of heart still:
In the autumn wind, risen from sickness.
There's always a place kept for an old horse
Though it can take no more to the long road.

(Tu, 1965, p. 48)

Han Yü (768–824)
from *The Pond in a Bowl*

In old age
I'm back
to childhood pleasures
A bowl in the ground
Just add water—
It's a pool!
Throughout the night
Frogs croaked
till it dawned,

as they did
when I fished
as a child at Feng-k'ou.

(Han, 1975, p. 185)

Wu Yü-pi (1392–1469)
from *Journal*

Entry 19 (1425 A.D., age 35) For several days now household matters have followed one upon the other. I cannot put aside my worries about my parents. My reading schedule has been interrupted and I have been harboring feelings of stinginess inside. It all makes me so ashamed of myself. The mind of the sage or worthy is like still water. Whether situations be favorable or adverse, he deals with both using principle and nothing else. How could he let what comes from the outside determine his inner sorrow and joy? Alas, how can I succeed in reaching this state? I must exert myself, yes, exert myself, without any forgetting.

Entry 102 (1426) Today I ran into an old friend along the road whose hair was already streaked with gray. Without realizing it, with a heavy heart, I asked him his age. He had just turned forty. He looked at me for a long time, for my hair too has been turning gray. We grew increasingly saddened. It was a long while before we parted. Later I thought how life is so disappointing: there is only this getting old and growing weak. How true it is that "when one is young, one doesn't exert effort, and when one is old, there is only sorrow." When I returned home tonight I recorded all this by the eastern window. Alas, it might be impossible to read all the books there are, but it may not be impossible to succeed in becoming a superior person.

Entry 109 (1429) Today I have been sitting outside the gate, my table filled with diagrams and books. Surrounded by my students, I take advantage of the shade of the trees and enjoy the clear breeze. The vital impulse of the manifold things fills my view. The beautiful mountain stands as guest and host. Looking at this glorious view, I feel a sense of expansiveness inside me.

Entry 211 (1454) Today I have been thinking how to reach the principle of "being at ease in all circumstances." "As long as there is any breath remaining, a person must not tolerate the least bit of negligence with respect to his effort of the will." How can I use the excuse of old age to feel wearied by events!

Entry 212 (1454) For several days now, I have been thinking how I've passed the days of my life as a fake [literally, an empty frame].

Entry 224 (1456) "The good person, in the pursuit of goodness, finds that there isn't enough time in life. The bad person, in pursuit of what is not good, likewise finds there isn't enough time."

Entry 265 (1462) Today I read the entries in my Journal from last year and the year before. Then I was tired and took a nap. [On my pillow] I was carefully considering how the strength of my learning is limited to just this. My vital spirit grows more enfeebled and weary with each day. Whether I look up or down, I am disappointed in myself that I've wasted much of my life in this world.

Entry 266 (1462) The Book of Odes says, "We should be apprehensive and careful as if we were on the verge of a deep gulf, as if we were treading on thin ice." Only now that I am seventy-two do I understand its meaning. Truly, to emulate the worthies is not an easy thing to do.

Entry 292 (1468) Today I was looking over a letter, a copy of which I have put up on the wall of my room. My deceased friend K'ung O, when he was inspector-censor of Kiangsi province, had written my father the following letter:

Sometime ago I had a talk with your son, Yu-pi, for several hours. In searching out his inner state of mind, I discovered that he was the type of person who could not be bent or moved by force or might, poverty or riches. While at the present moment he is beset with difficulties, at a later time he will certainly achieve something great. So don't worry about him.

I was startled when I read this, and so copied the letter in order to caution myself against laziness.

Entry 294 (1468) How lovely is the vital impulse of things evident after a rainfall! Taking this self of mine and letting it go amidst the myriad things in the universe, I look upon all things as the same, "deriving great pleasure in both the great and the small."

Entry 320 (1468) Today I was looking over some old papers of mine from the days when I was living in Wu-feng. Many painful recollections are bound up in these.

Entry 323 (1468) Today I was poring over the Book of Changes. In silence I tried to seek out its meaning and found myself overwhelmed with joy. I only regret that there is not much time left in my life.

Entry 324 (1468) After making my toilet this morning I have been occupying myself with my books in the eastern studio. The sun shining through the bamboo brightens the whole room. I find myself thinking back to the time when I first returned to my native village (in 1411). I had a poster on one of the pillars at my place in the Shih-Chuan, which read: "If I wish to reach the realm of the great worthies, I must proceed from the results of studying things on the lower level." Looking back, I realize that that was almost sixty years ago. When will I ever reach that realm of the great worthies? (Wu, 1982)

Ts'ao Hsüeh-Ch'in (?1715–?1763)
from *Dream of the Red Chamber*

[The New Year's party having begun in the estate of the wealthy Chia family], the Matriarch asked after one of her favorite maids: "Where is Hsi-jen? She's certainly getting conceited if she's only going to send the younger maids out to join us."

The Matriarch's eldest daughter-in-law, Lady Wang, rose to explain: "She couldn't very well come, madam, because she's newly in mourning for her mother."

The Matriarch gave a nod, but then commented, "A maid in service cannot really afford the refinements of filial etiquette. She would hardly absent herself at a time like this if she were still waiting on me instead of my grandson, would she? It's all because we're lenient. Since we have more than enough servants we're not so demanding, and things like this have come to be a habit.

Phoenix, the young mistress trusted with managing the estate, now hastened to give an explanation: "Even if Hsi-jen were not in mourning we would still need someone in the Garden this evening to keep an eye on the fireworks and prevent accidents. . . . so I told her to stay there to look after your grandson's quarters and see that everything is ready for his return when the party is over. That way we don't have to worry about whether the boy is being taken care of, and she can observe some of the proprieties of mourning. Isn't that better all around? Of course, if Your Grace wants her, then I will send for her."

"How right you are," said the Matriarch. "I can count on you to think things through. So we won't send for her. But, tell me, when did her mother die? And how is it I didn't know?"

Phoenix smiled, "Has it slipped your mind, madam? The other day she came to report it to you herself."

The Matriarch thought back and chuckled, "Oh my, yes, she did. What a memory I have!"

The other ladies smiled and said, "How can Your Grace remember every little thing?"

Now the Matriarch sighed, recalling: "She came here to be my maid when she was just a child. . . . Finally I gave her to that young demon king of a grandson, and what a dance he's led her all these years! Well, it's not as if her parents had been our bond-servants or received any special kindness from us. After her mother died I meant to give her some silver for the funeral, but somehow it slipped my mind."

Phoenix put in: "The other day she received forty taels, so that should have covered it."

The Matriarch nodded. . . .

One of the matrons brought in two women story-tellers who often visited the house, putting stools for them at one side. They were told to sit down and handed a fiddle and a lute. Then the Matriarch asked Aunt Li and Aunt Hsueh what they would like to hear, and they answered, "Anything will do." Then she asked the two women what new stories they had.

"One about the end of the T'ang dynasty and the Five dynasties," they replied.

"What is its name?"

"The Phoenix Seeks Its Mate."

"That's a good title," she remarked. "Why is it called that? Let's hear what it's about, and if it sounds good you can tell it."

"It's about a country gentleman named Wang Chung at the end of the T'ang dynasty," said one of the women. "His family came from Chinling. After serving as a minister under two emperors, he retired in his old age. He had an only son called Wang Hsi-feng. . . . One year, old Mr. Wang sent his son to take the examinations in the capital. Running into heavy rain on the way he took shelter in a village where, as it happened, there lived a gentleman named Li, an old family friend of Mr. Wang's, who put the young man up in his study. This Mr. Li had no son, only one daughter, Chu-luan, who was thoroughly accomplished in lyre-playing, chess, calligraphy, and painting—"

"Now I understand the title," the Matriarch interrupted. "You needn't continue. I can guess the rest. Naturally this Wang Hsi-feng wants to marry this Miss Chu-luan."

"Then Your Grace has heard the story before," the story-teller smiled.

The others explained, "Madam can guess the ending without having heard the story before."

"There's a sameness about all these tales," complained the Matriarch. "And they're so stereotyped—all about talented scholars and lovely ladies. Fancy describing girls who behave so badly as fine young ladies! Why, they're nothing of the sort. They're always introduced as girls from cultured families whose fathers are invariably high officials or prime ministers. In that case, an only daughter would be treasured and brought up as a real fine young lady, well-versed in literature and a model of propriety; yet the first glimpse of a handsome man, whether a relative or a family friend, sets her thoughts running on marriage. She forgets her parents then and gets up to all sorts of devilry, behaving quite unlike a fine lady. If she carries on like that she's surely no lady, no matter how crammed her head is with learning. If a man whose head is crammed with learning becomes a thief, does the court spare him on account of his talent? So these story-tellers contradict themselves.

"Besides, not only would the daughter of a good scholar-official family be well-educated and a model of propriety—so would her mother. And even if her father had retired, a big family like that would have plenty of nurses and maids to look after the girl. How is it that in all these stories, when such things happen, no one has any inkling of it except the girl herself and one trusted maid? What are all the others doing, I'd like to know? Isn't that contradictory?"

Everyone laughed.

"Madam has shown up their lies!"

"There's a reason for this," she continued. "Either the people who spin these tales envy the rank and riches of other families, or ask for help which isn't granted, and so they make up these stories to discredit them. Or else they're so bewitched by reading such tales that they wish they could get a fine young lady themselves, and so they invent these things for their own amusement.

"But what do they know about the ways of scholar-official families? Let's not talk about those great families in their stories—even in a middle-rank family like ours such things couldn't possibly happen. They're talking utter nonsense! That's why we never allow such stories here, and our girls have never heard any. Now that I'm growing old and the girls' apartments are some distance across the compound, I may listen to a tale or two to pass the time; but as soon as the girls come I put a stop to it."

Aunt Li and Aunt Hsueh approved; "That's a rule for a good family, madam. Even in our homes we don't let the children hear such frivolous nonsense."

Phoenix then stepped forward to pour more wine. . . .

The Matriarch was now in such high spirits that Phoenix suggested, "While the story-tellers are here, why don't we get them to drum for us while we pass round a spray of plum-blossom and play 'Spring lights up the eyebrows'?"

"That's a fine drinking game, and this is just the time for it," approved the Matriarch. She sent for a black-lacquered drum with copper studs which was kept for drinking games, asked the story-tellers to beat it, and took a spray of red plum-blossom from the table: "Whoever has the blossom when the drum stops must drink a cup and tell a joke."

In no time at all the room was crowded with maids. Then she ordered the drumming to start. The story-tellers, being old hands at this, varied the tempo and the plum was passed from hand to hand to its rhythm.

First slow as water dripping from a clepsydra, the drumming soon gathered speed like the patter of peas being poured into a bowl. Then, after a rapid tattoo like a horse stampeding or sudden flashes of lightning, the sound abruptly broke off just as the plum blossom reached the old lady's hand. A roar of laughter went up, and at once her cup was filled.

"Naturally madam's face should light up first," cried the others. "Then we shall be able to share in her happiness."

"I don't mind drinking a cup," she rejoined. "But I can't think of a joke."

"Why, Your Grace knows even more jokes than Phoenix, and better ones, too," they insisted. "Do tell us a good one, madam."

"I don't have any new jokes. I'll just have to brazen it out. Well, here goes," said the old lady. "Once upon a time a family had ten sons and ten daughters-in-law. The tenth daughter-in-law was the cleverest, so smart and well-spoken that she was the favorite of her father and mother-in-law, who kept finding fault with the nine others. This seemed so unfair to the others that they put their heads together, and said, 'We've been dutiful daughters-in-law. We're just not as smooth-tongued as that bitch. That's why the old couple keep on singing her praises. Who can we complain to about this injustice?'

"The eldest one suggested, 'Tomorrow let's go to the Temple of the King of Hell to offer incense and complain to him. We'll ask why, since we've all been born human, that bitch alone was given the gift of gab while the rest of us are so dumb?'

"The other eight approved of this idea. They all went the next day to the temple and offered incense, then slept there at the foot of the altar while their spirits waited for the King of Hell to appear. They waited for a long time but nothing happened, and they were growing impatient when they saw the Monkey King come somersaulting down through the clouds. At the sight of these nine spirits he raised his magic staff and threatened to beat them. The nine spirits knelt down fearfully to beg for mercy. Then Monkey asked what brought them there, and they told him the whole story. He stamped his foot.

" 'So that's the reason!' he sighed. 'It's a good thing you met me. If you'd waited for the King of Hell, he wouldn't have known.'

"The spirits of the nine sisters-in-law pleaded, 'Have pity and tell us, Great Monkey Sage. That's all we ask.'

" 'That's easy,' answered Monkey with a smile. 'The day you ten girls were born, I was visiting the King of Hell and happened to pee on the ground. Your youngest sister-in-law lapped it up. Now if you want the gift of gab, I have lots more pee you can drink if you like.' "

The whole company burst out laughing. . . . By the time soup was served the Matriarch remarked, "It's been a long night and I feel rather hungry."

"We've prepared some duck congee," Phoenix told her.
"I'd prefer something less greasy," was the reply.
"There's date congee too for the ladies observing a fast."
"One's too greasy, the other too sweet," complained the old lady.
"We have almond gruel as well. Only I'm afraid that's sweet, too."
Then the tables were cleared, fresh delicacies served, and after a small
collation they rinsed their mouths with tea and the party broke up. (Ts'ao,
1981, pp. 212–229)

Pa Chin, pen name of Li Fei-kan (b. 1904)
from *Family*

One afternoon, on returning home from a meeting of the Students' Federation, Chueh-hui was summoned into his grandfather's room. Well over sixty, the old man lay in a reclining chair. . . . As long as Chueh-hui could remember, there had always been a picture of a stern grandfather in his mind, a severe, forbidding man whom all feared and respected. Chueh-hui had seldom exchanged more than a few words with his *Yeh-yeh*. Except for the two times during the day, once in the morning and once in the evening, when he formally called to pay his respects, Chueh-hui had little opportunity to come into contact with him. . . . *Yeh-yeh* probably wasn't always such an irritable old stick, thought Chueh-hui. He recalled that many of his grandfather's poems had been dedicated to singsong girls, quite a few girls at that. He must have been a dashing sort then; it was only later he acquired his pious air. Of course that was thirty years ago. As he grew old, he turned into a crusty Confucian moralist. Yet even now, his grandfather played around with the young female impersonators in the opera. Of course, nobody looked askance at that sort of thing in Chengtu. Not long ago, a few old-timers who had been officials under the deposed Ching dynasty [1644–1912]—pillars of the Confucian Morals Society, too—made a big splash in the local press, publishing a list they had composed of the best female impersonators in the opera. Patronizing these actors was considered a sign of "refinement." Yet how could you reconcile this "refinement" with the defense of "Confucian morals"? Young Chueh-hui couldn't figure it out. His grandfather kept a concubine—Mistress Chen, a heavily made-up woman who always reeked of perfume and simpered when she talked. Mentally comparing his grandfather's elegant tastes in books and painting with his fondness for this coarse woman, Chueh-hui had to laugh. People are certainly inconsistent, he mused. The more he puzzled over it, the less he understood the old man. His grandfather was an unfathomable mystery to him.

Suddenly the old man opened his eyes. . . . He seemed to see many forms and faces drifting before him. Not one of them looked at him with any affection. There were his sons, indulging themselves in women and

wine, sneering at him, cursing him behind his back. There were his grandsons, proudly going their own new road, abandoning him, old and weak
and powerless to stop them.

Never had he felt so lonely and despondent. Had all his hopes been
nothing but idle dreams? He had built up the family until it was large and
prosperous. Ruthless, dictatorial, he had controlled everything, satisfied in
the conviction that the family would continue to flourish. Yet the results
of his strenuous efforts had only brought loneliness. Though he was tax-
ing his waning strength to the utmost to keep a grip on things, it was
obvious he could not. No question about it—the family was sliding down-
hill. He already had some premonition of how it would end. It probably
would happen very soon. He had no way to prevent it. (Pa, 1972, pp. 64–
65, 65, 282)

REFERENCES

Biographies of immortals (Lieh hsien chuan) (n.d.). Wang Shih-chen (Ed.). 16th cen-
tury.
The classic of filial piety (Hsiao ching). (1933). In J. Legge (Trans.), *The four books*
(Chap. 25). Shanghai: Chinese Book Company.
Confucius. (1933). *Confucian analects (Lun-yü).* In J. Legge (Trans.), *The four books*
(Bk. 1., chap 2, v.2; chap. 4; bk. 2, chap. 4, v.1–6; chaps. 5, 6, 7; bk. 8,
chap. 7). Shanghai: Chinese Book Company.
The great learning (Ta hsüeh). (1933). In J. Legge (Trans.), *The four books* (Chap.
10, v.1). Shanghai: Chinese Book Company.
Han Yü. (1975). The pond in a bowl (C. Hertman, Trans.). In Wu-chi Liu and
I. Y. Lo (Eds.), *Sunflower splendor* (p. 185). Garden City, NY: Anchor Books.
Li Chi. (1967). *Li Chi: Book of rites* (C. Chai and W. Chai, Eds., and J. Legge,
Trans.). New Hyde Park, NY: University Books.
Li Ch'ing-chao. (1965). Tz'u verse (Hsu Kaiyu, Trans.). In C. Birch (Ed.), *An
anthology of Chinese literature* (pp. 359–61). New York: Grove Press.
Lin Yutang. (1914). *Proverbs and common sayings from the Chinese* (A. H. Smith,
Ed.) Shanghai: American Presbyterian Mission Press.
Lin Yutang. (1963). *The importance of understanding: Translations from the Chinese.*
Cleveland: Forum Books.
Mencius. (1933). *The Works of Mencius (Meng-tzu).* In J. Legge (Trans.), *The four
books* (Bk. 1 [King Hui of Liang], part 1, chap. 3, 4; Bk. 4 [Lilou], pt. 1,
chap. 26,1; part 1, chap. 30,2. Shanghai: Chinese Book Company.
Meng Chiao. (1975). Autumn meditations, and Lament for Lu Yin (I. Y. Lo and
S. Owen, Trans.). In Wu-chi Liu and I. Y. Lo (Eds.), *Sunflower splendor*
(pp. 163, 185). Garden City, NY: Anchor Books.
Pa Chin (Li Fei-Kan). (1972). *Family* (S. Shapiro, Ed. and Trans.). Garden City,
NY: Anchor Books.
Ts'ao Hsüeh-ch'in (Ts'ao Chan). (1981). *Dream of the red chamber* (G. and Hsien-yi
Yang, Trans.). Peking: Foreign Language Press.
Ts'ao Ts'ao Ballad. (n.d.).
Tso-ch'iu Ming. (1979). *Tso-chuan.* B. Watson (Trans.). In Li Han (Ed.), *Ming*

ch'iu [The unenlightened seek, from the 8th century A.D.] (p. 104). New York: Kodansha International.

Tu Fu. (1965). *The Autumn wastes,* and *Yangtse and Han.* In A. C. Graham (Trans.), *Poems of the late T'ang* (p. 42, 48). Harmondsworth: Penguin.

The Twenty-four examples of filial piety (Erh-Shih-szu hsiao). (1933). In J. Legge (Trans.), *The four books* (Chapter 8). Shanghai: Chinese Book Company.

Wu Yü-pi. (1982). *Journal* (M. T. Kelleher, Trans.). In M. T. Kelleher, *Personal reflections on the pursuit of sagehood: The life and journal of Wu Yü-pi.* Unpublished doctoral dissertation, Columbia University.

FURTHER READING

Davis-Friedmann, D. (1983). *Long lives: Chinese elderly and the communist revolution.* Cambridge: Harvard University Press.

Ganschow, T. A. (1978). The aged in a revolutionary milieu: China. In S. F. Spicker, K. Woodward, & D. Van Tassell (Eds.), *Aging and the elderly: Humanistic perspectives in gerontology.* Atlantic Highlands, NJ: Humanities Press.

Ikels, C. (1983). *Aging and adaptation: Chinese in Hong Kong and the United States.* Hamden, CT: Shoe String Press.

Yang, Chiang. (1983). *Six chapters from my life "downunder"* (H. Goldblatt, Trans.). Seattle: University of Washington Press.

Index

About the Editors and Contributors

W. ANDREW ACHENBAUM, Research Scientist and Professor of History at the Institute of Gerontology at the University of Michigan, early in his career exhibited an interest in the issues of aging. His works include *Old Age in the New Land: the American Experience Since 1790; Images of Old Age in America: 1790 to the Present;* and *Shades of Gray: Old Age, American Values and Federal Policies Since 1920.* He is currently working on a history of gerontology as an intellectual field of inquiry.

JON HENDRICKS, until recently Professor of Sociology at the University of Kentucky, is currently associated with the Department of Sociology at Oregon State University. He is Associate Editor of the prestigious *International Journal of Aging and Human Development.* Among other works, Professor Hendricks is co-author of the landmark study *Aging in Mass Society: Myths and Realities.* His recent work, *Creating Dependency in Old Age,* will be published shortly. Professor Hendricks is Chair-elect of the Behavioral and Social Sciences section of the Gerontological Society of America.

CYNTHIA A. LEEDHAM is pursuing her doctorate with a focus on Social Gerontology at the University of Kentucky. Ms. Leedham has a degree from Oxford University in England, and has studied language, literature, and civilization at the University of Lille in France.

LOUIS ROBERTS is currently Dean of Arts and Sciences at Merrimack College and is former Chair of the Department of Classics at Syracuse University. Professor Roberts is the author of *A Concordance of Lucretius.*

RICHARD C. FALLIS, Associate Professor in the Department of English at Syracuse University, specializes in modern British and Irish literature and is the author of the *Irish Renaissance* and the editor of the Irish Studies series published by Syracuse Unviersity Press.

PAUL J. ARCHAMBAULT is Professor of French literature at Syracuse University and Editor of *Symposium*. His specific field of research is medieval chronicle writing and autobiography. His most recent book, co-authored with Marianna Mustacchi Archambault of Bucknell University, is *A Renaissance Woman: Helisenne's Personal and Invective Letters*.

GERD K. SCHNEIDER is Associate Professor of German at Syracuse University. Professor Schneider's research interests include nineteenth- and twentieth-century literature and culture along with literature and gerontology. Publications include works on Nietzsche and A. Schnitzler.

ROBERT H. STACY is Professor Emeritus of Slavic literature at Syracuse University. Professor Stacy's works include *Russian Literary Criticism,* and *Defamiliarization in Language and Literature*.

MYRON I. LICHTBLAU is Professor of Spanish American literature and Chairman of the Foreign Languages and Literature Department at Syracuse University. Among his works on Spanish American literature are *The Argentine Novel in the 19th Century; El Arte Estilistico de Eduardo Mallea;* and *Manual Galvez*. Professor Lichtblau is also the editor of *Emigration and Exile in Twentieth Century Hispanic Literature*.

ROGER ALLEN is Professor of Arabic at the University of Pennsylvania. He is a distinguished scholar of Arabic with many books, articles, and translations to his credit. He is a member of the editorial advisory board of *Literature East and West* and is the guest editor of the twentieth-anniversary issue of *Al-Arabiyya*. Professor Allen's works include *The Arabic Novel: An Historical and Critical Introduction* and *Modern Arabic Literature*.

VIRGINIA SKORD, who resided several years in Japan pursuing research interests, received her doctorate from the Department of Asian Studies at Cornell University in pre-modern Japanese literature. Doctor Skord is currently Adjunct Assistant Professor at Hunter College in New York City, specializing in medieval Japanese narrative.

EDWARD GUNN is Associate Professor of Chinese literature with the Department of Asian Studies at Cornell University. *Unwelcome Use* and *20th Century Chinese Drama* are included among Professor Gunn's several publications.

PRISCA VON DOROTKA BAGNELL is the Director of Academic Programs, All-University Gerontology Center at Syracuse University. Her previous works include *Information Resources in Social Gerontology, Special Collection: Gerontology and Geriatrics,* and she has assisted in a film on aging in the Soviet Union.

PATRICIA SPENCER SOPER is currently pursuing doctoral studies in composition and rhetoric at Syracuse University where she is an Instructor and Writing Consultant. She has presented papers at national conferences on research in the teaching of writing. She has several works in progress.